ONE FATHER, ONE BLOOD

ONE FATHER, ONE BLOOD

DESCENT AND GROUP STRUCTURE AMONG THE MELPA PEOPLE

ANDREW STRATHERN

TAVISTOCK PUBLICATIONS

First published in Great Britain in
1972 by Tavistock Publications Limited,
11 New Fetter Lane, London EC4

This book has been set in 11pt Monotype Bembo,
two points leaded and was printed and bound in
Australia at The Griffin Press Pty. Limited, Netley,
South Australia

Distributed in the USA
by Barnes and Noble Inc.
SBN 422 74050 0

PREFACE

The fieldwork on which this book is largely based was conducted during 1964-5 while I was a graduate student in the Faculty of Archaeology and Anthropology at Cambridge University. It was supported by grants from the Horniman Scholarship Fund administered by the Royal Anthropological Institute, from the Smuts Memorial Fund and the Mount Everest Fund, and by a William Wyse Studentship from Trinity College, Cambridge. I thank all the institutions concerned for their help. Between February and July 1965 facilities were kindly granted to me at the Department of Anthropology in the Research School of Pacific Studies, Australian National University, and the results of my writing-up there were presented as a Fellowship dissertation to Trinity College. The dissertation has been revised and rearranged to form this book. My Research Fellowships at Cambridge and, subsequently, the Australian National University have enabled me to visit New Guinea again on shorter trips in 1967, 1968, 1969, and 1970, and so to follow the affairs of the book's main subjects, the Kawelka people, through to the present.

The Kawelka are a tribe of some 860 persons who live in the northern part of Mount Hagen Sub-District in the Western Highlands of Australian New Guinea. Their language is Melpa (other spellings are Metlpa, Medlpa), which has more than 60,000 speakers, mostly settled north of Mount Hagen township. South of the town are 30,000 Gawigl speakers, closely related to their northern neighbours. My term 'Hageners' includes all Melpa- and those Gawigl-speakers who come from parts fairly close to the township. However, most of my detailed work has been done with Melpa-speakers and my generalisations about 'Hageners' should be taken as referring in the first instance to these. More background to these points is given in an earlier book, *The rope of moka* (1971); and it may be in order here to explain the relationship of the present book to that one.

In *The rope of moka* my main aim was to describe the Hagen *moka* system of ceremonial exchange and to show how it is predicated on competition between groups and individual leaders or 'big-men'. Although it includes a single chapter (chapter two) in which I set out a skeleton account of group structure as a necessary basis for my later account of group activities, it does not examine in detail the internal constitution of any of the Hagen clans. Thus it largely bypasses the issue raised in 1962 by Barnes on the applicability of African 'lineage models' to New Guinea Highlands societies; and it is this issue which I take up in the present book. It centres on the internal composition of groups and on the ideology which reflects their co-operation and competition in the external dealings of *moka* exchange. The two books will, I hope, complement each other, providing readers with an opportunity to cross-check my suggestions, in one or the other, about big-men and group structure.

My wife's book, *Women in between* (in press), is also relevant to the present one. It takes as its central focus the position of women, moving as wives and mothers between groups of males and retaining ties with both natal and affinal kin. Mothers, on widowhood, divorce, or separation from their husbands, are often instrumental in bringing back children to their brother's clan group, as I show here in chapter six. *Women in between* provides a more comprehensive picture of women and their roles in Hagen society than I am able to include here. Finally, in one other book, *Self-decoration in Mount Hagen* (1971), we have attempted to convey something more of the feel of life in Hagen than can readily be incorporated into a monograph on social structure, by describing dances and ornaments worn at festivals and sketching out the colour symbolism which seems to underlie the choice of decoration for different ceremonies. Some of the persons whose photographs appear in *Self-decoration* and whose case-histories are discussed in this book also appeared on BBC television in the series *The Family of Man* during 1969.[1] Two at least are my close friends and sponsors in Hagen: the big-men Ongka and Ndamba.

I wish to thank here all those who have steered me along the roads of fieldwork and the analysis of material. I must mention especially Professors Ralph Bulmer, who read and commented extensively on my Fellowship dissertation, Meyer Fortes, John Barnes, Paula Brown, and Roy Wagner, and Drs Jack Goody and Clive Criper, all of whom discussed problems with me during 1965-9, and my wife Marilyn, who contributed many comments on a draft of the original dissertation and has given me some material for this revised version. I thank also officers of the Administration in Mount Hagen and the staff of the Lutheran Mission at Kotna and Ogelbeng for material aid and kindnesses; in particular I am grateful to Rev. Hermann Strauss for early help with grammatical materials on the Melpa language and for anthropological discussion, especially on questions relating to Melpa religious concepts. Finally, I wish to thank Mrs Dorothy Aunela of the Anthropology Department, Australian National University, for her assistance in typing the manuscript of the book.

True names of persons, groups, and places are given in this book, as in *The rope of moka*. It is an ethical question whether the anthropologist should identify his subjects directly. The solution adopted here has been to omit names in some cases, rather than using pseudonyms, but otherwise to include them, because it is hoped that in the future the book may help to provide for the Kawelka people a record of themselves, and that 'their names will remain'.

My field station in Hagen is Mbukl (see Map 1), overlooking from its altitude of over six thousand feet the depths of the Wahgi and Baiyer Valleys. It was at Mbukl that we first met the Kawelka, and came to know especially well Ongka, Ndamba, Nykint, Ru, and Kont. To these, and to many others, my thanks in closing.

Andrew Strathern
Canberra, March 1971

CONTENTS

Preface		v
Tables		xi
Illustrations		xiii
Note on the Text		xiv
Introduction		1
1	Idioms	6
2	The Kawelka	31
3	Settlement Patterns	54
4	Settlement and Warfare	73
5	Affiliation	91
6	Choices	129
7	Status	188
8	Conclusions	213
	Appendix	234
	Notes	236
	References	252
	Index	259

TABLES

1 Kawelka population, February 1965 — 64

2 The composition of Kawelka settlements — 66

3 New homesteads — 68

4 Occupants of Tipuka settlements within old Kawelka territory — 84

5 Affiliation changes to and from Kawelka clan-groups over a period of 2-3 generations — 102

6 The Kawelka clan-groups, February 1965 — 104

7 Non-agnates of Kawelka and their hosts — 107

8 Choices relevant to the affiliation of Kawelka non-agnates — 109

9 Stages in life at which residence or affiliation changes are made, and reasons given for moves — 112

10 The situations of uxorilocally resident men and their children — 121

11 The incidence of wife-taking from other groups by Kawelka men over two generations — 133

12 Wife-taking from traditional allies and enemies — 135

13 Residence and affiliation changes between the Kawelka and other tribes and between Kawelka clans over two to three generations — 141

14 Numbers of non-agnates in Kawelka clan-groups who were taken in by big-men — 166

15 Material on ten bridewealths observed during 1964 to early 1965 — 195

16 Unmarried men in Kawelka clan-groups, February 1965, who were over the usual age of marriage 197

17 Whether hosts of incomers had sons of their own or not 201

18 Numbers of current wives of Kawelka Kundmbo men, February 1965 202

19 Numbers of marriages made by Kawelka Kundmbo men 207

20 Whether non-agnates have lost their links with extra-clan kin or not 208

21 Incidence of payment of bridewealth for, and previous marital status of, wives of agnates and non-agnates in Kawelka 210

ILLUSTRATIONS

FIGURES

1 'One blood' ties   14

2 Kawelka segments   35

3 Kawelka Kundmbo Roklambo sub-clan   45

4 The descendants of Tilkang, according to Kawelka
  Membo Kont   48

5 The fit between genealogy and *rapa* divisions in Kawelka
  Membo clan   49

6 Genealogical account of Oyambo ingk *rapa* in Membo   50

7 Maepna settlement-place: genealogy   61

8 A Kawelka Kurupmbo lineage   88

9 'Agnate' and 'non-agnate'   203

MAPS

1 Site of field station (Mbukl) within the Hagen Sub-District   33

2 Kawelka clan territories around Mbukl   79

3 Part of the Tipuka-Kawelka boundary area   83

NOTE ON THE TEXT

The special symbols I employ are:

 ø = a mid, open, front, rounded vowel

 ə = a mid, close, central, unrounded vowel (the schwa —
  in some contexts this may be phonemically redundant)

There is also a symbol similar to y, a high, close, front, rounded vowel which appears only in the word *nyim*, big-man, and in the proper names Rying and Nykint, and is therefore represented by an ordinary y.

The group name which appears as Ngglammbo in *The rope of moka* is here written as Klammbo.

Abbreviations of kinship terms are used occasionally, as follows:

F	=	father
M	=	mother
S	=	son
D	=	daughter
B	=	brother
Z	=	sister
H	=	husband
W	=	wife
e	=	elder
y	=	younger
ch	=	children

INTRODUCTION

Europeans discovered the New Guinea Highlands in the late 1920s and early 1930s. Administration officers, gold prospectors, and missionaries moved in with their separate aims of pacification, commercial activity, and conversion. Some of the missionaries were anthropologists, and to them we owe accounts of Highlands peoples in the 1930s, for example the study by Vicedom and Tischner (1943-8) on the Mbowamb or Hagen people, who also form the subject of this book. Professional anthropologists began to work in the Highlands in growing numbers from 1950 onwards, and in 1962 J. A. Barnes published his penetrating survey on 'African models' which has since been taken as a starting point by many investigators. Barnes examined the question of whether models based on descriptions of corporate lineage structure in acephalous African societies were fully appropriate to the analysis of group-formation in the Highlands. Before going to the field in 1964 I had come to suspect, from reading Barnes's treatment of the ethnographic material and from other available literature (most importantly, perhaps, Reay 1959, Glasse 1959, and Brown 1962) that a solution to some of the apparent anomalies in accounts of Highlands societies lay, not so much in understanding discrepancies between ideology and practice, as in comprehending what the ideology of the Highlanders in relation to their social groups was and how it might fit the contexts of social activity, for example warfare and other expressions of inter-group competition, in which it was found. Langness (1964), Scheffler (1964a, 1965, 1966), Barnes (1967), Sahlins (1965), and de Lepervanche (1967-8) have since provided support for this viewpoint. The central point of the analysis which can be developed from this initial notion is that we must distinguish the descriptive statements and idioms in terms of which Hageners refer to the solidarity, continuity, and segmentation patterns of their main social groups, from the rules which they say apply to processes of recruitment to these groups.[1] Whereas Hageners lay stress on idioms which at least resemble patrilineal dogmas when talking about the former, about the latter they speak only of obtaining membership through either one's father or one's mother. To the extent that the first mode of recruitment is more common than the second and has rather more normative justification we can speak, as Barnes (1962) has, of 'cumulative patrifiliation'. To concentrate only on the rules and processes of recruitment would be, however, to miss out from one's analysis the other sector of ideology in which Hageners use a number of 'native models' to describe and con-ceptualise their own groups. Whether at the end of an analysis of group structure this or that Highlands society is declared to exhibit overall a greater emphasis on 'patriliny' than others do is likely to depend simply on how many elements of meaning are included in the definition of patriliny (elsewhere, 1969b, I argue that this consideration complicates evaluation of Meggitt's well-known hypothesis linking a stress on patriliny with pressure on agricultural resources). The important initial task is to see what the ideology is about and to discover its function in the society being looked at.

A classic case of such a functional analysis of descent ideology in an African society is provided by Evans-Pritchard's study of the Nuer, alluded to in Barnes's initial article on African models in the New Guinea Highlands. Although Barnes cogently shows in this article how many features of Highlands societies mark them off from alleged African counterparts, it is my contention that in one respect the Nuer do indeed provide us with important parallels. Barnes perhaps foreshadows this possibility when he writes (1962:5) that 'It has been easy to make the mistake of comparing the *de facto* situation in a Highlands community . . . with a non-existent and idealized set of conditions among the Nuer, wrongly inferred from Evans-Pritchard's discussion of the principles of Nuer social structure'. He points out that among the Nuer, just as in many of the Highlands cases, the people we find actually living together in local communities are unlikely all to be agnatically related members of a given lineage. It does not follow from this, however, that the lineage principle is unimportant to the Nuer. Evans-Pritchard has turned such an idea on its head by arguing that it is actually the 'clear . . . lineage structure of the Nuer which permits persons and families to move about and attach themselves freely . . . to whatever community they choose' (1951:28). Schneider (1965:74), applauded by Buchler and Selby (1968:75), has dubbed this statement as one of 'those special gems of paradoxical obfuscation for which Evans-Pritchard is justly famous'. If, despite this damning tribute, we persist in believing that Evans-Pritchard's argument makes some kind of sense, we can defend it as follows. It is quite true that Evans-Pritchard's account of the Nuer social system emphasises the importance of 'the lineage principle' (1940:265). Yet, as Marie de Lepervanche (1967:138) points out, he also stresses that the *form* of the lineage system is a reflection of 'the form of the territorial system within which it functions'. Named lineage segments among the Nuer correspond to named territorial groups whose political relations are conceptualised in lineage terms. In actual composition these groups are not simply agnatic lineages; they are communities of persons related by a variety of agnatic, cognatic, and affinal ties and focused on leaders who are usually agnates of the 'dominant' lineage which gives its name to the local group. Lineage member-ship is given by birth and cannot be changed; local group membership depends to some extent on choice and can be changed, for example in accordance with economic circumstances. At the same time local groups themselves are spoken of as if they were lineages. In reality there are two 'lineage systems': one comprising a set of dispersed, agnatic units whose members recognise prohibitions on inter-marriage and killing among themselves, the other a set of territorial, political groups named after the lineages of prominent men within them. Evans-Pritchard thus distinguishes in his analysis between lineage ideology as it relates to territorial, political groups and actual processes of recruitment to such groups. A similar set of distinctions can be applied to Highlands societies, although I am not, of course, suggesting that Highlands societies are like the Nuer in all respects. Nuer ecology differs markedly from that of the Highlands; there is no equivalent, at least in Hagen, of the Nuer *dil* or aristocrat; and Highlanders use other idioms besides that of the lineage to conceptualise inter-group relations.[2] Evans-Pritchard's central analytical point, however, does apply, at least to some levels of structure, in many Highlands societies: lineage ideology provides 'a conceptual skeleton on which the local communities are built up into an organization of related parts, or, as we would prefer to state it, a system of values linking tribal segments and providing the idiom in which their relations can be expressed and directed' (1940:212). For the Highlands we need only add that it is better to speak of 'descent' ideology in general than of a specific, elaborated, lineage ideology, although the Mae-Enga (Meggitt 1965) appear to have developed a lineage system.

This formulation, then, enables us to place 'descent dogmas' in the Highlands in a proper perspective. It does not help us to examine the factors involved in actual processes of affiliation and recruitment to groups. Scheffler (1965) and Barth (1966) provide concepts which are useful in this domain of analysis. Scheffler quotes Leach's contention that 'social structures are sometimes best regarded as the statistical outcome of multiple individual choices rather than a direct reflection of jural rules' (Leach 1960:124; cp. Keesing 1967:15 on 'decision-making' models). Modifying this, Scheffler argues that to explain statistical patterns we must construct 'mechanical models of behaviour-generating and constraining mechanisms'. Norms themselves, he says, should not be taken as the only factors generating behaviour. Instead it is better 'to regard the introduction of norms or rules into social transactions as a form of social action in itself. Norms are not just static ideological entities ... they are also strategic resources in the process of social organization' (Scheffler 1965:292, 294). As an example he points out that among the Choiseulese it was an ideal that descent groups were open to all legitimate descendants of the founder, but it was also understood that this held only if a candidate for admission was 'a good kinsman' and also 'provided the group is not too full, [and] provided it is in our interest'. Such considerations 'protected the interests ... of those within whose power it was to exercise closure' (1965:295). The same pragmatic, contingent conditions affect attitudes to group-membership in the Highlands. Scheffler's remark on the importance of rhetoric ('rhetoric is, after all, one of the ways of ... organizing and steering action'—1965:300) is also very relevant, since Highlands big-men are noted for their use of rhetoric in disputes and it is on these occasions that norms are most frequently promulgated.

Scheffler sees 'social structure' as emergent from transactional processes. Barth (1966) presents a similar view. He argues for a continual feed-back from transactions to norms. He would probably agree that certain basic values can sometimes be taken as given. For example, he discusses processes which generate different social forms among societies which all place some value on patrilineality (1966: 22-32). In the present context we can suggest also that the value placed on patrifilial recruitment to groups, say, in the Highlands is dependent on the transactions which surround this process: that is, on payment of bridewealth, maintenance of marriage, exchange relations between affines, and the requirements for labour of particular men and their groups.

For Hagen we can posit certain basic values—individual and group strength, wealth, and prestige—and we can also point out that it is only certain men who fully realise these values: the big-men. They most regularly promulgate, manipulate, and even break norms in pursuit of these values; and they have a definite influence over *de facto* patterns of group composition. Looking at big-men and their transactional relationships with others helps us to understand many— although not all—of the processes relevant to group formation and continuity.

Starting then, from a discussion of idioms and ideology, the following chapters outline group structure and settlement patterns and show the influence of warfare in the past (chapters one to four), before embarking in detail on the question of affiliation and on an analysis of case-histories which will, I hope, indicate both the influence of big-men and the use of norms in action (chapters five to eight).

CHAPTER 1

IDIOMS

In approaching the analysis of a society whose language and culture are clearly very different from his own, the anthropologist has two main tasks: one is to find an adequate means of translating terms in the language he is studying into the language in which he himself is writing; the other is to bring to bear on the material he collects concepts which have proved of value in the analysis of similar societies elsewhere. Both tasks carry many semantic difficulties. In both the anthropologist is essentially attempting to find a reference language which he can employ to speak about a people's view of themselves and his view of them. The problem of whether to describe the group structure developed by a given people as 'patrilineal' or not exemplifies all these difficulties. The anthropologist is trying to understand what his informants are saying to him in their own language, and at the same time he is gathering material intended to test, for example, whether persons are regularly affiliated to groups in accordance with a rule which he defines in analytical terms as 'patrilineal'. The distinction which anthropologists make between jural norms and statistical patterns is, of course, crucial here: there can be rules which are not followed in practice, and practices which are not reflected in rules. Rules, again, may carry differential jural, moral, or affective weight, and there may be different rules for different contingencies, so that one can meaningfully speak of 'flexible' attitudes to, say, the incorporation of persons into groups. Despite these complications, in principle the anthropologist has a clear procedure which he can follow: first, he can define the analytical concepts which he hopes to apply to his society; second, he can examine the people's own concepts to see how accurately his analytical concepts can be used as translation terms for these; and third, he can investigate processes of social life to see whether the people's actions correspond to their own rules, to his analytical concepts, or to both, should they happen to coincide.

Unfortunately, following this procedure is not so simple as it sounds. Difficulty begins with the definition of patrilineal descent. Leach (1962), following Rivers (1924:86-8), has argued that the term should be used to refer only to descent *groups*, and that these are groups to which recruitment occurs automatically by virtue of birth alone. In addition, he says, the term can be useful only if the groups are discrete and do not overlap, so that in practice a descent group should always be a unilineal descent group. Leach maintains that neglect of these suggestions made by Rivers has since led to the creation of a 'tortuous taxonomy' of so-called descent groups, resulting not in 'the language of science but of gobbledygook' (1962:131). In a similar vein Fortes (1969:280) writes: 'I regard the diffuse and discursive usage of such key concepts as "descent" and "descent groups" as conducive to analytical confusion as well as to misinterpretation of the empirical data of kinship and social organization.' Fortes, however, has also provided us with a definition of descent which does not link it indissolubly with descent groups and unilineality: 'descent refers to a relation mediated by a parent between himself and an ancestor, defined as any genealogical predecessor of the grandparental or earlier generation' (1959:207, also quoted in 1969:281). It can be seen that this formulation enables us to separate the question of whether there is some cultural recognition of descent in a society from the question of whether the society's main formal groups are best described as descent groups or otherwise. Scheffler, in a painstaking article (1966), has pointed out that this can potentially confer a considerable advantage, for it enables us to escape from whole-system typologies in which 'descent' is embedded in models of total lineage systems and their ramifying jural correlates. Scheffler himself favours the definition of descent as 'relationship by genealogical tie to an ancestor' (1966:542), and suggests that wherever such relationships are recognised we can speak of 'descent-constructs' (1966:543). In some cases these constructs are relevant to rules determining (in theory) membership of corporate groups; in other cases they may be relevant to social action in some other way.

The definitional problem, then, stands as follows. One position is that the term descent should be restricted to a rule of recruitment to corporate unilineal groups; the other is that the term should be defined as widely as possible and should include any genealogically-reckoned relationship with an ancestor. The latter alternative is chosen here, not because I believe that the theory of corporate unilineal groups has failed to produce significant generalisations,[1] but because Fortes's distinction between descent and filiation, altered to accommodate a more broad meaning of descent, does prove useful in the empirical analysis of group structure and composition in Mount Hagen. Earlier, I distinguished between 'the idioms in terms of which Hageners refer to the solidarity, continuity, and segmentations patterns of their social groups' and 'the rules which they say apply to processes of recruitment to these groups'. The former are couched at least partly in a way which enables us to call them descent-constructs, whereas the latter have to do with ties of filiation.

To justify this usage I must now present some of the Hageners' own ideas on kinship relations and the phrases which they apply to their social groups. As Salisbury has put it, following Leach, 'there should be an examination of different peoples' conception of the category "kinship" ' (1964:170). It is only after this has been done that one can say how far it may be useful to translate peoples' own ideas as 'descent-constructs', and how far such constructs are predominant in their conceptions of kinship relations.[2]

Melpa ideas about procreation provide a convenient departure-point for investigation of their concepts of kin-relationships in general, as well as the touchstone for their view of what kinship is. In English we refer to the act of 'bearing a child'. This idiom, derived from the fact that a mother carries her child in her womb, has its Melpa counterpart in the verb *mei*, which can be applied to the physical act of carrying something, to paying compensation for a killing (*wuə metemen*, 'they bear the man', i.e. give payments which can be used to obtain new wives for the victim's group and so replace the person they have lost with new children), and to the act of giving birth to a child. However, *mei* is applied to both sexes, so that in Melpa the father as well as the mother is said to 'bear' the child. This does not mean that Melpa speakers are unaware of, or deny, differences between the roles of the sexes in procreation! They distinguish between the father's initial work, i.e. his intercourse with the mother, and the mother's later work of carrying the child in her womb and giving birth to it.[3] As a result of intercourse a man's semen surrounds a woman's menstrual blood and forms a package (*kum ronom*). Several acts of intercourse are required to make a child, since the function of the semen, according to Hageners, is to bind the menstrual blood so that it can no longer flow in its monthly cycle, and a considerable quantity of semen is needed to fix the blood in this way.[4]

When the mother's belly is large, intercourse should stop, for otherwise the semen will now block the road along which the child must travel to be born. The child forms inside a kind of tissue in the womb. At first it is a *mel pim*, unformed and without limbs or orifices.[5] Mothers-to-be sometimes take care to wash frequently in streams, for this action, they say, helps to form their child's limbs.

Another term for procreation, in addition to the simple *mei*, is *kaklpa tii*, 'to straighten, or fashion, and obtain'. This refers to the process whereby children are physically made in the womb, and it is used predominantly in reference to the physical coalescence of semen and blood. Most frequently, I heard it employed in relation to putative male ancestors of particular groups: thus *Kawelka wamb kaklpa titim-e-nga ik teman-e*, 'the story of how the Kawelka group originated'. It can thus be contrasted with *mei*, when this is used specifically of the female action in bearing a child. Both terms contrast with a third, *etepa pindi*, 'to make and place', which refers to the action of ancestral ghosts in implanting a soul (*mini*) into a foetus which is newly formed. In a person's lifetime his *mini* appears as his reflection or shadow. It can slip out of him when he is asleep or suddenly frightened, and at his death, feeling that his body has become cold, it leaves him finally, 'goes outside', and becomes a ghost (*tipu* or *kor kui*). The *mini* may be implanted by either paternal or maternal ghosts or by both sets in concert, and each child has a new *mini* made for it: so far as I have established, there is no notion of conception being caused by the entry of a deceased spirit into a woman.

A child is thus thought to be physically formed by the conjunction of its father's semen and mother's blood and in some sense metaphysically quickened by its soul, which is bestowed upon it by ancestral ghosts. These ideas, relevant as they are to notions of filiation, do not so far carry us into the realm of descent-constructs. However, one Melpa informant (Ru, of Kawelka tribe) told me that agnatic male descendants of an ancestor are said to have his *ndating* (a word which is discussed below), and are known as 'men of one *ndating*'. Only sons take their father's *ndating* and pass it on to their sons in turn. When a daughter marries, it is her husband's *ndating* which makes children in her. The father's *ndating* shows in the son's body and head hair, his genitals, and in his manly ability to make speeches and fight.[6]

Another way of expressing this is to say that he has his father's 'bone' (*ombil*). A big-man's son is also expected to inherit his father's *ndating*. Here, then, the *ndating* is something which is particular to his father, not shared by the father's agnates. Such an idea, of course, has to be adjusted to the real world, in which sons are not always as capable as their fathers and vice-versa. If the former, people ask 'Did his father's *ndating* really bear him?'; if the latter, they say that his other dead kinsfolk have helped him to succeed.

This notion of *ndating*, which is recognised by Melpa-speakers generally, cannot quite be equated with their idea of semen (*noimb kopong*), since both male and female children are said to be made from a mixture of semen and mother's blood. It is clearly an idea which approximates to the anthropologist's analytical concept of patrilineal descent, although it differs from this in one respect. In descent theory the daughters of a man share his identity as a member of a descent group, although they do not transmit that identity to their children; whereas in Ru's formulation, which is exactly parallel to the Orokaiva concept of *ivo* as quoted by Schwimmer (cf. note 6), daughters do not even share their father's *ndating*. The reason for this slight disparity between the analytical concept of descent and the Hageners' concept of *ndating* is not far to seek. The concept of descent was developed by anthropologists as one of a number of terms intended to deal with jural entitlement to statuses obtained through kinship. It is thus a jural concept, as Fortes has stressed. The idea of *ndating*, however, like that of *ivo*, is a cultural dogma which expresses not only the notion of continuity in lineage membership but also the notion that males are different from females. It explains why only males can theoretically transmit lineage membership, by stating that they have a special physical strength which marks them off from females. In jural terms, it is quite true that in Hagen women are natal members of particular lineages and they retain this membership throughout their lives. But they do so *as women*, lacking the *ndating* which only males can possess.

In fact, however, Hageners' notions about *ndating* are not entirely clear, and they cannot be regarded as saliently expressed dogmas. Most informants speak only of a father's 'grease' (*kopong*, semen) and equate this with the 'grease' of his group. In one context a man of the Kawelka tribe declared that they should take the names of all the men of their sub-group who had gone to live with other groups and demand pay from the groups of their wives, at whose places they were living, for their *kopong* had been used to increase the numbers of alien groups. His suggestion was made at an annual tax-paying occasion when the group-membership of each person is symbolised by his paying tax along with his group mates. The context was thus rhetorical: the speaker was deploring the loss of men to his sub-group, which in fact is not very large, and was complaining that other groups had taken the men away. The Kawelka men living uxorilocally were acting like brides: just as a woman's group receives bridewealth for her, so, the speaker implied, should a man's group if he reverses the normal rule by living at his wife's place and procreating children for her kin. Commenting on this case, Ru declared that the reference to the men's 'grease' was really a reference to their *ndating* also, so that here *ndating* and *kopong* were equated.

Since the *ndating* of an ancestor is passed on continuously through his male descendants, the concept clearly encompasses more than a notion of patrifiliation: it is a notion of 'paternal substance' (cf. Wagner 1967) shared between agnatically related males. It correlates, however, with a stress on physical paternity. For example, a widow may take her children with her when she re-marries, and in some respects her second husband acts as their father, but their original paternity is not forgotten. If one of the children is a girl the new husband arranges her marriage and receives bridewealth for her; but he is supposed to cook a pig as a specific sacrifice to her original father's ghost, for otherwise the ghost, annoyed not to have received bridewealth for the daughter, will make her sick. The presumptive genitor of a child is usually the husband of the mother at the supposed time of conception, since normally it is considered that only the woman's husband has sufficiently regular access to her to induce conception. Even if the woman is estranged from her husband and living with another man, her lover cannot readily gain unequivocal custody of children she may bear to him unless she becomes divorced and he eventually pays a new sum of bridewealth for her to her kin. If a woman becomes pregnant at a time when she has no husband, a vigorous attempt is made, usually under the leadership of a big-man, to discover the presumed genitor and to obtain a standard bridewealth payment from him, thus converting him into a legitimate pater.

There is some pressure on widows to allow themselves to be 'reallocated' to a man of the same small group as their dead husband. The members of this group are likely to have contributed a good part of the bridewealth for the woman and feel they have a claim on her. If a widow passes in this way to a group-mate of her first husband, no problem about the group-identity of her children arises. However, she may choose instead to return to her natal kin or to remarry elsewhere. In such cases her sons are spoken of as 'being with' the *ndating* of a group other than their original one. Ru pictured the situation of a boy meeting his original father's brothers, and their telling him: 'Now you have gone to stay with the *ndating* of another group, but you should remember that your original *ndating* is with us. If you want to take part in ceremonial exchange (*moka*) you should come for part of your time at least and help us with ours.' A boy approached in this way can admit his agnates' claims if he wishes, but he need not always go back to join them as a group member.

I have argued so far that Melpa ideas about procreation reveal a concept of filiation which is clearly bilateral; but that, equally clearly, the contributions of the parents to the child's body are differentiated: the father provides 'grease', the mother 'blood'. Grease and blood are thus potentially contrasting symbols of male-ness and femaleness. 'Grease', transformed into the idea of *ndating*, is also a symbol of unity and continuity between agnatically related males. These ideas are reinforced by others which Melpa speakers sometimes make. Thus, a daughter has her mother's bones, blood, and 'breast grease' (milk, *aem kopong*), while a father's grease (i.e. semen) and strength make his sons. A son takes his mother's blood and drinks her milk, but the father's *ndating* makes his bones. Other informants also told me that a son has his father's disposition, *noman*, which men declare is 'single' and strong; whereas a daughter takes her mother's *noman*, a weak and 'multiple', i.e. unreliable, thing (cp. Wagner 1967:65). To explain the fact that some women have a strong *noman* men argue that sometimes an unborn child begins to become a male and develops a strong *noman*, but then changes and becomes female, retaining her male *noman*. (The opposite process, incidentally, could be invoked to explain cases of men with a weak *noman*, but men did not make this point to me.)

The function of all these contrasts is evidently to claim that men are superior to, and different from, women, a dogma similar to that which Meggitt has particularly stressed for the Enga (Meggitt 1964:219). But Melpa dogmas are not free from ambivalence. First, sons are thought to take their mother's blood. It is this blood which they share with their mother's kinsmen, and ties with mother's kin are socially important: correspondingly, mother's blood and cognatic or 'one blood' (*mema tenda*) ties are accorded some value in men's remarks. Second, after a child is born, its dependence on mother's milk for its growth and continuing health is fully recognised (milk can be described as *aem kopong*, 'breast grease', or simply as *aem*). Indeed 'payments for the mother's milk' form one category in the schedule of payments which should be made to a child's maternal kin. Hence ties with the mother are by no means entirely denigrated. Concomitantly the mother's male kin are often recognised as strong big-men who can help their sisters' sons in exchanges. Friendly relations are facilitated by the pattern of marrying into allied rather than major enemy groups, and this pattern may have had some influence on attitudes towards maternal kin. The Melpa seem to posit a less sharp opposition between paternal and maternal kin ties than do the Mae-Enga, whose view of themselves is that they marry their enemies rather than their allies (Meggitt 1964:218).

Just as the notion of 'grease' is made a symbol both for immediate filiation and for the physical identity of close agnates with each other, so the idea of 'sharing blood' is extended beyond the immediate mother-child relationship. Cross-cousins are spoken of as *mema tenda*, because they share the blood of a single grandmother, distributed among all her descendants (Figure 1). In the figure, those

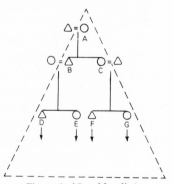

Figure 1. 'One blood' ties

enclosed in the dotted triangle are said to share blood; and the triangle could be prolonged another generation or so until the blood of the original ancestress is said to be 'finished' and her descendants no longer regard themselves as related. The 'one blood' idiom in this context thus refers to a range of cognatic relationships

traced back to a single female ancestor. As such it effectively contrasts with the *ndating* idiom. But the important further point to
make here is that this contrast is dramatically broken down in
expressions which refer to *agnatic* kin as sharing blood and to
segments within a clan as 'one blood people' (*mema tenda wamb*).
People are aware that this latter usage is loose, and one informant[7]
explicitly stated that members of the same group should not be
called 'people of one blood', but 'people of one father' (*tepam
tenda*). But in terms of social action this confusion of idioms is
highly significant. It enables Melpa speakers sometimes to argue
that their groups are agnatic, as distinct from cognatic, and at
other times to refer to them as simply cognatic, with the implication
that agnatic and cognatic ties are in any case similar. The usefulness
of this double idiom, which alternately separates and equates one
father and one blood ties, is that it allows Hageners to maintain
both that the males in their groups 'are' agnatically related and that
persons can obtain membership of such groups through their
mothers as well as their fathers.[8] How these assertions are related
to actual cases of affiliation will be shown in chapter six. Here I
continue with discussion of *mema tenda*, 'one blood', ties as a preliminary to outlining Melpa ideas about group affiliation in general.

Cognatically related one blood people may not marry each
other.[9] The paradigm which Melpa speakers usually think of in
this context is as follows. Female members of a group marry out
into other groups, and their blood, here conceived of as blood
shared by their group, 'makes branches' (*paka-maka etim*)[10] in their
affinal groups, for it is transmitted to their children and by these to
their children in turn. My informant Ru instanced a relationship
with a FFFZDDS, pointed out that this is beyond the usual degree
of recognised genealogical kinship and that for this reason there
is no standard kin term which is applied to the category, but added
that nevertheless it can be recognised as a kin relationship and that
it can also be used for establishing exchange partnerships:

> from a single female ancestor one line has come down here straight to
> ourselves, while of the line that went out from here you are now the
> living descendants, so we are one blood people. We are not simply friends,

we are people of one stock. We are of one root of blood, which has been carried out, out, and out, until now the place is full. You must not think of this place, then, simply as a place of friends, for you understood that this was the place of your own blood that you were coming to, so now we want to make a gift to you before you leave us.[11]

In addition to showing how one blood ties are in practice calculated, this text indicates that a distinction is made between exchange relations based on kinship and those based solely on friendship between non-relatives. It implies that once a kin tie has been demonstrated, persons feel they *should* make a present to their visitor, so that the presumed fact of sharing blood converts a person from a stranger into an exchange partner. A joke which I was told played on this point, telling how a man met a woman, who was a complete stranger to him, on the road, as she was returning from a pig-festival with a leg of pork. Wanting the pork, the man accosted her as 'cousin'. She asked what he meant. He said 'You and I are of one blood, we're distant cousins. Our parents were separated during warfare and went their different ways and so you and I have never met before, but I have been told we are definitely kin to each other.' 'Oh', said the woman, 'My cousin!' and she gave him the leg of pork as a present which he happily accepted.

As implied by this cautionary tale, second cousins who do not belong to the same group or live near to each other may remain strangers and unaware of their genealogical links; and this may help to explain why the classification of such cousins in Melpa kinship terminology is rather uncertain.

I have discussed Melpa kin terms elsewhere,[12] and, although this chapter is about kinship, it would not be relevant to the wider theme of the book to present a detailed analysis of the terminology here. The classification of cousins, however, is relevant to my theme, in the following way. First cross-cousins are distinguished from parallel cousins, who are equated with siblings. They are *pelpam*, which I gloss as 'cousin', as opposed to *øngin/kimun*, = same-sex/opposite-sex sibling. This cross/parallel distinction, clear as it is when applied to first cousin relationships, is not applied consistently to all cousin relationships involving longer strings of genealogical nodes. If all the nodes connecting an ego and an alter in a string are of the same sex, then there is no ambiguity: the relationship is classified as parallel, and sibling terms are used between ego and alter. In the case of all other strings there is often some doubt in informants' minds whether to apply a 'cousin' or a 'sibling' (i.e. a cross or a parallel) term. At first, when investigating this problem, I thought that usage would turn out to be consistent if I could discover the rules informants were actually following. Further discussion led me to suspect that there was genuine uncertainty over the classification of these kin types; and in 1969 Ru, my intellectualist informant, himself generalised that the question 'What do you call your second cousins?' was 'hard to resolve' (ik-e tikrɔk enem). However, most of the usages which I in fact obtained were either Iroquois-cross in type or contextual conversions of Iroquois-cross into parallel categories.[13] No informant gave responses which regularly followed Dravidian rules. Particular usages are likely to be explained by informants in terms of whether the kinsfolk in question maintain exchange relations with one or live nearby. Thus Ru told me that sibling terms are most likely to be used if ego and alter know, and live close by to, each other; and he gave me the case of FFZSch: if these live near to ego, and *a fortiori* if they are actually current members of the same group as ego, he calls them siblings. The rationale for this is interesting: if the FFZ had been a man, then her *son's* children would ordinarily have been of ego's group anyway; hence if they live nearby they may be called siblings out of courtesy. By contrast FFZ daughter's children are less likely to be called siblings, for the same reasoning cannot be applied to them. They are *mema tenda* people simply, and one perhaps does not use a specific kin term for them at all.[14] This example is interesting, as it adumbrates conceptual reasons for the easy incorporation of sister's sons into their mother's group. The sex contrast between brothers and sisters is neutralised and the sister is regarded potentially as a 'sociological male'. Correspondingly with these usages, the children of one's first cross-cousins can be addressed by 'child' terms, and they may reciprocate with 'parent' or 'parent's sibling' terms.[15]

This example, then, has brought us directly to the question of recruitment to groups. In Hagen persons belong to an elaborate set of progressively more inclusive named groups, and I have labelled these group levels, from the largest to the smallest, as: great-tribe, tribe, tribe-section, clan, clan-section, sub-clan, sub-sub-clan, and lineage (cf. *The rope of moka*, chapter two). Each lineage is a segment of a particular sub-sub-clan, each sub-sub-clan is similarly part of a sub-clan, and so on, up the segmentary scale. Further, the different group levels carry characteristic functions: the tribe (which corresponds to the level of group which other writers have labelled 'phratry', e.g. Meggitt, Reay, and Cook, on the Mae-Enga, Kuma, and Manga respectively) is the maximal group whose members feel they should have some unity in warfare and in holding festivals; the clan is in most cases the exogamous unit, is important in *moka* exchanges[16] and was previously important in warfare; sub-clansmen consider they have an obligation to assist one another with bridewealth payments; and lineage mates most regularly expect to inherit land rights from one another. Particular descriptive idioms are applied to the different levels also. Thus the clan is spoken of as *tepam tenda*, (descendants of) 'one father', (or as 'people of one blood', as we have seen), the sub-clan is *manga rapa*, 'a men's house group', and the lineage is *tepam-kangemal*, 'a father and his sons'. Other idioms apply to the whole range of group levels; thus *mbo tenda*, 'one stock', or *mbi tenda*, *reklaep tenda*, 'one name, one line', which can be used for a unit as large as a tribe or as small as a lineage. In addition, groups at all levels are regularly paired together as allies. So, for example, one regularly hears the Tipuka and Kawelka tribes referred to as *Tipuka Kawelka rakl*, 'the Tipuka-Kawelka pair'. Now individual members of lineages are usually classifiable as either *wuə-nt-mei* or *amb-nt-mei*, 'man-bearing' or 'woman-bearing'.[17] Man and woman in this contrasted pair are not husband and wife but brother and sister, and the idiom relates to the fact that, although a sister normally moves into patrivirilocal residence at marriage, if she subsequently returns to her own natal group and brings her children with her, they can become *amb-nt-mei* members of her group. If her sons stay at her

natal place and become *amb-nt-mei* members *their* children in turn
become *wuə-nt-mei*, 'man-bearing' members, just as are those who
are putatively descended from a longer genealogical string of male
group members. These are the two main formal terms relating to
the recruitment-status of group-members, (although they are not
of course the only ways in which Hageners reckon continuity of
group membership),[18] and the fact that the children of individual
amb-nt-mei members become *wuə-nt-mei* indicates that the idiom of
recruitment is couched in terms of immediate filiation, not of
descent.

It is important also to notice that these two terms refer to consanguineal kinship relations rather than to any other principle. It is
sons and sisters' sons of current male members who are expected
to perpetuate the group; and their jural position is theoretically
different from that of others. For example, an uxorilocally resident
husband has no good prior claims to membership of his wife's
natal group. He may, especially if he is forceful and successful in
exchanges, gain *de facto* recognition as a member of his wife's local
community, but he is less likely to obtain full membership of her
clan. Those who obtain, or attempt to obtain, acceptance as members of a clan group to which they do not have a direct filial tie
can be described by a number of idioms. They are *təpa røndi wuə*,
'taken and (re-)planted man', *təpa mundi wuə*, 'taken and made-to-
be man', *təpa pindi wuə*, 'taken and placed man', *omba mul wuə*, 'an
arrival', and *eta*, which is one of the terms for a refugee.[19] The first
phrase, *təpa røndi wuə*, is the one I have heard used most frequently,
and, like the others, it has a latently pejorative edge to it. The first
three phrases all refer to the act of a sponsor in changing the group
affiliation of a man and giving him a place to live at in his own
settlement. That the incomer is spoken of as 'planted' in his new
area is important also. Whole groups are often referred to as of one
stock (*mbo tenda*) or one root (*wamb pukl*), an idiom for common
ancestry which is clearly derived from the model of vegetable
growth of trees and plants in general, and which reflects the empirical
importance of residing continuously and working in an area for
making good one's claims to membership of the group which

owns it. This idiom shows also in ideas about the position of sister's sons, who are explicitly exempted from the category of *təpa røndi wuə* when they join their mother's brother's group, and are regarded as having a definite potential claim to his land, which they can make good by giving their allegiance to his clan. A mother's brother sometimes emphasises his close connection with his sister and her children by pulling at his chest and saying '[these children are fed by] my breast' (*nanga aem*). Ongka, a major big-man of Kawelka tribe, gave a figurative explanation of the sister's son's position, as follows:

> There are big trees of the forest, *kraep* trees [*Nothofagus*], with moss hanging from them. Birds which have eaten the berries of other trees alight on the branches of the *kraep* and deposit seeds on the moss in their faeces. Later the seeds sprout, but they have no ground of their own to grow in and so they wind their way down the tree in vines to reach the ground. It is especially seeds of the *koma* and *kipa* trees which grow in this way as parasites on the big *kraep* tree. We liken this situation to that of our sisters' sons (*amb kangemal*). Men who quarrel with their kin and go to stay with another group we call 'replanted men' (*təpa røndi wuə*). But a sister's son is like a strong *kraep* tree. If he comes to our place and makes a garden or builds a house there we say we must not be cross, we must let him do this. Sisters' sons are not like *koma* and *kipa* seeds which grow on the *kraep* tree, they are like the tree itself with roots in its own ground. It is replanted men who are like *koma* and *kipa*. To other men, including affines, we may say no, you can't make gardens or a house here, and when he says 'Where shall I go then?' we fight. But the sister's son says he has come to his mother's ground and we agree to this.

Here the sister's son is thought of as having roots (*pukl*) in his mother's land, just as he has a kin-tie (also spoken of as a *pukl*) with his mother's people.

This relationship between the sister's son and his mother's people is set into the context of payments which should customarily be made between affines. One side of the relationship is that which I have delineated so far: the claims which the sister's son has on his mother's brothers. The other is the set of claims which the mother's brother has on the sister's son and his father. A father should make a number of payments on behalf of his children to their maternal kinsfolk. The general reason given for these payments is that they ensure a good disposition (*noman*) on the part of the affines. Were the payments not made, the affines would be angry and would call on their dead relatives to visit sickness on their sister's children. A man thus safeguards his children's health by making the payments. When his children grow up they may begin their career in the exchange system by themselves making prestations to their maternal kin in order further to ensure that their 'skin is good', skin condition being taken as a sign of health or sickness. Again, if a husband fails to make these payments, his wife, identifying with her kin, may decamp to her natal place, taking her children with her. Her kin may encourage her to do this, in expectation of eliciting payment from the husband. The payments are thus supposed to ensure for a man both his children's health and his effective custody of them. They are not always made nowadays, and some men claim that the Christian missions disapprove of them. Most men, however, make some gifts under this rubric to their affines, perhaps only for their first child; big-men may make much larger gifts and turn these into ongoing reciprocal *moka* exchanges with their wives' people, especially if one of the latter is a big-man also.

Payments are customarily made when a child's hair is first cut, and when a child is weaned. The latter payment is called *wakl te kng*, 'child faeces pig' (or, in the Central Melpa area near to Mount Hagen township, *maepkla kng*). Both haircutting and weaning indicate that the child has successfully grown, and payments should be made for the mother's milk which has nurtured it. If a woman bears a number of sons, when these are grown up her contribution to the strength of her husband's group may be made the rationale for larger, concerted gifts to her natal clansmen, and these again become part of protracted *moka* exchanges. At a more general level, pairs of groups which are closely allied and inter-married speak of themselves as *apa-pel*, 'mother's brothers, sister's sons, and cross-cousins', to each other.

It can be seen from this brief outline that the mother's brother-sister's son relationship is as important in Hagen as it is in the classic

African cases which prompted Fortes to produce his distinction between descent and complementary filiation. An element, however, which Hageners stress and which perhaps appears with less force in African examples, is the requirement that payments should be made to the mother's brother and the idea that these can be converted into mutual exchanges of wealth objects between the sister's son and his mother's people. It is worthwhile to turn aside from our examination of Melpa concepts at this point, and compare them with those of the Mae-Enga, their western neighbours, and the Daribi, a people who live close to the Southern Highlands and who have been described by Wagner in his book *The curse of Souw* (1967).

Among the Mae-Enga, who appear to have a highly developed patrilineal system of descent,[20] close kinsmen in the mother's clan nevertheless retain an interest in their sister's children, just as they do in Hagen. Mae emphasise the acquisition of a spirit by a child from its father's clan ghosts, while its body and corporeal vitality (Meggitt 1965:168, 174) are maternally derived. Hence, in Mae thinking, payments should be made to compensate maternal kin whenever a person's body is harmed. The maternal kin are, in a sense, owners of their sister's children's bodies for all time, despite the fact that the children are usually affiliated to their father's, not their mother's clan. This part of Mae dogma is reminiscent of Daribi ideas, although Wagner explicitly denies that the Daribi should be regarded as 'patrilineal'. Daribi speak of maternal kin as 'base' or 'cause' people (*pagebidi*). The *pagebidi* must be adequately paid if a father is to secure custody of his children and their affiliation to his clan. Daribi clansmen, and especially sets of male siblings within the clan, 'share wealth', i.e. contribute to each other's child payments, which oppose the claims of *pagebidi* and recruit the children to the clan. This definite recruitment function of the payments to maternal kin, which forms an important feature of Wagner's model of Daribi social structure, seems to be less prominent in the case of both the Mae-Enga and the Melpa; although I have already mentioned that non-payment may lead to a mother's removing her children among Melpa, and Meggitt mentions

(1965:177) that men try to maintain claims over their children by a divorced wife who is living with her own people through continuing 'to make injury compensations' on the children's behalf. Payments to maternal kin can thus function to secure a father's rights over children, just as they do among Daribi. Does Wagner's Daribi model apply, then, to Mae and Melpa as well? His model is based on the propositions 'exchange defines' and 'consanguinity relates'. A child is related by 'substance' to both of its parents, and this holds whatever group the child is recruited to. In addition maternal kin, especially mother's brothers and father, are 'owners' of the child, since it is said to be their blood which the child shares. The father's semen helps to make a child, hence he has a claim on it, but the claims of blood have to be opposed by special payments. It is particularly these payments which Wagner refers to in his proposition 'exchange defines'.

This recruitment function of the Daribi payments is not the only possible function of payments to maternal kin in other Highlands societies. The Mae, as I have mentioned, accept that a person has a permanent tie with his mother's clansmen because his flesh is derived from them (the flesh being opposed to his agnatically-acquired spirit). Thus, whenever his flesh is harmed, he must pay compensation to them, for they are its 'owners'. The clan affiliation of the man may not be in question at all, especially as payments are continued into adulthood and indeed are completed only after his death when final compensation is paid to his maternal kin. Similarly, in Hagen people emphasise both that payments are made in return for mother's milk which has made a child grow and that payments ensure a child's continuing health, i.e. that maternal kin will not ask their ghosts to send sickness to the child. Neither of these functions has specifically to do with recruitment, although they are, in a general sense, to do with opposing the claims and influence of maternal kin. The possibility, however, of maternal kin recruiting sisters' children to their group is a real one, as Melpa concepts of filiation reveal.

Wagner argues that 'patriliny' among the Daribi 'is only an idiom and we cannot speak of descent here' (p. 76). Here he is

regarding descent as a rule of recruitment. Since the Daribi recruitment rule is not phrased in descent terms but in terms of the father's
option to 'buy off' the claims of the mother's brother, 'patriliny' is
no more than a contingent result of recruitment-payments. It
does not in itself have the jural force which it is said to have in some
African lineage systems.

If one were to free the term descent, as Scheffler has done
(Scheffler 1966), from what Wagner calls its 'loaded' implications,
i.e. free it from its 'strict' meaning as a rule of recruitment (Wagner
1967:xxvii), the objection to speaking of descent-constructs among
the Daribi would disappear. Unlike the term consanguinity, which
refers simply to the 'sharing of blood', 'descent' focuses attention
on the transmission and continuity of kin relationships from specific
ancestors over a period of generations. It is for this reason that I
shall retain Barnes's phrase 'the dogma of descent' (Barnes 1962) in
this book. I do not mean to imply by this usage that descent is
important as a jural rule of recruitment to groups among the Melpa,
but simply that it is a useful term for referring to Melpa ideas of the
transmission of kin ties within named groups; and that it is an
idiom in terms of which the unity and continuity of such groups are
symbolised. Both of these conditions may also be true of the Daribi.
Moreover, the term 'filiation' is also useful, as a means of referring
to Melpa idioms of recruitment, in which the point of reference is
the immediate parent of a child, rather than the child's connection
with an ancestor.

So far I have outlined Melpa notions of procreation and shown
how these relate to concepts of extended kin ties and of modes of
recruitment to groups. I have not attempted to say whether *the*
system *is* strongly or weakly patrilineal or even whether agnatic
attitudes are pervasive or otherwise. Such enterprises, as others have
shown (e.g. Lewis 1965, Barnes 1967), are hazardous, and potentially
useful only if they are undertaken in conjunction with some
explanatory hypothesis (as in Meggitt 1965). I have been concerned
only to argue that it is appropriate to retain the terms descent and
filiation, promulgated as a linked pair by Fortes and used extensively
by ethnographers of African lineage systems, to refer on the one

hand to ideas about group continuity and on the other to rules of recruitment. I realise that my usage is scarcely consistent with the specific models of lineage systems developed by Africanist anthropologists, in which a person's group-membership is fixed by his descent, while he is distinguished from his descent group mates by his complementary filiation. In my model, by contrast, a person's group-membership is obtained through filiation and group unity is symbolised through an assertion of common descent. The disjunction between the bilaterality of filiation and the unilineality of descent is mediated, in Melpa usage, by the equation of 'one father' with 'one blood' ties.

Although, because of analytical complications of this kind, I shall not attempt finally to label the Melpa as either strongly or weakly patrilineal, I do wish to suggest further that there is one cultural sphere in which we could profitably compare Highlands societies in terms of their stress or lack of stress on agnatic ties, and that is the sphere of beliefs about the influence of ghosts on the living. One of the implicit assumptions made by many social anthropologists since Durkheim wrote his *Elementary forms of the religious life*, is that religious beliefs have a close connection with actual social relationships. A sociological version of this assumption, stated strongly, would be that religious activities symbolise and support important principles of social structure; a psychological version might be that religion depends on the ability and propensity of the human mind to make projections and that the raw material for these projections is to be found in social relationships. Neither of these versions, of course, gives or is intended to give a full 'explanation' of religion, yet both give us at least an approach to the problem of understanding religious beliefs and symbols. If, then, agnation were important as 'a principle of social structure' in a society, we might expect to find this fact in some way reflected in religious cults (cf. Lienhardt 1961:135). Indeed, to be more accurate, we might expect to find that the native concept of 'descent' or 'agnation' *is* ultimately couched in mystical or religious terms, as Salisbury (1964) finds among the Siane. What do we find among the Hageners, and do they contrast in any respects with the Mae-Enga, who appear to emphasise patriliny? Rather than attempting to give an outline of Hagen religious ideas in general (for which see Strauss and Tischner 1962), I shall pin the inquiry down to statements about sickness sent by ghosts.

Melpa speakers consider that ghosts are of considerable background importance to the living. They give support or hindrance, ensure success or failure of enterprises, visit sickness or health on their kinsfolk. In the past invocations were made to ghosts at a whole range of public and private occasions of sacrifice. The public invocations are no longer held, owing to disapproval expressed by evangelists of the Lutheran Mission, but specimen examples were spoken for my benefit by informants (not without some trepidation, for they were unaccompanied by the customary sacrifices and the ghosts could be expected to be annoyed at being summoned for nothing). It was traditionally important men (the big-men) who made prayers on behalf of their group, and correspondingly prayers were particularly addressed to the ghosts of dead big-men, asking them to help their kin just as they were supposed to have done in life. In one specimen invocation (given to me by Ru), an appeal to guarantee success in a range of activities was made severally to ancestors of current small lineages within one section of a clan, to ghosts of agnates of these lineages who had left no male descendants, to the ghost of a non-agnatic member, and also to a pair of dead cross-cousins of senior living men, who, as neighbours of the group and as big-men, had in their lifetime helped the group in its exchanges with others. All the ghosts invoked were at the generational level of fathers of living old men. The prayer ended with an invitation to little spirits of good luck (*kor kil køi*) at the places of affines or maternal kin, and ghosts of children of the group who had died, to come and share in the pork provided for them. All the ghosts should come and 'walk at the head' of their people, and help them to kill enemies, make exchanges, and obtain wives.

It is clear, then, if we may judge from this example, that sacrifice was not made simply to founders of lineages within an agnatic lineage system. The ghosts of big-men of one's group were singled out for mention, whether they were lineage founders or not; and ghosts of cognatic and even affinal kin could also be mentioned. In divining for the causes of sickness, a diviner similarly extends his questioning to a range of close bilateral kin. (The most common method of divining is to push a divining stick into the floor or wall of one's house and to call the names or kin relationship of suspected ghosts. When the right one is called, he or she is supposed to seize the stick and hold it tight, and the diviner then asks the reason for the ghost's displeasure in sending sickness to its living kinsman and what colour, sex, and size of pig it requires as a sacrifice.) One man of the Kawelka group, himself a ritual expert, generalised:

> We people of Hagen are bitten by sickness, and we say it is our mother who sends this. The reason is as follows. When we first think of having children we lie with our wives in the bush, we lie with them all the time and they become pregnant. We men watch them while they are pregnant, and when they bear children we say this is dirty, we find some of our men-friends and we go away, leaving the mothers to it. The mother looks after the child and cleans its urine from its leg, gives it the breast all the time, carries it about as she harvests the sweet potato, and she feels the pain of this. She takes it to the gardens and brings it back, all day and every day, until it is big. She may bear only a few children and then die, or she may bear many children, and die when she is old and sits beside the fire. 'Your father neglected you, and if you wanted to touch the fire or fall in the water or play in the hot sun I saw to you and brought you back, and now you have grown big under my care. Your father had nothing to do.' This is what the dead mother says, and so we say that it is our mothers only who send the sickness. They have hard work in bringing us up, and when they die they are frustrated because of this, and send us sickness.

The same informant emphasised that it is one's dead parents who in general are likely to make one sick (thus including the father as well as the mother), giving as his reason that 'in life it is our real parents who punish us, and so who else could it be that sends sickness to us after they are dead?'[21]

This informant had a special reason for stressing the likelihood of sickness being sent by a mother's ghost. He and his elder brother had deprived their mother of a large leg of pork which she wished to eat not long before she died and they presumed she was upset about this, perhaps had even died of frustration, and thus was likely to punish them with sickness for their misdemeanour. It is interesting to note that he often acts as a diviner on behalf of members of his small group, and in a list of diagnoses which he gave me matrilateral ghosts are as well represented as patrilateral. I have obtained lists from other diviners and heard of isolated cases as well, and the ascription of sickness to matrilateral ghosts occurs in these also. Usually the ghosts are closely related to the victim. The victim may well have known them as living persons, and reasons for sickness are sought either in past disagreements between victim and ghost or present trouble between the victim and a kinsman or associate. Ghosts may be jealous: one idea is that a brother who dies before he is grown up and can marry is jealous of any of his brothers who succeed in doing so, and may send sickness to, or even kill, their children. Ghosts can also make persons sick out of pity: for example, in one instance a man cooked a pig belonging to his old father, and the ghost of the father's father, sorry for his son, was said to have visited sickness on the grandson.[22]

The Appendix lists some details of diagnoses given by diviners. Part (a) cites the diagnoses which my Kawelka informant gave to me. Part (b) is a comparative list from a ritual expert of the Ulka tribe in the Nebilyer Valley south of Mount Hagen (the expert spoke Gawigl, which is closely related to Melpa). This part refers to divinations done for adult married men only, since, according to the expert himself, 'it is married men with children who are most likely to get sick', and he declared that he did not divine on behalf of women and children. His statement is intriguing. Perhaps it is married men with children, whose social obligations are more complicated than those of young men, that are most likely to interpret their sickness as due to their own or a ghost's 'frustrated anger' (*popokl*). It is also, we may note, they who are most likely to own pigs which can be used for sacrifices to appease the ghost responsible for a sickness. Experts receive a fee, primarily in pork, but sometimes also in shells (or Australian currency nowadays). The expert here was a middle-aged man of the group, who had begun to divine after the death of the previous expert (who was of a different sub-group) in about 1960; my list was taken in 1965, but refers only to divinations which had taken place within the preceding year.

What seems to be significant in these ascriptions is not so much the laterality of the ghost's relationship to the victim, but the fact that the ghost is usually a past member of the victim's domestic group. Further, children, as well as siblings, wives, and parents of the victim may cause sickness: clearly we are not simply dealing with a prolongation of authority relationships after death, but with a complex of imputed frustrations, perhaps reflecting guilt feelings on the part of the victim which are also known to the diviner. Meggitt (1965:172) has commented on a similar pattern which he found among the Mae-Enga, and explains it cogently in terms of conflicts which can arise within the immediate family of a man. (His discussion does not, however, cover cases in which the ghosts of children who died young attack their parents or siblings. Parents, of course, have to socialise children from an early age and 'frustration' can be imputed to children for that reason as well as on the assumption that the ghosts of dead children are upset because they have not been granted a full life.) Meggitt points out that among the Mae it is the father who controls his wife and children and argues that hence it is reasonable that the father's ghost also 'is seen as minatory' (p. 172). He notes that informants ascribe malignity 'to the ghosts of the mother and siblings' as well, and that this seems to stand in contrast with relationships between the living, in which mothers and siblings are usually supportive rather than punitive. From actual cases, however, he finds that it is agnatic ghosts who are most likely to launch attacks. The fact that the mother is *said* to attack he ascribes to 'the strength of the identification of the woman with the agnatic group into which she marries'. For the Melpa, as we have seen, such a structural explanation may be unnecessary, since ghosts are held to attack out of anger or frustration and a mother's ghost is expected to be angry because of disappointments in her lifetime. Moreover the cases in the Appendix suggest that the mother is held to attack fairly frequently. The material in the two tables is not exactly comparable, since (a) does not give statements of frequencies with which sickness was ascribed, and (b) does not state whether the parents of the victim were alive or not. Hence attempting to sum up the tables may not be profitable. But it is clear, at any rate, that the mother appears often as a cause of sickness in (a) and rather less often, but still as frequently as most other categories, in (b). (In (a) the mother is the most frequently cited single category, in (b) the father; but one should note also the joint category mother plus father.) Among the Mae the mother seems to be cited less often (Meggitt 1965:174); instead the father and siblings predominate.

On two counts, then, the Melpa cult of ghosts appears to lack an agnatic emphasis: prayers and sacrifices are not especially directed towards putative lineage founders, and both paternal and maternal ghosts are regarded as important in influencing sickness and health.

In conclusion, the basic paradigm underlying Melpa statements about descent is that of the supposed physical contributions of the two sexes to the creation of a child. From the idea that the father provides semen and the mother blood, the two dogmas of 'one father' and 'one blood' relationships are elaborated. Both dogmas can be used to refer to named groups, to which all Melpa-speakers belong, although the 'one father' idiom is most prevalent. A juxta-position of ideas is found in the sphere of recruitment also, in the phrases 'man-bearing' and 'woman-bearing' which refer to the kind of filiative tie a person has with his group.

The next chapter turns from the general discussion of kinship to the particular examination of origin myths and group segmentation in one tribe, the Kawelka.

CHAPTER 2

THE KAWELKA

In this chapter my main concern is to compare the terms in which Hageners refer to their groups with specific facts about group composition in a single tribe, beginning with an account of the tribe's origin myth, and proceeding from this to consideration of the relationship between genealogies and group segments. My argument is that certain kinds of genealogical statement must be looked on as reflecting 'structure' rather than 'composition', as expansions of the descent idioms which are used to conceptualise group structure rather than accurate accounts of how groups were founded in the past. Such an argument is scarcely novel; indeed, a disjunction between genealogy and demographic fact is implied in much of the writing on African lineage systems. The Nuer, for example, are clippers, patchers, and telescopers of genealogies (cf. Evans-Pritchard 1940: 246). In the present case, however, there is a further point to be made: that, in addition to the descent idiom, which provides them with a set of elements which they can manipulate to make structural models of their groups, Hageners also use a functional idiom, which explains to them what the smaller group subdivisions are for and why they came into being. This idiom gives them an alternative way of talking about groups, separate from their descent constructs, and I suggest that it thus helps to bridge the conceptual gap between mythological genealogies which relate to the foundation of the main segments in each tribe, and genealogies closer to demographic facts which indicate the relations of persons to one another within small lineages. The idiom is that of the 'men's house group' (*manga rapa*). I shall look first, then, at the group's origin myth, and later at some details of the constitution of its smaller segments.

'Kawelka' (Kaulka, Kauliga are alternative spellings)[1] is the name of a tribe whose men live chiefly on the mountainous slopes north of the Sepik-Wahgi Divide within the Mount Hagen Sub-District, in what since 1962 has been Dei Local Government Council area (Map 1). In 1964 the Kawelka numbered about 860 persons, including women and children co-resident with the male adult members (Chapter 3, Table 1). In the last twenty years some of the Kawelka have re-colonised an area which their tribe occupied before, many miles away from their present main territory, in the Wahgi Valley.

The Kawelka are not a large tribe by Hagen standards. A few tribes in the Central and Western Melpa areas reach sizes of 5-7,000 people, and the segmentation pattern of these is correspondingly more complicated than that of the Kawelka. An overall average size for Melpa tribes is c. 1,060 persons; within Dei Council the figure is 820. These averages are reduced by the fact that a few tribes have shrunk to a very small size, sometimes to fewer than 100 persons. In the Northern Melpa area (Dei Council plus some Baiyer and Jimi Valley groups) there were two tribes in 1964-5 with 2-3,000 persons; four with 1-2,000; and thirteen within the range of 68 to 1,000. (These figures include inmarried wives and children and exclude natal female members who have married into a tribe other than their own.)

Gross overall population density within Dei Council is not high by comparison with some other parts of Hagen Sub-District or the Mae-Enga and Chimbu areas (Brookfield and Brown 1963; Meggitt 1965). It amounted in 1964-5 to only 67.81 persons per square mile (with a population of 14,323 persons in an area of 2,112 square miles). Since 1965 Melpa-speaking groups in the Jimi Valley have joined Dei, making the Council population up to about 16,000 persons. Population is relatively sparse in the Jimi, so this addition has probably lowered the gross density further. Tracts of forested land in the Jimi and stretches of sometimes marshy land in the Wahgi within Dei are unoccupied because of malaria or cultivation problems. Effective

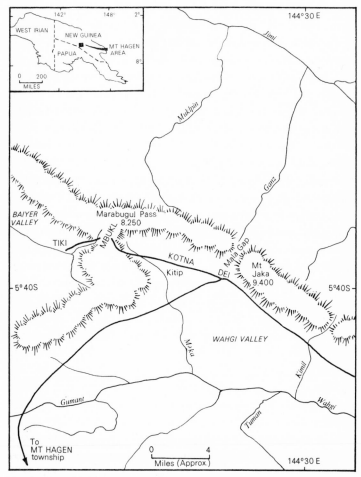

Map 1. Site of field station (Mbukl) within the Hagen Sub-District (adapted
from Australian Geographical Series 1 : 1000000)

density in the territory of the Kawelka is probably between eighty and a hundred persons per square mile, not very different from the average density for the Central Melpa area (in the early 1960s) of 118.1 persons. The Kawelka do not consider themselves to be *en bloc* short of land, although certain sub-groups have from time to time found themselves in difficulty and men living in the re-colonised area in 1969 became embroiled in a dispute with men of a neighbouring segment of the large Ndika tribe, which was ostensibly over land. The development of cash cropping, which requires garden land to be removed from the ordinary cultivation processes and to be planted with semi-permanent coffee trees, has in recent years increased both people's awareness of the material value of land claims and the possibility of land shortages. Most of my material on group composition was collected in 1964, before these problems were serious. It will be interesting to see what effect they will have on ideas about recruitment of persons to groups in the next few years (post-1970). Here we may note that the apparent lack of overall land pressure and concomitant inheritance problems (until, perhaps, very recently) may well have enabled the Kawelka and other Melpa groups to maintain flexible attitudes to the incorporation of 'outsiders'. This does not, however, explain why they should want to maintain such attitudes nor why they favour particular categories of persons rather than others. The answer to the first problem is, of course, that where land is not scarce people are valued because they can swell the group's strength (Reay 1967:14) or can be of advantage to individual big-men. The second question I relate to features of kinship structure and values which seem to be common in the New Guinea Highlands, viz. a stress on brother-sister ties and the importance of the mother's brother-sister's son relationship. (I am not arguing that these are in any way immutable or irreducible features, but that they appear, with variations, and are empirically important in a number of Highlands societies.)

I begin discussion of the Kawelka material by looking at versions of the Kawelka origin-myth which defines the group's *mi* or mystical divination-substance, and at other assertions about the definition and inter-relationship of segments within the tribe. The formal segmentary paradigm of sub-groups within Kawelka is given in Figure 2, down to the level of sub-sub-clans. Below this level are what I call lineages, sets of persons described as 'the sons of' a particular named

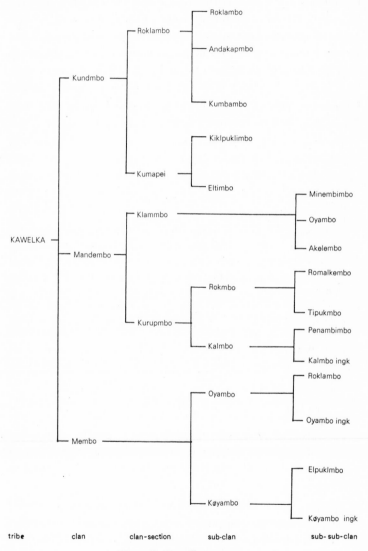

Figure 2. Kawelka segments

ancestor. Each sub-sub-clan usually comprises two or more of such lineage sets. I give examples of lineages later.

Before discussing how each of these apparent segmentary levels is defined and described, I shall give the tribe's origin-myth, in order to see how this relates to the segmentary paradigm.

A full version of the myth was not given to me until 1969. The version I received in 1964-5 began with an ancestor of the group arriving from the Wahgi area to the Kawelka's current main territory. In 1969 Ongka, the Kawelka Local Government Councillor, told me that this version had begun in the middle of the story only and he gave the earlier part, as follows.

> The Kawelka origin-place (*kona wingndi*) is at Kimbapukl, close to Keltiga [which is a few miles out of Hagen in the Nebilyer Valley]. Kimbapukl is a little hill, topped with red earth (*kela møi*: men who are on their home territory say 'I am on my own red ground'). At this place was a *wuə mam* (large man, old man, ancestor). His son fell sick and the old man had no pigs with which to make a sacrifice. He hunted for bush rats (*kui kuimbuk*) and cooked these, near to a tall limbum tree. The son saw an old man crawling down this tree head first, like a *konda* snake. He pointed the old man out to his father, but the father could not see him and thought the son was lying, and he went off to the bush to relieve himself. The spirit visitor then came over to the son and said 'Boy, what is it you're cooking?' 'We're cooking some rats' he replied. 'Why are the two of you not cooking your best female pig?' the visitor said. 'In future if you are cooking meat as a sacrifice and a cordyline leaf (*nde køya omong*) falls on it, you will know that what you are doing is true [i.e. that the sacrifice is heeded by ancestors]. Now go and tell your father this.' The visitor took two large cordyline leaves, bound them together, and placed them on the cooking pit [an earth oven]. 'Tell your father' he said 'that I don't eat rats, and I have put a *mi* [divination-stuff of the tribe] on this oven to mark this. I eat only pork.' With his stone axe the visitor hit the boy on his temples, but without causing blood to flow. Later, when the son told his father about these events, the father again disbelieved him, as there was no blood showing on his head. Next morning the boy died. The old man cried for him and cooked a large sow for the funeral. Now he thought of the boy's story about a spirit visitor and realised that the visitor must have been his own father, so he took the head of the pig and cooked it at the spot where the spirit had appeared. As he did so, the wind rose, and a dry cordyline leaf fell on the oven-place. He thought 'My father has sent the cordyline leaf again, he must be cross. I cannot stay here, I shall

go to the place Kim' [in the Wahgi]. And so he did. He was angry with
the ghost of his father for killing his son and hoped to leave the ghost
behind him. He left the oven containing the pig he was sacrificing
unopened, and declared that from that time on he would look at the tall
limbum tree by which he had buried his son only from a distance.

He and his wife arrived at Kim, and there they had many more sons:
Møndimbo, Køwulmbo, Kundmbo, Uyambo (Oyambo), Kumømb-
mbo, and Akelembo. The groups named after Møndimbo, Oyambo, and
Kundmbo are still in existence, the others have all died out. Taken all
together they were called Kawelka Kumapei, 'the Kawelka who live
[*petemen*, infinitive form *pei*] at Kuma' [i.e. the Central Melpa area].
Around Kim they lived, in settlements called Roklwa, Kwamb, Møtil,
Røu, Kenta, Køikundumul, Mapa, Kuk, Kuning, Ep, Pokløk, Ropri, and
Rakorong. They expanded and made new settlements. They were
divided into two sections, Kiya-ngom-mul ('those who live at the place
of the cane-grass') and the Rua-ngom-mul ('those who live at the place
of the banana leaf').Within these there were numerous small groups. They
spread, and men gave them more room to live in. Then a Mokei man
died and the Kawelka were said to have played games and made merry
at this time. The Mokei suspected that the Kawelka had poisoned their
man. Mokei and Kawelka were allies at that time, and in fact belonged to
a single large group called *Paklnur* [which included two other contemporary
tribes, the Elti and Penambe]. Now, however, they fought, the Kawelka
killed the Mokei men, and the two groups split and went their separate
ways, leaving some of their settlement places unoccupied. The angry
Mokei declared that they would kill the Kawelka's pigs, take their women
and steal their crops. Ndika, Yamka, Kukilika, and men of other tribes
came to steal as well [looting of this kind was fairly common in warfare].
The Kawelka in turn were angry and fought back, but the other groups
were too strong. Kawelka men were chased into a swamp, where some
drowned and others were cut with the axe as they waded in it. Some
escaped to the top of Ep hill and others to Pokløk [to the side of the main
settlement area]. One ran to Kuk to warn a big-man called Koi who
lived there, with his wives, houses, pigs, cassowaries, bamboo tubes of
decorating oil, and so on. Koi said 'I'm not a boy, I can't leave at once,
I'll straighten my possessions and come tomorrow morning.' That night
he slept in his little shelter house [probably used for making sacrifices].
Kukilika men heard that he was still at Kuk and surrounded the place. In
the morning he put on his feather head-dress, took up his shield, and
stepped outside. He was stabbed by a cassowary-claw-tipped spear and
fell. His women cried out to the big-man Kaepa, who was over at
Rakorong settlement. [Kaepa was the reciter's father: we are firmly in the

realm of oral history now.] Some of Koi's followers and wives escaped and ran to Rakorong, where they rubbed themselves in ashes and mud. The Kawelka thought 'Koi, our big-man, has been killed. We can't stay here, let us go'. Meanwhile their enemies divided into search parties and went to each settlement, burning the valley grasses as they went to smoke out fugitives, and finally reaching Pembki where the Kawelka had mustered. Two men of Kawelka Kundmbo clan, Pilip and Maninge [the latter is cited as founder of one of the Kundmbo sub-clans] fought hard, protecting weaker men. Maninge was struck on the nose and killed; they put him in the grass and covered him up, hoping the enemy would not find him. They were hungry and thirsty. There was no water, only a muddy place where pigs paddled. 'Let us go now' they said. 'We are not strong. Koi is dead.' The son of a woman of Kawelka Oyambo clan came to Ep with a large pig. The Kawelka had withdrawn to the hill-top, and Kaepa suggested they kill the pig as a sacrifice before splitting up. He held the rope to which the pig was tied [as a big-man does before a sacrifice], and spoke: 'Where will you go now, my brothers? Those who can, may go to their wife's or their mother's group. Those of you who cannot do that, I shall take you off to Mbakla [where some Kawelka were already living].' He called the names of all the settlement places they were leaving: 'Now they are driving us out and we must leave you, our places, only a few of us are left and we are going. I am sorry for you, my land, and am killing this pig for you [i.e. for ghosts of the group buried there]. Now we are going to Mbakla, our sister's sons will show us the way.' And so they came down to Mbukl and Mbakla where we live now.

Before, when they were still living at Kim, there came a hot, dry time. A man, Kipilya [Uip, in a version given to me in 1964 by a man of Kawelka Membo clan; according to this version, Uip was 'the father of all the Kawelka', but this was the version which 'began in the middle of the story'] went hunting for marsupials in the forest near to Miti Kuk. He went over to Maem, then to Pɔkli, then up to Nggolke hill, and looked over to Tap Manga [one of the present-day Kundmbo settlements]. He saw that it was a good place. People had been burning off areas of garden-land there and only at Mbakla Eimb Manga ('Mbakla fertility place') were there trees standing. So he went down and slept at this place [which is now recognised as an origin-place, cemetery, and old cult-place of all the Kawelka]. There were marsupials there, and these he caught, cooked and ate, along with wild greens. A woman of the Tipuka tribe came, also looking for greens. She asked him how he had arrived. He said he was from Kuma and had come down here looking for marsupials and wild foods. They became friends. She told her relatives, of Oklembo clan [special present-day exchange partners of the reciter's clan, Mandembo], returned, and offered to plant sweet potato vines for him, as he was clearing ground for a garden. They lived together, and the woman bore a son. The father said 'I call my son Klaem, after the name of the ground on which I first settled here.' Klaem later had two sons, one light-skinned (Kund), one dark (Pønd), and the two lived at Mbakla. Kund went back to Tap Manga to see this place, Pønd went off to Mbukl. Pønd founded the Pøndimbo comprising Mandembo plus Membo [these two are paired together as especial allies in opposition to Kundmbo], Kund the Kundmbo. Pønd had many sons. The smaller sub-groups were named later as the numbers of men grew. All the Kawelka living at Mbakla were known as Mbakla-pei, 'Mbakla-dwellers', as opposed to those at Kuma. That was how much later Kaepa knew that he could go to Mbakla to join them. In fact a man, Tilkang, had visited Mbakla earlier and men had begun to go back and forth between the two areas, especially at festival times, just as they do now.

This story provides, from one man's point of view, a complete account of how the Kawelka have settled their territory, as well as gaining their mystical divination substance, the cordyline. Three points, perhaps, are important to note. First the story-teller is a big-man, son of a big-man before him, and his knowledge and skill are unusually great. The story cannot be considered a charter in the sense of a tale known to men of the group as a whole; but it does explain Kawelka 'history' and validate their settlement for the big-man himself, and it is he who is likely to be called on by others if the group's origins and settlement are questioned. Other big-men maintain slightly different and less copious but essentially similar versions.[2] Second, in the middle of the story we find an account of fairly recent fighting; the story-teller, Ongka, was a young boy when his father fled to Mbakla. This part must be distinguished from the first and last parts of the narrative, which are mythical (although Ongka himself would not make this distinction so sharply). These two mythical parts do not fit together perfectly. In the first we are told one version of the origins of the groups Mandembo and Kundmbo, in the second another version is given. The reason is, I think, that usually these two stories are told independently: each validates Kawelka settlement in its own way. The first story is, I think, known to few people, so that its slight discrepancies in relation to the second are unlikely to be a matter for anyone's concern.

The first story also clearly merges into history, and the numerous settlement places mentioned in it were genuinely occupied by the Kawelka in the past. The third point to make is that the mythical parts of the account are concerned with the establishment of the tribe's main contemporary segments and also, at one point, with a marriage between a Kawelka ancestor and a Tipuka woman which clearly represents[3] the contemporary generalised alliance between the Kawelka and Tipuka tribes—an alliance of great importance in warfare, current marriage patterns, land use, and ceremonial exchange. The myth is not concerned to 'document' particular genealogical relationships of living men to the original ancestors nor to explain how smaller segments of the main segments were created. Ongka, the story-teller, specifically refers to this latter process by remarking that 'they made the smaller names as their numbers became greater'.

The cordyline leaves which the spirit visitor places on the oven in the story would be recognised at once by Kawelka hearers as their tribe's *mi*, or divination substance. Strauss (Strauss and Tischner 1962) has emphasised the importance of the *mi* concept in Hagen culture. The origin myth of each Hagen tribe contains a reference to its *mi*, explaining how this was revealed to a tribal ancestor either by Sky Spirits or by a ghost, as in the version of the Kawelka story which I have quoted. The *mi* is also called the tribe's *tei-mel*, its 'thing laid down', that is laid down from the beginnings of the tribe for all time. In the tribe's myth it is often described as revealed to an early ancestor in the tribe's *kona wingndi*, 'creation-place', and its appearance is taken by the ancestor as a sign that he has entered the place where the first founder of his tribe sprang up. The *mi* is thus intimately related to the ultimate origins of its tribe and so to its tribesmen's unity and singularity, founded on the supposed fact of their common origins. The notion of a *kona wingndi* peculiar to each tribe in which the tribe's founder is considered to have first appeared seems to express the linked importance of locality and descent to the Hageners. It is not just that there are local groups, whose men conceptualise their unity by claiming common descent, as we, the outside observers, are likely to put it. From the Hageners' point of view it is rather that each tribe originates both from a particular place and from a particular ancestor, so that place and ancestor are indissolubly linked. In the Kawelka story the original *kona wingndi* is said to be at Kimbapukl, far from the present Kawelka territory; a compromise with the fact of migration from their first territory is made in the story by naming a new site, Mbakla, within the current territory, as the successor to the first *kona wingndi*. The Kawelka *mi*, however, is traced firmly back to Kimbapukl.

In the story the spirit visitor lays the cordyline *mi* on an earth oven as a sign that it is indeed he who has come and that in future only 'true' sacrifices, of pork, must be made to him. In contemporary social contexts also the *mi* is used as a touchstone of truth. Challenged in a dispute, a tribesman may swear by his *mi*, touching it or eating it, as a sign that he is telling the truth, and, by implication, others are lying. If he perjures himself, it is thought that the *mi* will 'eat' (kill) him. (Interestingly enough, a tribe's *mi* is said also to have influence over sisters' sons of the tribe in other groups, so that, if they swear falsely by it, it can attack and kill them too.) Thus the *mi* is associated on the one hand with the most distant origins of the tribe and on the other with the conscience of each individual tribesman. It is an overarching symbol of identity, strongly reminiscent of the totems which are important to the African Dinka and Tallensi (Fortes 1967. See especially p. 17, where Fortes writes: 'Herein lies the reminder of the corporate unity and identity of the lineage which binds him [the individual] as the ultimate condition of his existence as a person.').

Mandembo, Membo, and Kundmbo at the present time are exogamous, localised clans, units which could act independently in warfare in the past and may do so nowadays in alliance-making for ceremonial exchange. Their co-resident male members belong to the Kawelka clan groups, together with some sisters who have returned to their natal kin along with their children. All three clans can intermarry, although there are fewer marriages between Kundmbo and the rest because of past enmities. There is a preference for marrying into friendly, allied groups. Membo and Mandembo, as I have mentioned, are paired as allies, just as, at a higher level, Tipuka and Kawelka are, and as groups at the sub-clan and sub-sub-clan level may also be. The principle of alliance by pairing is thus important at successive levels of group structure.

The segmentation patterns of the three clans differ in certain respects. It appears possible, from accounts, that some of the Kundmbo sub-clan names have been invented within the last twenty-five years, and that the two contemporary clan-sections earlier functioned as sub-clans.[4] (Sub-clans establish themselves by a measure of independence in exchanges; clan-sections are marked by a greater mutual opposition and by the fact that their men may marry each other's sisters' daughters.) In Mandembo clan the process of separation between sections has proceeded further than in Kundmbo, partly because its two divisions have had section status for longer, partly because of the separation of activities of two prominent big-men, who belong to Klammbo and Kurupmbo sections respectively. The Klammbo are currently rather few, and their subdivisions are not marked, functioning more as sub-sub-clans ('little men's houses') than as sub-clans. Membo clan, which is the largest of the three, is, surprisingly, not divided into sections at all. It has expanded in territory (and numbers probably) within the last thirty or forty years and has proliferated new groups at a lower level without changing the status of its two sub-clans.

At Mbikl the Kawelka clans and clan-sections have separate territories, and, in addition, recognised pockets of settlement within other clan areas. In the Wahgi settlement area territories are not so established, but there are still separate places associated with Klammbo, Kurupmbo, and Membo. Sub-clans and smaller groups may also effectively occupy areas of their own, but this is not always the case.

It will be noticed from the Kawelka paradigm that all of the segment names end in -mbo, a suffix meaning 'stock' or 'shoot', 'something planted'. The formal ideology here is that each group can be looked on as founded by a single ancestress, wife of the group's male founder. The name of her tribe, it is said, is taken and -mbo added to it to form a new segment name. Segments are 'planted by' women of different tribes who married into the Kawelka tribe. Thus, for example, Klam-mbo and Kurup-mbo derive from ancestresses of Klamakae and Kurup tribes respectively. In some cases the tribes are now extinct as corporate groups. Thus the Membo are said to derive from the Kopalike Mea-ke, and the Mandembo from the Mand-ke tribe, both defunct and little spoken of nowadays.

The -*mbo* idiom provides a useful model of differentiation, and it is often linked to the notion that the clan had a single father who was a polygynist and whose wives founded separate sub-clans. In the case of the smaller groups, sub-sub-clans especially, it is often possible to cite the name of the ancestress eponymous to the segment; but on inspection it turns out often that she is not literally the founder of the segment, but merely mother of some of its men.

Strauss (Strauss and Tischner 1962:76-80) has listed terms which, he says, are applied to different levels of grouping within the tribe in the Central Melpa area. The tribe and its major sections (if it has these) are distinguished as *mbo tenda* ('one stock') and *mbo kats* ('separate sub-stocks'). The clan level is *pana-ru* ('field-ditch', an expression which I discuss later), and succeeding levels below it are *anda-noimp* ('grandfather penis'), *rapa* ('men's house'), *anda-kangêm* ('grandfather and son'), *önginödl* ('brothers'), and *tepam-kangemadl* ('father and his sons'). Strauss's paradigm is an elaborate one, and for many Hagen tribes it is not necessary to recognise so many hierarchical levels, nor indeed to isolate separate terms as corresponding to the levels in an exclusive fashion. Thus I found, for example, that the contrasting pair *mbo tenda/mbo kat(s)* could be used for any two levels where the aim was to contrast a whole group with its segments. Again, I did not find *anda-noimp* (or *anda noimb*) and *anda-kangêm* regularly used for definite levels of subdivision within the clan, although both terms were certainly recognised by my informants as possible ways of referring to a clan itself or to one of the small lineages within it. *Anda-kangêm*, in the shortened form *andakam*, can actually be used with a wider meaning, to refer to natural as well as social divisions. Thus the phrase *andakam andakam* or *andakam elpa elpa* means 'of all different kinds'.

Kawelka tribe and its clans can be spoken of as *mbi ou tenda*, *mbi kel elpa elpa*, 'a single big name, different small names', and in fact the big/small contrast, like that of *mbo tenda/mbo kats*, can operate right down the segmentary scale, higher levels being 'bigger' than lower ones. The group's single name can be appealed to as a rationale for unity. Another idiom frequently used is to say that the tribesmen are *unt tepam tenda*, 'long ago of one father', while clansmen are *tepam tenda*, 'one father', i.e. their ancestor is a more recent one. The 'one father' in question is not always known to all of the group's male adult members. In Kundmbo clan, for example, male informants of Kumapei section suggested, after some casting around, that Maninge (mentioned in Ongka's origin story) was the clan founder; but some men of Roklambo section declared that Maninge was not their ancestor, and in fact Kundmbo men had different ancestors, not a single one. Yet the same men, in certain contexts of action, would assert that they were all *tepam tenda* and for that reason 'brothers'. The same contrast between dogma and literal fact shows in the idea that men of Roklambo sub-clan (inside Roklambo section of the Kundmbo clan) were descended from a woman of the Roklaka tribe. The actual situation seems to be that *various* men of this group married Roklaka wives and moreover Roklaka men at one time came as refugees to the group, so that it was considered appropriate to dub the sub-clan by this name. Figure 3 gives some genealogical material on this sub-clan.

The small units in the sub-clan are listed as (a), (b), and (c). They are spoken of as separate *tepam-kangemal* ('father-son') units. None of their founders is represented as having been a man of the Kawelka Kundmbo clan by birth. The founder of (a) was a man of the Mile tribe, who must have come to the Kawelka via his marriage link with Klammbo clan-section;[5] the founder of (b) a Tipuka man who married into Roklambo sub-clan; and of (c) a Roklaka tribesman who came as a refugee. It is clear that there is no single apical ancestor cited for the whole sub-clan.

In this, as in other examples, there is a strong contrast between the native model of the clan as a unit founded by a single father, whose sons, perhaps by different wives, found sub-clans, and the apparent realities of sub-clan formation. It is very hard to be sure on a matter of this kind, yet I have the impression that informants are themselves aware of the discrepancy, but that it does not

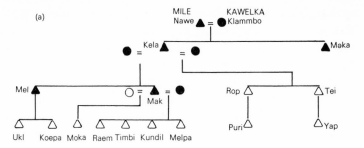

(a)

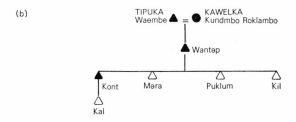

(b)

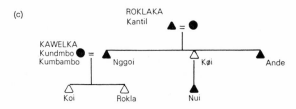

(c)

Figure 3. Kawelka Kundmbo Roklambo sub-clan
Note: tribe names are in capitals.

trouble them much, since they do not seriously present the dogmatic model as a statement of the same order as the genealogies I have given in Figure 3. My impression is derived from conversations in which the creation of new sub-clan names has been described. For example, in Yelipi clan of the Minembi tribe (neighbours of the Kawelka) three new sub-clans were made after the group had re-settled in a fresh territory. Two Yelipi men, both ancient by 1964, told me that they had arranged these divisions. They called one set of men *Rokmbo*, 'the long ones'. No form of descent model was advanced as an explanation of this. My two informants simply said that some of these men were tall, hence the name. It is the case that most men of the *Rokmbo* sub-clan are currently clustered together in a single part of the clan territory, so that possibly they were also initially grouped together on the basis of co-residence also. The other two sub-clan names were called after the tribal or clan affiliations of two women who were mothers of some, but not all, of the men involved. These two thus became *Tipuk-mbo*, 'Tipuka stock people', and *Nambakae-mbo*, '(Minembi) Nambakae stock people'. Talking of their divisions in public contexts, Yelipi men may refer to the two sub-clans as founded by a single ancestor who married a Tipuka and a Nambakae wife, but the older Yelipi, at least, are quite aware that this is not a literal representation of historical fact but a way of referring to the contemporary fact of subdivision within the clan. The idiom of the polygynist father with his descendants by different wives states that sub-clans are formally equivalent, separate groups within the clan. By contrast, the relationships recorded in Figure 3 are relevant only to the internal affairs of the sub-clan, for example to processes of land inheritance, daily co-operation, and co-residence.

There is another idiom which can be applied to the clan level and should be noticed here. This is the term *pana ru*, 'garden ditch'. Strauss (Strauss and Tischner 1962:77) comments on this, pointing out that the name brings into focus the concrete interests of clansmen in land by contrast with the terms for the level of the tribe, which are primarily to do with 'mythologisch-religiöse Selbstverständnis.' He adds: 'die bezeichnung ... ist also von der Feldeinteilung hergenommen, gemeint ist aber die Aufteilung des Siedlungslandes.' In Hagen sweet-potato gardens are divided into grids by cross-cutting trenches used both for drainage and to produce soil for the actual garden beds. Certain of the trenches in a garden can thus form convenient marking-points for divisions between sections planted by different persons, for example, co-wives of the garden owner. There is another type of garden, in which taro, sugar-cane, bananas, and a variety of greens are grown. This type is trenched less systematically, but may be cut through by one or two deep drainage ditches which again can be used as markers of different sections. The whole garden area is enclosed by a fence and sometimes by a large perimeter ditch as well, which helps to keep out pigs. The exact referent of the ditch/trench term (*ru*) in the phrase *pana ru* is thus not quite clear, but I suggest that it refers to internal *ru* made within a garden rather than to the perimeter ditch. If this is so, the sense of the term, as a symbol for the clan, would be that the clan is part of a larger unit, the tribe (the whole garden), but has its separate territorial area (marked by a *ru*) within the total 'Siedlungsland'. Whatever the precise symbolism involved, however, it is clear that the term *pana ru* refers to land and locality rather than to descent, and, as Strauss has suggested, it is appropriate that it should be applied to the level of the clan, for the clan is a significant territorial group, whose members fought together in the past to maintain or expand their boundaries.

In some clans descent models are more elaborately conceptualised, and provide the clan with a genealogical skeleton which duplicates the division into different *rapa* ('men's house') groups. This is so for the Membo clan of the Kawelka, although not all Membo men are equally knowledgeable about the clan's genealogy. The version which I shall give was cited by Membo Kont in 1964. Kont is a big-man, and his father (who was killed in warfare) is reckoned to have been a big-man also. He gave his account as *the* genealogy of Membo clan, specifically starting with the founder and working down to himself and others.

Kont said that Uip was the first father of all the Kawelka. (He is not recognised as such by men of Kundmbo and Mandembo clans; cf. Ongka's myth, given earlier.) Uip married a Klamakae girl and bore Tilkang, ancestor of Membo clan.[6] Some of Tilkang's descendants are given in Figure 4. It will be noticed that Kipilya and Lklaem appear in the genealogy, but the position of these ancestors is different in the two versions. Ongka makes Kipilya the first ancestor of the Kawelka at Mbakla and Klaem (Lklaem) his son; whereas

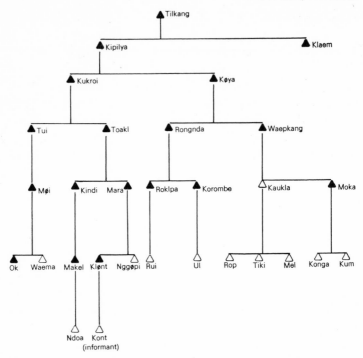

Figure 4. The descendants of Tilkang, according to Kawelka Membo Kont

Kont has Kipilya and Lklaem as brothers, sons of Tilkang.[7] The top generations in Kont's genealogy show a marked binary arrangement, and perhaps the representation of Kipilya and Lklaem as a brother-pair is influenced by this. The position of Lklaem in Kont's version is certainly anomalous, as he is given no descendants, and this again suggests that he may have become displaced from a position as a son of Kipilya.

The binary structure of the genealogy at levels 3 and 4 fits with the segmentation of the clan into named *manga rapa* or 'men's house groups' (cf. Figure 5). In this case then, there is a correspondence between the descent dogmas and actual social divisions; whereas in Kundmbo clan the correspondence is less exact. However, one *rapa*, Elpuklmbo, is not provided for at all in Kont's scheme. Moreover, if we consider the fuller internal genealogies of any one

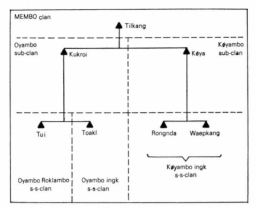

Figure 5. The fit between genealogy and *rapa*
divisions in Kawelka Membo clan

of the *rapa*, we shall find deviations from the agnatic model, just
as we found before in Kundmbo clan. Figure 6 indicates the pattern.
Toakl is not in fact apical to the whole of Oyambo ingk *rapa*, as
Figure 5 would suggest. The *rapa* divides into lineage sets named
Kindi-Mara *kangemal*, 'the sons of Kindi and Mara', and Mbe-
Raplka *kangemal*, 'the sons of Mbe and Raplka'. As Figure 6 shows,
Toakl is apical to Kindi and Mara, but not to Mbe and Raplka, who
did not appear on Kont's genealogy-scheme at all. Figure 6 includes
a number of persons affiliated to the lineages by other than agnatic
links, as well as showing putative lineage founders who are uncon-
nected genealogically with Toakl. Some of these were said by Kont's
father's brother, Nggøpi, to have been men of Kawelka living in
the old Wahgi territory who migrated down to the present territory, either before or as a result of fighting with the Mokei, and
fitted themselves into existing *rapa* groups.[8] In other cases the origins
of incoming lineage founders are not even known now. Versions of
genealogical connections are quite often simplified. This is usually
done by asserting that co-ordinate ancestors were brothers, and the
result is that the simplified versions look more agnatic than the
complicated ones. But there is no systematic effort made to eliminate
the representation of non-agnatic links or to ensure an exact correspondence between lineage names and the positions of their epony-

(1) Kindi-Mara Kangemal

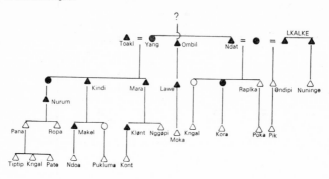

(2) Mbe-Raplka Kangemal

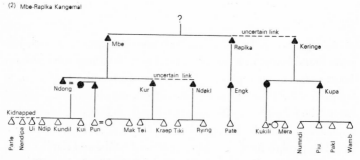

Figure 6. Genealogical account of Oyambo ingk *rapa* in Membo
Note: another formulation is that the descendants of Ndat, Mbe and Raplka,
are known as Oyambo Kundumbo or *amb-nt-mei* ('borne by the woman') and
Kindi-Mara Kangemal (apart from Ndat's sons) as *wuə-nt-mei* ('born of the man').

mous 'founders'. Kindi and Mara, for example, are patently not
lineal ancestors of everyone in the set of persons named after them.
In further cases where a lineage set takes its name from two ancestors,
the ancestors are invariably paired as brothers. As in the case of
Mbe and Raplka, the name of the father of the two may not be
known. It is not needed, for the pairing of ancestors as brothers is
itself an adequate charter for the lineage.

The lineage should not be thought of as an entirely fixed unit.
Lineage alignments probably shift more than sub-clan divisions do.
If lineage sets dwindle in numbers of men they can be re-
amalgamated to bring them up to par with other sets. For a par-

ticular occasion, also, readjustments may be made. Thus, when Kawelka Mandembo clansmen were cutting up a steer presented to them at a *moka* ceremony in January 1965 they coalesced some of their small lineages in order to match the numbers of lineages with the number of the steer's ribs. And in general lineage divisions are said to be made by clansmen internally among themselves 'for dividing out meat and vegetable foods' which they may receive at prestations. Men of other clans may not know the small lineage, and also perhaps sub-sub-clan, names at all. They will, however, know the sub-clan names, for men of a sub-clan act together publicly as donors and recipients in exchanges.

Rather than a descent model of a clan's segmentation being given as an explanation of why it is divided into sub-groups men will often reiterate the function of these as sufficient reason for their separate existence. As Ongka, the most important big-man in Kawelka Mandembo clan, put it to me: 'when we have ten men here and ten men there, we call them by separate *rapa* names and they can give and receive separately in exchanges.'[9] From such a statement we can infer that it is the exchange system, geared to the activities of big-men, rather than any principle of descent, which actually generates segmentation in groups. The descent idiom is applied *after* the fact of segmentation. In fact, so powerful is the *rapa* idiom itself that Hageners do not feel it necessary retrospectively to adjust all their genealogies to a neat unilineal lineage calculus. Earlier, we saw that in Kawelka Membo clan Elpuklmbo *rapa* is not fitted on to the agnatic skeleton genealogy which my informant Kont gave me at all. This in no way affects the ordinary functioning and status of Elpuklmbo as a sub-sub-clan within the clan. Since Elpuklmbo men are recognised as a separate *rapa*, they do not need to be fitted into an elaborate lineage framework; and this underlines the point that Kont's genealogical picture of the clan and (some of) its segments does not constitute the prime calculus for all jural relationships within the clan.

It is interesting, moreover, that it is precisely at the sub-clan level that the *rapa* idiom, as an alternative to the descent idiom, operates most strongly; for the sub-clan level is the level at which genealogies which are reasonably close to demographic fact tend to merge into mythological genealogies, where these exist, of the clan founder and his sons. It is my suggestion, then, that conceiving of the sub-clans as 'men's house groups' rather than as 'descent groups', helps to mediate between clan mythology and the relatively accurate genealogies which record the complexities of relationships between sets of clansmen over spans of a few generations. The clan myth may be grandly agnatic; the demographic facts of group composition, influenced by a multitude of factors including the ambitions of big-men, are likely to be untidily cognatic. The *rapa* divisions, blueprinted over this untidiness, give order and organisation to the clan as an assemblage of separate decision-making units. Thus sub-clans can be described also as *ol tenda*, groups of men who confer privately together on plans for making *moka* or bridewealth payments. While the descent idiom is stressed from time to time as a charter for the unity of the clan as a whole group, the *rapa* idiom tends to be used in contexts where the pragmatic activities of its segments are being referred to, for example when clansmen are receiving gifts of pork or shells and each sub-clan or smaller subdivision wishes to be recognised by receiving its separate share. Indeed, in describing how new subdivisions are created, men often stress that the aim of making new segment names is specifically to impress outsiders, to make them think that the group is large and therefore requires gifts of substantial size in inter-group transactions.

But if, as I have argued, the *rapa* idiom is a powerful and appropriate way of referring to clan segments and their functions, why, one might ask, are descent-constructs employed at all? I think that the descent idiom, as a symbol, adds certain elements of meaning which the *rapa* idiom does not encompass. These elements are, first, the notion of continuity in the clan's occupation of its territory, and second, the notion of linkage, as well as separation, between sub-clans. The image of the polygynist founding father and his sons provides, as I see it, a perfect symbolisation of these two elements of meaning. Its implication is that clansmen are united as descendants of the original father, while the separate sub-clans in the clan are divided, but linked, just as are the sons, by different mothers, of the same father. It is the descent idiom, also, which provides the explicit rationale and framework for the use of kinship terms within the clan. Because of their imputed descent from a single founder clansmen are, in a general sense, 'brothers'. Within the small lineages generational distinctions can be accurately reckoned by their members, so that a young man, for example, calls senior men 'father' (*tepam*, reference form, as are all forms which follow) or 'grandfather' (*andakouwa*), and men of his own age 'brother' (*angin* or *øngin*), while young boys he calls *kang angin*, 'boy brother,' or *kangəm*, 'son'. Within the clan as a whole he applies these terms similarly, judging by the age of each clansman which generational term to use. For women he has a parallel set of usages: *mam*, 'mother', applicable to all the women married to men whom he calls 'father'; *wendape*, 'grandmother' (women married to *andakouwa*); *kimun*, 'sister', extended to natal females of his clan of roughly his own age; and terms for father's sister (*øtin*), brother's wife (*kimøm*,) and daughter (*mboklam*). It is for these reasons that I argue that the notion of descent provides a useful structural model for the Hageners, while the *rapa* idiom conceptualises their view of the functions of their group segments.

The next two chapters look in more detail at an important empirical dimension of the Kawelka groups, the dimension of settlement patterns and co-residence.

CHAPTER 3

SETTLEMENT PATTERNS

The Hagen countryside is dominated by contrasts between mountain ranges, river valleys, and rolling plain lands. The mountains are forested above a certain height and are known as *ndepana*, 'tree-gardens'; plainlands and valley, covered with stands of sword- and cane-grass, and swampy in places, are both known as *kwipana*, 'grass-gardens'. Seen from the point of view of their settlement by people, areas are classified as *oa-kona*, 'clearing-places', *kwi-kona*, 'grass-places', and *ran-kona*, 'hot valley-places'. Most of the Kawelka live in *oa-kona* and openly say they prefer it to other environments; but many have within the last twenty years colonised or re-colonised grassland and valley areas, in search of fertile land and ample pig-pasture.

Each settlement-place, whatever its environment, is likely to be surrounded by a stand of planted casuarina trees, mingled with cordyline bushes (used to provide rear coverings in men's dress) and perhaps one or two Highlands breadfruit trees, the leaves of which help to line earth ovens on ceremonial occasions of cooking pork. If the settlement contains an important man, he is quite likely to have laid out his own dancing ground in front of the main men's house in his place. At the least he will have a front yard (*mangketa*, 'house-mouth') where visitors can congregate and discussions on bridewealth and other exchanges can take place. Men and women have separate houses, and it is the men's houses which usually occupy the central part of the settlement place. The women's houses, which they share with their pigs and children, are likely to be down from the men's house area or tucked away behind it.

Men's houses are round, with a pointed roof, sometimes packed at the top with earth. Inside, the rafters are blackened with soot and sugar-cane leavings are scattered over the floor; the men's sleeping compartments are at the rear behind the central fireplace where food is sometimes cooked and men warm themselves in the chilly evenings. Food is more often cooked and eaten in the women's houses, which are long, low, and divided usually into a separate compartment for the pigs—each of which has its stall—a main living room with a fireplace and perhaps an earth oven as well, and a smaller sleeping room to the side of the main room. A little distance away from the other houses there is the menstrual hut, where women eat and sleep during their periods and for a few days afterwards; or there may be a menstrual seclusion-room built into one of the main women's houses. The houses are surrounded by fences which ensure that pigs cannot break into near-by gardens, will enter and leave their stalls by the proper doorway, and can find their way out to pasture in the mornings.

Hageners, then, do not traditionally live in large, consolidated villages, but in settlement-places scattered over clan-territories. Each clan is likely to have its own territory, probably contiguous with that of at least one other clan of its tribe, although it may also share a part of its land with another group. In the past clansmen fought to defend their whole territory and abandoned it only if they were overwhelmed by a superior coalition of enemies determined to expel them.

This pattern of dispersed settlement within politically defended territories is common in the Western Highlands and Chimbu Districts, and contrasts with the prevalence of villages in parts of the Eastern Highlands, for example among the Siane[1] (Salisbury 1962) and the Gahuku-Gama (Read 1966). There is some evidence that settlement in the Northern Melpa area was in the past affected by warfare, such that men tended to live together in large men's houses more than they do now, but the basic pattern of *Streusiedlungen* rather than villages was reported both by early explorers (Leahy and Crain 1937) and by the missionary-anthropologist Vicedom (Vicedom and Tischner 1943-8).

The broad ecological limits on settlement throughout the High-lands area have been examined by Brookfield (1964), who estab-lishes that altitude, weather, and agricultural resources all place restrictions on the distribution of populations. In particular, settle-ment is inhibited above a certain altitude by the possibility of frosts, which has to be combated by mounding and mulching techniques; and below about 5,000 feet the dangers of malaria and, in places, snake bite have restricted settlement or at least population growth. Groups displaced from mountain territories have sometimes been forced into the valleys; and this process of involuntary migra-tion has more recently been paralleled, in the Hagen area, by the voluntary expansion of tribal segments out from mountainside areas to both the Wahgi and Baiyer valleys. These moves have occurred as a result of the imposition of colonial peace in the area and have been prompted by the desire to find good pig-pasturing grounds and, lately, to find tracts of land suitable for planting with coffee trees. Migration is facilitated by the fact that the groups occupying valley areas tend to be the depleted fragments of clans or tribes previously decimated in warfare and currently suffering from endemic malaria and other diseases. It is tempting to see this new drift from mountainside to valley as exemplifying Stanhope's suggestion with regard to Highlands populations in general: 'It is possible that a Highland model before contact would have consisted of an ever-expanding centre spilling over into an ever-dying periphery' (1970:38).[2]

Throughout most of the heavily settled central parts of the Highlands populations depend largely on sweet potatoes for their staple subsistence and for feeding the pigs which are important sources of both protein and prestige. Sweet potatoes take about six to nine months to mature at altitudes between 5,500 and 6,000 feet; thereafter the tubers can be harvested for many months, but Highlanders do not have techniques for storing them, so that harvesting work has to take place daily or almost daily. In Hagen agricultural work in general continues for most of the year. Season-ality in the Wahgi Valley and Hagen is low (Brookfield and Brown 1963:21-2), and men are able to do work on clearing garden areas in most months, intensifying their activities of burning under-growth in the drier months of June to August.

Brookfield and Brown (1967) have studied residence patterns in Chimbu in some detail, and have advanced conclusions which take into account sweet-potato agriculture, pig-keeping, and modern cash-cropping. They cite the Chimbu's own explanation that 'men congregate on high points for observation and defence, and disperse their women, children and livestock in order to hide them'. To this they add that nowadays, although warfare has been stopped, it is still convenient for men to live close together, in order to take part in discussions on group plans; while women are dispersed nearer to gardens and fallow or bush areas which they can exploit for human subsistence and pig-rearing. Moreover, they add (p. 149), 'Chimbu gynaecophobia is significant in keeping the sexes apart', so that women may still have separate houses even though they are 'nowadays drawn increasingly into centrally located activities as a result of the new cash economy.' In Chimbu large garden areas are enclosed and women's and pigs' houses have to be placed at the periphery of these in order to provide grazing grounds for the pigs. Brookfield and Brown contrast the Raiapu Enga area, in which garden sites are more permanent and family holdings less dispersed, and men's house groups are smaller than in Central Chimbu (cf. Waddell 1968).

Settlement among the Kawelka tends more towards the Raiapu Enga than to the Chimbu pattern. First, although the growing of coffee for cash has developed considerably since the 1960s, it has probably not gone as far as it has in Chimbu and in parts of the Hagen area closer to Mount Hagen township. Kawelka settlements have not been drawn uniformly closer to the roads, which nowadays cut through their clan territories, simply to exploit marketing possibilities. Persons have, however, become baptised as members of the Lutheran church, and these are required to live in a mission-oriented 'line-village' beside the road and to give up traditional pursuits in favour of Christianity and cash cropping: hence these men are likely both to live near the road and to grow at least some coffee for sale.

Second, large communal men's houses are not, at least nowadays, found among the Kawelka, although, as we have seen, the idiom of the 'one men's house' is employed as a term of reference for clan segments.

Third, women's houses are not normally widely separated from the men's house or houses, but form part of the same settlement-complex. In some other parts of the Hagen area, particularly within the Wahgi Valley, there are special pigs' houses, cared for and resided in by women, and these may be a long way from men's houses. Such pig-houses are useful for keeping good stock away from both diseases and the eyes of exchange partners and for securing ample grazing ground. They may also form outposts of settlement: after a pig-house is built a man may shift the site of his own house to the new area if he finds it attractive and if garden land is available around it. In their Wahgi Valley territory the Kawelka have established a few large permanent settlement places and smaller offshoot settlements in grassland areas around these. The latter usually have a men's house as well as a women's house and thus tend to follow the pattern of the main Kawelka territory.

Kawelka gardening methods, however, are not so intensive as those of the Raiapu. There is no equivalent of the Raiapu permanent-field, mounded sweet-potato cultivation. However, although garden areas are exploited only for a limited number of years before they are allowed to revert to either short or long fallow, the same general area around a named settlement-place continues to be exploited as long as the settlement-place itself is occupied. Some gardens are maintained at places where men have previously resided, and good sites, which can be used for growing mixed vegetables as well as sweet potato, are re-cultivated even if they are half a mile or so away from the owner's current settlement. Moreover, through their extra-clan ties, men can obtain use of garden strips in areas further away. Women may be given such strips by their natal kin even after they are married, and can harvest the strips when they wish. Nevertheless, there are always important gardens near to the settlement-place itself, although I cannot document the extent to which families depend on these home gardens.

Pigs are put to graze in old fallow land beside current gardens, or in gardens newly turned to fallow, or in forest areas or swamps within clan territories. It is convenient, therefore, to have such grazing areas not far from each women's house where pigs are kept, and the practice of fallowing gardens around the home settlement helps to ensure that this condition is met.

Following Brookfield and Brown's discussion, one can see residence patterns in the Highlands as affected both by the separation of men's from women's houses and by agricultural and stock-rearing requirements. Women do much of the daily harvesting of food and caring for pigs, so it is expedient for them to live fairly close to gardening and grazing areas. If men live in large, communal houses, women's houses are likely to be dispersed; where men are dispersed, women's and men's houses can be combined in small settlement-places. Men can meet and discuss issues at ceremonial grounds, and a big-man may perhaps live at the ceremonial ground itself, thus ensuring that he is at the centre of public discussions. This is the pattern for Hagen. Another possibility is the 'pulsating' settlement pattern described for the Maring (Rappaport 1967), in which families disperse in order to raise pigs over a number of years, then coalesce into a single village to hold their pig-festival, at which the bulk of their pigs are slaughtered. They can then continue to live in the ceremonial village until the pig population rises again, when the process of re-dispersal may begin. In Hagen, however, *moka* festivals often involve live pigs and may not deplete the donor group's herd so decisively. Participants simply use a central ceremonial ground for the duration of a festival, returning by night to sleep in their separate settlements.

It can be seen, then, that there must be optimal limits on settlement size. Each settlement needs amounts of cultivable, fallow, and bush land not too far away, and the more the persons that require gardens the further afield they may have to go. Given the condition that men's and women's houses are built near to each other, and on the assumption that people will not wish to walk too far to reach their staple gardens, one can suggest that settlements will either split if they grow too large or move as whole units if the land around them becomes exhausted.

Each settlement-place in Kawelka territory is named; in fact each small part of a clan's territory is given a locality name, taken from the names of streams, types of trees, plants, and so on which flourish or once flourished there. There are locality names which cover a wide area, and include smaller named areas within them. Locality names do not correspond exactly to social groups; their function is to provide clansmen with a conceptual 'grid' by which they can refer to each part of the territory which is so important for their subsistence and for their group identification. Hence we cannot simply identify separate settlements by means of locality names themselves. We can, however, obtain an adequate enough guide by considering which sets of houses are referred to by the people them-selves as different *mangkona* ('house-places').

Even so, because of tendencies towards aggregation (1) of the houses of men who belong to the same sub-clan, (2) of houses of men who are living in pockets of settlement as refugees, (3) of houses in sub-groups which are relatively short of land, and finally (4) of the houses of baptised men who are all supposed to live in a 'house-line', it is not always easy to state where one 'house-place' ends and another begins. There is quite a range of consolidation, from the single house or man's house plus woman's house, occupied by a man, his wife, children, and pigs, up to hamlets, clustered near to a main ceremonial ground. There is one such hamlet in the Minembi Papeke clan area. In it lived in May 1964 most of the men of a particular sub-sub-clan. It consisted at that time of twenty-five dwelling houses (nine men's, sixteen women's houses), occupied by fifteen men (two of whom were bachelors), nineteen wives, twenty-three unmarried sons and thirteen unmarried daughters. Apart from mission house-lines there were no hamlets as large as this among the Kawelka in 1964-5.

Mangkona can be classified according to the number of married men resident in them, and the relationships between these. I dis-tinguish (1) homesteads, normally occupied by an elementary family or by a polygynist with his wives and unmarried children, and (2) settlements, in which there are two or more adult married men. Homesteads have a single head, usually the husband-father of the family. In settlements consisting of a man and his married son or sons, the father continues to hold most authority until he is senile. Otherwise the senior men are likely to be formally equal to each other, although often one is a big-man whose influence is recognised by the others. In addition, as I have mentioned, there is frequently some kind of consolidation of settlements into locality areas, and where such settlements are numerous and closely associated we can recognise them as constituting a hamlet. Locality areas, again, are not in themselves to be equated with precise subdivisions of a clan, although the members of such a subdivision may tend to cluster together and so to form these areas.

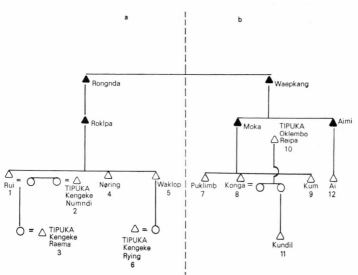

Figure 7. Maepna settlement place: genealogy
Note: tribe names are in capitals.

Most homesteads are associated with others within a locality area, and indeed in some cases such areas can be looked on as equivalent to expanded settlements. My division into homesteads and settlements can only, then, be an approximate one. To illustrate the difficulties involved here I consider the place Maepna. I have split this into two 'settlements', which we may call a and b. However, there is considerable sharing of activities between these two. Some of the genealogical relationships between the men of Maepna are given in Figure 7 (cf. also Figure 4). It can be seen that there is a genealogical break between a and b; but we have to compare this with separations made in activities. Here I shall consider a pig-killing event, gardening, and actual house-sharing.

A pig-killing took place on 8th May 1964. At it Membo men presented pork to kinsmen as part of a funeral cooking, and to exchange partners from the Roklaka tribe who had come to receive a prestation of pearl-shells; they also exchanged pork internally, Køyambo presenting to Oyambo sub-clan as part of a sequence of gifts between them. Maepna men killed pigs as follows:

a Waklop   4 ⎱ = 7, killed jointly
  Nøring   3 ⎰
  Rui   10, by himself
b Kum   2 ⎫
  Puklimb 3 ⎪
  Konga   2 ⎬ = 9, killed jointly
  Ai   1 ⎪
  Kundil   1 ⎭

In addition, Mang, a ZH of Puklimb, cooked 1 pig along with Puklimb's, making a total of 10 for b.

Settlement b thus emerges as a unit (plus an extra helper) whose men spoke of themselves as co-operating in the work of killing and cooking their pigs. In a, however, there was a division between Rui, who is a (now ageing) minor big-man and cooked 10 pigs by himself, and Rui's two younger brothers.

There is some sharing of the cultivation of gardens between a and b. In one garden where Puklimb (b, no. 7) holds the clearing rights and which required a good deal of work to prepare as it lies high in a forested area, Puklimb gave in 1964 shares to his two brothers (nos. 8 and 9), but also to Waklop and Numndi (nos. 2 and 5) of settlement a who had helped with the work. (In addition he allocated strips to a married daughter of his wife, by a previous husband; and to a co-resident affine of his sub-clan who lives in a homestead near to Maepna.) In another garden cleared jointly by Maepna men and planted with sugarcane, strips were taken by:

a : nos. 1, 2, 3, 5, and 6
b : no. 9
others: another Køyambo man and a man married to a woman of the same clan as no. 5's wife.

And in a third garden:

a : nos. 1, 2, 3, 4, 5, and 6
b : nos. 7 and 11
others: a ZH and a WB of 1; and an affine who lives in the same locality area.

Sharing of the use of gardens between a and b is thus quite extensive.

Men's houses within the two settlements are formally shared by:

1. Reipa (b:10) and Kundil (b:11). Kundil was cared for by his grandmother, 10's wife, while he was still suckling, after his mother's death. Later Reipa came to live with his son-in-law and brought Kundil with him.

2. Waklop (a:5) and Rying (a:6). Rying in 1964 was spoken of as on an extended visit with his father-in-law; he was not said to have 'become a Kawelka' (he belongs to Tipuka Kengeke clan).[3] However, he was a member of the Maepna work-force. The minor big-man, Rui (a:1), was said to have called him and other Kengeke men in when Maepna had been depleted by an exodus of men to theWahgi territory.

3. Rui (a:1) shares with Numndi (a:2) and Konga and Puklimb (b:7 and 8).

4. Kum (b:9) has his own men's house.

The three brothers, 7, 8, and 9 are thus separated; two share with a minor big-man, while the youngest and most apparently ambitious, Kum, has an independent house. Sharing of men's houses thus does not correspond exactly to the genealogical break between a and b. Nevertheless, Puklimb and Konga were often spoken of as belonging with Kum, Ai, and Kundil, so I have assigned them to settlement b. To indicate the close networks of interdependence between a and b I speak of Maepna as a single settlement *place*, containing two roughly discrete 'settlements'.

As a preliminary to discussing the distribution of Kawelka men in homesteads and settlements I give some population figures for the separate clans (Table 1). The figures list non-clansmen who are resident on Kawelka territory, as well as resident clansmen and other categories of persons.

In discussing settlement composition, I concentrate on the bulk of the Kawelka, who live at or near to Mbukl. In this territory-area there were in 1964-5 forty-five occupied homesteads and forty-one settlements. Homesteads numbered fourteen among Kundmbo, twenty among Membo and eleven among Mandembo; settlements

TABLE 1: KAWELKA POPULATION, FEBRUARY 1965

(a) KUNDMBO CLAN

	All residents on clan territory		Resident clansmen + attached women and children	
	At Mbukl	At Mbukl and Wahgi	At Mbukl	At Mbukl and Wahgi
	(a)	(b)	(c)	(d)
Married men	57	62	50	54
Wives	62	68	55	59
Unmarried men, including widowers	37	41	33	36
Widows, separated, and divorced women	13	13	11	11
Children—male	62	63	56	57
—female	43	44	39	40
	274	291	244	257

(b) MEMBO CLAN

	(a)	(b)	(c)	(d)
Married men	62	86	55	79
Wives	76	103	68	96
Unmarried men, including widowers	8	18	8	18
Widows, etc.	8	11	8	11
Children—male	94	111	82	99
—female	71	77	63	70
	319	406	284	373

(c) MANDEMBO CLAN

	Klammbo section—resident clansmen + attached women and children		Kurupmbo section—resident clansmen + attached women and children	
	At Mbukl	At Mbukl + Wahgi	At Mbukl	At Mbukl + Wahgi
Married men	13	15	17	26
Wives	15	18	17	29
Unmarried men, including widowers	2	5	7	9
Widows, etc.	3	3	6	6
Children—male	14	16	13	24
—female	17	22	19	27
	64	79	79	121

(d) SUMMARY, CLANSMEN + WOMEN AND CHILDREN

Clan	Living at or near Mbukl	In Wahgi area	Total
Kundmbo	244	13	257
Membo	284	89	373
Mandembo	170	59	229
	698	161	859

Note: in 1(c) I omit certain residents who are not clan members, since these have effectively been granted territory of their own; and also certain clan members who reside away from the clan's territory areas. The latter (numbering, with their wives and children, 29 persons) are included in 1(d), since they are group members.

seventeen, thirteen, and eleven respectively. Homesteads consisted mainly (thirty-one cases) of a married pair plus children; others contained also a mother of one of the married pair (four cases) or certain other incorporated members (four cases); or they consisted of a widowed person plus children and others (two cases), an old married pair and other kinsfolk (three cases), or a father-in-law and his dead son's wife (one case). For comparison with the homesteads, I give details on the composition of settlements in Table 2. The table indicates that classificatory as well as immediate kin may live together. In fact the number of settlements in which more distantly related 'brothers' (i.e. lineage, sub-clan, or clan mates) are associated as senior members equals that of settlements where the senior members are immediate brothers. However, there are more settlements with a single senior member than of any other single type, and the senior member is usually the immediate or lineage father of junior members.

TABLE 2: COMPOSITION OF SETTLEMENTS

(a) SENIOR MEMBERS OF SETTLEMENT

Type	Number
1. Settlements with a single senior member (F ± married sons + others)*	15
2a. Settlements with two married brothers as senior members	7
b. As 2a, but with more than two brothers	4
3. Settlements with two lineage mates (not immediately brothers) as senior members	6
4. With two sub-clan or clan mates as senior members	5
5. Doubtful or aberrant cases	4

(b) RELATIONSHIP OF SENIOR TO JUNIOR MEMBERS OF SETTLEMENTS (TYPE 1)

Relationship	Number
Immediate father or lineage father to all junior members	5
Immediate F or lin. F to some, elder B to others	4
Mo's 2nd husband, F to some, s-s-clan F to others	2
Immediate F to some, host to non-agnatic incorporated kin or affines	4
	15

* In one case a MB with his married ZS.

Homesteads may develop into settlements as the sons of a man grow up and marry. Eventually, when the father dies, the settlement becomes a dual one (Type 2 in Table 2(a)). At this stage some juniors may leave and found new homesteads or join other homesteads or settlements, thus forming dual settlements in which members are related by classificatory ties. These processes are modified by moves about clan territory made by adult men whose fathers are dead or by sets of fathers and sons together. In the past, particularly, there were opportunities of moving into areas vacated by persons defeated in warfare; and nowadays, as I have mentioned, men can occasionally colonise areas belonging to groups which are short of men and welcome settlers.

Land claims and allegiances to big-men are perhaps factors which induce junior members to stay with their seniors, although a son sometimes decides to abandon his paternal land claims and goes to join another clansman or his mother's brother. Cases where married sons live away from their 'fathers' (lineage F, etc., if the immediate F is dead) may be the result of a number of factors. For example, widows are often remarried within their first husbands' clans: if a son is grown-up at the time of his mother's remarriage he may remain on his first father's ground and not go to his mother's second husband's place. In one case, a son was ordered to leave his father's place by a big-man who lived nearby: the big-man wished to rid the neighbourhood of the son, who was a noted pig-thief. Nowadays, also, sons may be away for periods at work on plantations, or the father himself may leave his sons and move into a mission village in order to be baptised before he dies.

Leaving the father's place does not necessarily mean giving up the right to resume garden claims there later. The wives of men away at plantation work have garden strips allocated to them, often by their fathers-in-law. Men who have left the main Kawelka territory to live at the Wahgi have made a variety of arrangements: an immediate brother may act as trustee for their rights or they may have distributed their gardens to settlement mates. There is some question whether the main territory could now accommodate them all if, following disputes, they should be required to return. One big-man at Mbukl told me he would be glad if they returned, since he is 'short of men' for both exchange activities and Government work. Those, however, who have a stake in the new territory are reluctant to leave it, as they have developed good gardens, coffee-tree patches, and pig herds there.

If a man has more than two married sons in his settlement, after his death the third or fourth brother may move out to establish a new homestead and separate garden claims, or he may build a house for his wife away from the main settlement but continue to share a men's house with his brothers. He is likely, unless he changes his clan affiliation, to continue working claims belonging to his lineage, perhaps at a settlement-place previously occupied by his father. Separate residence does not preclude brothers from maintaining interests in each other's gardens, especially the valued mixed-vegetable gardens which are usually more extensively divided than sweet-potato gardens and are considered to require a more fertile type of soil. Table 3(a) summarises some information on place of establishment of new homesteads, although I cannot estimate distances of moves as Brookfield and Brown (1967:140) have done for Chimbu. Five of the nine cases listed under 2(a) in the table concern men moving into the mission village area, although such moves could also be made in the past when a clan was expanding in population and using up more of its territory. The men who initially went back to Kawelka territory in the Wahgi almost all moved into places with which they had only a general association through their clan membership; subsequent movers have joined them in the settlement-places they established.

TABLE 3: NEW HOMESTEADS

(a) PLACE OF ESTABLISHMENT OF NEW HOMESTEADS

Place	No. of cases
1. Same locality area	9
2. Different locality area	
(a) with which only clan-association or extra-clan kin association previously existed	9
(b) to which a tillage claim had previously been established	4
(c) which belongs to the mover's sub-clan, uncertain whether he had previous tillage claims there	4
(d) uncertain cases	4
	30

(b) RUMP AND PIONEER HOMESTEADS

Type	Clan			Total
	Kundmbo	Membo	Mandembo	
Rump homesteads	5	5	5	15
Pioneer homesteads	9	12	6	27
Non-classifiable (mission teachers away from home territory and living with Kawelka)	—	3	—	3
	14	20	11	45

(c) SEPARATION OF PIONEER HOMESTEADERS FROM KIN

Separated from	No. of cases
Father (or place of F some time after his death)	5
Brother	3
Father and brother $\pm$ others	2
Pair of brothers	5
Son or sons (men moving into mission-village)	3
Lineage mate(s)	3
Clan-section mates $+$ others	4
Other kinsman	1
Uncertain cases	4
	30

Men who make a move within clan territory may found their own homesteads or join others. There are thus homesteads which are the 'rumps' of depleted settlements (a settlement can also, of course, be depleted by the death of a senior male), and others which are 'pioneer' places. Table 3(b) gives the relative incidence of rump and pioneer homesteads among the Kawelka at Mbukl. It should be noted that some of the homesteads which I classify as 'pioneer' have in fact been built by the Christians near to or at the mission-villages. These moves could have been analysed separately from the others and seen as moves into an 'expanded hamlet' rather than a 'homestead' situation.

Who are the persons left behind when a man moves to build a

homestead of his own? Table 3(c) examines this point. As with previous tables, we find that we are not simply dealing with sets of full brothers who split up at determinate points in a domestic cycle of development. Such a cycle certainly occurs, but it is complicated by the association of other than immediate kin in settlements and by movements which occur at random to it: men moving to associate with a different sub-clan, to become a supporter of a big-man, to find better garden ground, and so on.

The degree of ease with which men can move from one settlement-place to another is affected by the situation over housing. In a settlement, a father and his married sons may share a single men's house (ten cases out of a total of fifteen settlements with a single senior man); or the father may have his own house (five cases). When the father has his own house, his sons may share a house with other settlement members or may have their own houses also. When a father does not share with his married sons, there is usually a particular reason. The son may not like the hot smoke from the indoor fire in his father's house, or may want to protect his dancing decorations from soot without having to wrap them elaborately; while the father may want to keep his resources in shells and Australian currency to himself, or may wish to share his house occasionally with a favourite wife if he is a polygynist. However, many men continue until they are very old to share a men's house with their married sons, and this is a mark of the relative unity of the settlement up till the father's death. Where a settlement is headed by two senior men there is a tendency for them to have separate men's houses, and this tendency is greatest where the senior men are more distantly related. Distantly related settlement mates are less likely to have grown up in a single settlement together as boys, and are perhaps correspondingly less likely to share housing when they decide to form a single settlement as adults. But we cannot say that immediate adult (i.e. married) brothers always share a men's house when they belong to the same settlement. Developmental processes seem to be involved here. In three cases where brothers share a men's house,[4] none of the brothers has a son who is himself married; whereas in the four cases where brothers have separate houses within the same settlement, five of the eight senior men involved have married sons, two others have married (but not co-residential) daughters, and only one is still relatively young. We may argue, then, that as men sharing a settlement grow older they tend to separate from each other and to share their housing-arrangements with their own families of procreation. The fairly marked degree of sharing men's houses which exists between fathers and their married sons shows also in the sharing of houses occupied by their women and pigs: fourteen of twenty-two married sons who lived in the same settlement as their fathers shared 'pig-houses' with them. In addition, both men's houses and 'pig-houses' are readily shared with other men who come to join a settlement, either as established clan-members or as non-agnatic kin seeking to change their clan-affiliations. An unmarried incomer can be accommodated particularly easily; he is simply allocated a place to sleep in one of the men's houses of the settlement and fed by the (or a) wife of his host, just as temporary visitors are. An incomer may be initially accommodated in this way and later may build his own house or houses. In most parts of the main Kawelka territory materials (timber, bark, cane, and grass) for house-building are to hand within each clan-area, and neighbours are willing to help gather the materials and build a house, provided they are rewarded with meals of steamed sweet-potato and other vegetables. A man who wishes to move from one settlement to another thus does not usually find that housing presents him with great difficulties, although it may take him some time and effort to provide himself both with a men's house and with a 'pig-house' for his wife, children, and herd of stock. The main necessity is for him to be accepted by his host group, for acceptance gives him access to the material resources and labour which they control.

Thus, in summary, the main form of settlement within Kawelka territory, and in the Hagen area generally, can be seen as an outcome of a number of factors. Most important, perhaps, are the requirements of shifting cultivation and of providing grazing areas as well as surplus crop-foods to support a large pig-population.[5] Rights in areas once cultivated which have gone into fallow are retained and are likely to be activated by the original cultivator or his inheritors. This is consistent with the fairly intensive methods of exploitation. In addition, Hageners prefer to keep men's and women's houses fairly close together, a pattern which may have become intensified since the ending of warfare, although it is sometimes broken by polygynists, who find it convenient and conducive to harmony to separate the houses of their wives from each other. The result is a tendency towards compact settlements, shared by a few men and surrounded by their garden and fallow areas.

An examination of the relationships between men who share settlements and the situation of men who live in homesteads of their own made it possible to discern in outline certain processes of developmental change in settlement composition. A man's married sons are quite likely to remain in the same settlement with him, and even if they move out they may not go far away, as it is convenient for them to maintain land claims at their father's place. When the father dies, the brothers may also continue to live together, but if there are more than two one is likely to leave. At all stages in family development this simple process may be overlaid by the incorporation of extra-familial members into the settlement, facilitated by sleeping arrangements in the men's houses. Settlements may be shared, in fact, by senior men who are not close lineage kin to each other at all. A major influence on this situation which is not shown by my tables so far is the tendency of big-men to draw persons to their settlements, in order to gain supporters and helpers for their enterprises. They may encourage married sisters with children to return to their natal place and bring the children with them, and they also recruit grown men sometimes as their low-status 'assistants'. These are points which will be examined again in later chapters.

In the next chapter the effect of warfare on settlement patterns is discussed. Warfare was one of the major factors modifying the stability of a clan's occupation of its territory, and many of my individual cases of changes of clan-affiliation also relate to the period when the Kawelka were still fighting against neighbouring groups, so the involvement of the Kawelka in warfare must be considered before looking at the cases themselves.

CHAPTER 4
SETTLEMENT
AND WARFARE

In chapter three I have concentrated on the internal composition of settlements and homesteads, while also pointing out that the dispersal of dwelling houses over group territories makes for an adequate ecological adjustment to the problems of gardening and pig-raising. In the past, however, there was an added requirement: clansmen not only had to adjust to their natural environment but were also regularly engaged in warfare against other groups. They had to maintain their joint hold over their group territory; or, if they could not do so, they had to have places of refuge to which they could go, temporarily or permanently. The alternative was loss of life and extinction of the group. Empirical patterns of settlement and affiliation to groups were thus considerably influenced by the fact of warfare.

Many anthropologists (e.g. Barnes 1962, Langness 1964) have stressed the importance of warfare in pre-contact Highlands societies. Berndt (1964), in reviewing this theme, has pointed out also that there were certain differences between these societies in terms of their stress on warfare and the extent to which large-scale, stable alliances were contracted between political groups within them. He points to other dimensions of contrast also: for example, the degree of nucleation of settlement, and whether there is a preference for marrying into friendly groups or not. He suggests, as a generalisation, that 'the more stable the alliances, the more highly developed and formalized the system of economic exchange' (1964:184).

These are all variables which are capable of fairly accurate assessment. Nevertheless, the empirical evidence is complicated, and it may be helpful to begin with two contrasting models, which may not correspond exactly to any given society.

The first model (1) has the following characteristics: there are stable alliances between clan groups; the groups are localised and territory-holding; the alliances are reinforced by close intermarriage and by important ceremonial exchanges; and allies afford each other refuge on both a group and an individual basis following defeats in warfare. The second model is constructed out of contrasts with the first. Its exact construction depends on the number of features which we choose to vary. As one sub-type (2a) I hold constant the existence of localised clan groups, but posit that there are no stable alliances, intensive rates of intermarriage, or large periodic exchanges between them, and they do not especially give each other refuge in warfare. Instead marriages are dispersed, and refugees correspondingly must usually disperse to their individual relatives if their group is defeated. Relations between individual extra-clan kin and affines are maintained by exchanges, and large-scale ceremonial prestation occasions are held, but at these the gifts are not channelled significantly between groups as military allies. By positing further changes, we can take the trends of this sub-type further (2b). We can specify that political responsibility rests primarily with individual men and not with groups *en bloc*. A man recruits allies entirely on a network basis from more than one local area, via his individual ties (this feature corresponds to the 'proliferation of ties at the individual rather than the group level' which Barnes (1962) posited). Similarly, he exchanges with his network only and is personally responsible for paying indemnities to men from a number of groups who have helped him in fighting.

These models correspond roughly to (1) Hagen society, (2a) Mae-Enga, and (2b) Huli society as described by Glasse (1968). They do not account for all features of these societies. Thus in Hagen there was a distinction between minor and major enemies, and allies could on occasion be minor enemies. Moreover, ad hoc alliances for particular battles were sometimes contracted; and there was some degree of intermarriage with clans other than one's close allies, so that refugees might disperse to a number of clans, particularly if their allies were also hard-pressed or were rather short of land, or if all previously neutral groups had turned against them. However, the presence of a stable alliance between Tipuka tribe and the Kawelka, for example, did facilitate a certain amount of sharing of territory between them, and the results still show in settlement alignments around Mbukl nowadays. The presence of this alliance had, I suggest, two separate effects on clan-affiliation: first, given the rate of intermarriage between Tipuka and Kawelka, and the fact that most changes of affiliation resulted from an adult person joining his maternal kin or a woman returning with her children to her natal kin, quite a number of Tipuka individuals have 'become Kawelka' and vice-versa; second, where numbers of adult men fled as refugees to the land of their allied tribe, they have subsequently retained their original tribal identity although they are living on the other tribe's land, and remain valuable as exchange-partners of their hosts. This maintenance of a separate identity is tolerated because of the alliance between the two tribes (effectively, the alliance between the particular clans involved, although notionally the two tribes are allied as whole units).

This latter situation may contrast with that which existed, or exists, in societies closer to the second model. In these there are no strong inter-group alliances. Hence men are likely to scatter individually and to be absorbed into their new groups. They may have difficulty in obtaining membership of a new community if its men feel they are short of land. Effective access to membership may depend on individual status. In the case of the Huli potential access to co-residential membership of a number of parishes seems to have been institutionalised; among the Mae-Enga it was, and is, strongly restricted.

Cross-cutting these possibilities there are others, which apply equally to Hagen and the other societies I have mentioned. First, an alternative to dispersal and absorption would be to colonise a new, unclaimed area, if such were available; another would be to claim the area of a group long ago defeated in warfare which had not returned, or to return to one's old area if it were not claimed by victors. A further possibility would be to obtain a special niche, equivalent to a new territory, via a kin-tie with, or an approach to, an important man of a community with enough land to spare, perhaps one itself short of men. This possibility was certainly exploited by big-men in Hagen. Watson (1967:69-70) shows that it could have been in the interests of a big-man to be credited with the personal decision to grant land to such outsiders and to look after their interests in return for their special support within his own community. They would to some extent act as his 'clients', supporting him more strongly than others of his group less obligated to, or perhaps actually in rivalry with, him. Watson's example, the big-man Matoto, belonged to Tairora, in the Eastern Highlands, but the possibility of such arrangements being made, in societies both with and without marked inter-group alliances, is clear. Watson himself suggests (1967:70) that 'the mutual relationship of collective and individual interests suggested [by Matoto's actions] is probably a classical instance in the politics of pre-contact New Guinea'.

Changes in Kawelka settlement over the last fifty years or so illustrate these processes. The general point is that settlement has never been static. By their own account, and so far as can be determined, Kawelka groups have continually been expanding in some directions, giving way in others to share territory with their allies, and migrating back and forth between their Wahgi and their Mbukl territories.

Informants' accounts of settlement history are no doubt simplified and incomplete, but their statements that both Kundmbo and Membo clans have increased the sizes of their territories at Mbukl seem reliable. Kundmbo men say that 'after the Kawelka migrated down from the Wahgi to Mbukl' they all lived close together, the Kundmbo sharing territory mainly with Mandembo. Quarrels which resulted in Kundmbo men moving to their present separate territory are placed within the lifetime of the father of an old Kundmbo man, Tei.[1] Tei's father, Kela, is said to have lived initially at Mbukl itself, then to have moved through a number of settlements, finally living at one of the present main Kundmbo places, Purlpana. One very old Kundmbo man remembers cutting into forest areas and roofing houses with leaves from the *yakla*, a forest tree, before there was secondary re-growth grass available for this task. The implication is that the impression given in the Kawelka myth of settlers entering an unoccupied or lightly occupied area has some foundation in fact. It accords also with the general view of Northern Melpa-speakers that the area they call Kuma or Koma, i.e. the plains-land south of the Gumant river, was occupied before the Kopon ('bush') area north of the Gumant. (In a funeral song a dead woman is called *Kuma amb mam*, 'Kuma mother', because the dead are like ancestors and the ancestors originally lived at Kuma.)

From their settlement-places near to Mbukl the Kundmbo moved out further. At this time, according to one account, they were divided into the two sub-clans Kumapei and Roklambo only, and men of these sub-clans lived close together. There are various versions of the disagreements which developed between them. One is that the Kumapei were friendly with Tipuka Kengeke clan (a view perhaps coloured by the informant's own friendly ties with this clan), while the Roklambo were not. A Roklaka tribesman, who was living with the Roklambo, lured a Kengeke man up to a point near Kundmbo territory on a pretext of giving him a bundle of salt; he ambushed and killed him, claiming pay from another clan which had hired him for the job. The Kumapei were angry at this and drove the Roklambo out.[2] Another version suggests that disputes occurred over garden claims, and that the fighting was only with sticks. In any case both sub-clans later combined to drive away from their borders two clans of the Kombukla tribe. They contracted alliances with Membo clan and with a clan, Kimbo, of the Minembi tribe which lived nearby, and with the aid of these drove away the Kombukla. This eased their situation in more than one way. They were being marauded by other Minembi clans at their backs and could now move away from these, and the feuding between their two sub-clans was settled by dispersal, although stick-fighting and pig-stealing continued between them. These minor enmities encouraged the Roklambo to move even further away from the Kumapei, and at the same time two big-men of Kundmbo contracted marriages with the Kombukla on their borders and converted relations with them from enmity to friendship. (One of the two big-men, Roltinga, actually captured a Kombukla woman from her previous husband and gave her to his clan-mate, Ai, the other big-man, as a basis for friendship. The two belonged to opposite sub-clans, now clan-sections, and Roltinga seems to have done this to secure his position *vis-à-vis* Ai, as a Kumapei man living close to the Roklambo.) After this, other Roklambo men moved into areas around the two big-men, thus completing the present pattern of settlement. It was apparently not till later that the further segmentation of the clan (described in chapter two) took place, but the grounds for it were laid in this expansion into a number of new settlement-places. Before the segmentation occurred, gardens of Kumapei and Roklambo men were more interspersed than they are now; since it, sub-clan territories have begun to emerge, but within what are now the two clan-sections there is still a good deal of interdigitation of gardens.

The Kundmbo expansion is paralleled by that of the Membo clan. At the time when accounts of specific fights and particular settlement-places begin, most of the Membo were living high on the hill of Rokle (see Map 2) with some outcrop settlements nearer to the Mɔka river in an area occupied mainly by Mandembo clansmen. Accounts suggest that the Membo were compacted within a small area. Fighting began between the Klammbo section of Mandembo clan and Tipuka Oklembo clansmen, and the Membo came in as allies of Mandembo.[3] As a result of this fighting some, but not all, of the Membo men settled near to the Mɔka moved back to Rokle or further west of it. One stayed 'on the boundary' between Tipuka and Kawelka settlements for some years after the fighting, until he too moved west. He was actually the son of an Oklembo clansman and had been adopted as a very young child by his Kawelka mother's brother when the mother died. Quite possibly he did not feel threatened by the Oklembo because of his original patrifilial tie with them; perhaps he even maintained a position of neutrality in the fighting. Following these fights with the Oklembo and the Membo withdrawal, further battles developed on the Membo's western front, against a clan of the traditionally hostile Minembi

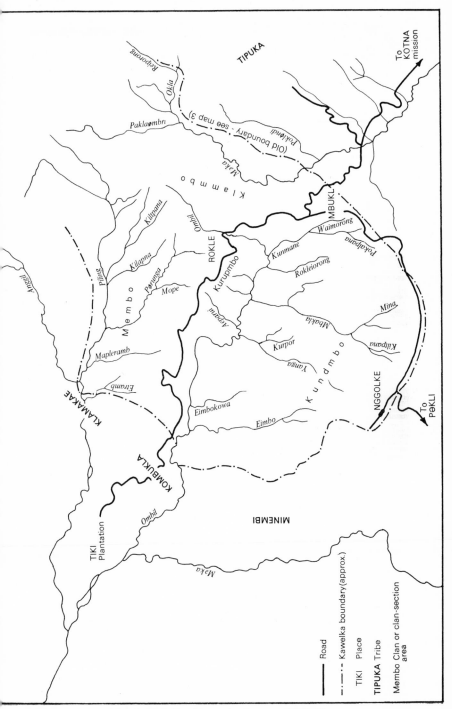

Map 2. Kawelka clan territories around Mbukl

tribe. Membo men speak of these as part of an ongoing series of hostilities; but in this case one of the results was that they ejected their enemies (Minembi Ruprupkae clan and men of the Klamakae tribe), and Membo settlement moved forward into five new places. They were aided by Tipuka clans and both Mandembo and Kundmbo *and* by another Minembi clan, the Kimbo, and thus formed a stronger alliance-set than their enemies. It was only from this time that the two Membo sub-clans began to occupy discrete settlements. Køyambo sub-clansmen nowadays say that a particular river (the Pørunga) is the boundary between themselves and Oyambo men, and except for one small homestead this held good in 1964. However, they shared a part of their territory with two Klammbo men, and these two also shared gardens with Oyambo men, so we cannot speak of a hard boundary between Oyambo and Køyambo. We can say no more than that there is a tendency towards the local clustering of settlements which belong to men of the same sub-clan. The degree to which they share with men of other sub-clans depends on ties of friendship and on the magnitude of work-requirements for bush-clearing, fencing, and tilling.

After moving forward into areas of land formerly occupied by the Klamakae, the Membo re-established friendship with these (just as Roltinga and Ai did with their Kombukla ex-enemies). In fact, they allowed some of them to return and take asylum when they were further defeated in warfare against another tribe, the Andakapkae. All the Klamakae who took refuge in this way were either close cognatic kin or affines of the Membo, and many were related to a single Membo lineage which included at least two big-men. These two welcomed the immigrants (who were returning to their previous territory, but on a dependent basis), helped them to obtain wives, and so bound them closely to themselves. Since warfare was stopped, some have returned to Klamakae territory while others have remained. Both some of those who have returned and those who remain keep, by their own account, a kind of 'double affiliation', making gardens with both Klamakae and Kawelka men, helping the Kawelka to make *moka* prestations and receiving *moka* from them, and so on. In fact, of course, they help only the small lineage whose big-men in the past helped them, and together they and the Kawelka lineage form a local association of neighbours, kinsmen, co-workers, and exchange partners. Here is a case, then, where big-men took in immigrants from an ex-enemy (but not major enemy) group, probably in order both to stabilise border relations and to gain helpers and supporters for themselves. The Membo big-men's actions paralleled those of the Kundmbo and actually went further, precipitated by the facts that the Klamakae were not their major enemies, had many ties of kinship with them, and suffered a further defeat in warfare which made it exigent for them to obtain refuge. The Klamakae also became a buffer between the Kawelka and their Minembi enemies (although a different Kawelka big-man also made friends with a Minembi big-man who lives not far from him). Their special position was sharply marked in 1964, when Waema, a Membo big-man and one of their patrons, fell sick: the Minembi were suspected of poisoning him, while his Klamakae friends helped to carry him in to hospital.[4]

Although both clans expanded westwards at least partly under the threat of warfare on their eastern borders, the pressure on the Kundmbo seems to have been more severe, and their situation was complicated by internecine quarrels, which do not seem to have occurred in the Membo case. Both clans were aided by special alliances to drive out other groups and take over their territory, although they do not emphasise that the fighting was actually undertaken in order to acquire land. After the take-over big-men re-established friendship with the defeated enemies, thus securing friends for themselves and a stable border situation for their group. This friendship has gone further in the Membo case, for reasons I have already suggested. Both Membo and Kundmbo have taken in numbers of non-agnates, in the Kundmbo case from a scatter of tribes, in the Membo mostly from Klamakae and Tipuka, and the expansion of their territories has clearly facilitated this process. By contrast, Mandembo clan has not expanded, and may even have declined in numbers. Correspondingly it has a lower intake of non-agnatic members. Instead it has accommodated a number of Tipuka settlements within its territory area and these Tipuka men have retained their original identity: a process which fits one of the arguments made at the beginning of this chapter. Tipuka men, coming in numbers from an allied tribe, have remained Tipuka, and in fact are valuable exchange partners of two of the Kawelka clans. I shall consider the history of their re-settlement in further detail.

The first territory the Tipuka Kitepi clan occupied in the Məka Valley area lay near the borders with the Kombukla tribe at a place called Kitip (marked on Map 1), and the Kitepi (or Kitipi) derive their name from this place. Kombukla enemies drove them away from Kitip (since Administration control some have re-settled there, just as Kawelka men have returned to the Wahgi), and they settled with two other Tipuka clans, Kendike and Oklembo. The latter had suffered an epidemic of sickness and lost many men, and were quite willing to give the incoming Kitepi ground. Perhaps the special alliance-pairing between the two dates from this time. Kendike and their allies of Kengeke clan then pushed their Kitepi guests out in a bout of minor warfare, and at this point some of the Kitepi took refuge in their present locations around Mbukl. Many of the original refugees were still living in 1964-9, and they told me they came along with their fathers when they were mostly unmarried boys. The same men were courting or newly-married when European explorers passed through their area in 1933, so this would place the Kitepi influx probably in the 1920s. With the Kitepi came some men of a small clan, Tipuka Eltimbo. Other Eltimbo stayed in association with Oklembo clansmen near the Məka river. Indeed the Eltimbo are in danger of losing their existence as a separate clan at all, living together with and closely related to men of the more powerful Kitepi and Oklembo clans.[5]

The Kitepi men now living at Mbukl arrived as individuals or sets of brothers, and each was granted a place to settle in by his particular kinsfolk. Map 3 indicates the locations of Kitepi settlement inside what was previously territory of Mandembo clan in the Kawelka tribe. Each location is marked with a letter, A–F, and Table 4 lists the occupants of the locations in 1964 and their links with the Kawelka. As the second part of the table shows, many of the settlers strengthened the ties they already had with the Kawelka

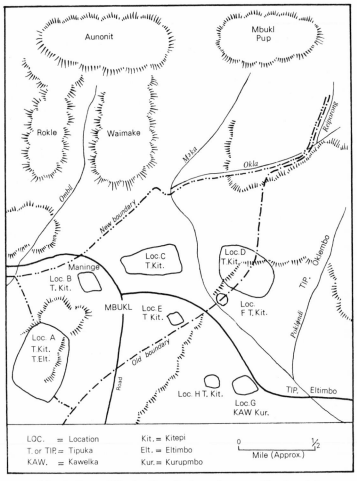

Map 3. Part of Tipuka-Kawelka boundary area (sketch only)

TABLE 4(a): OCCUPANTS OF TIPUKA SETTLEMENTS WITHIN OLD KAWELKA TERRITORY

Location; name of man	Sub-clan or clan	Rough age in 1964	Circumstances of arrival
A 1. Nditing (big-man)	K. Rulkembo	45-50	Came with no. 7. At first, two other men of Rulkembo came too, both since returned to the main territory.
2. Ok	K. Rulkembo	55-60	Came as a young married man, with his father.
3. Pana	K. Rulkembo	40-45	Came as a boy, with his elder brother, no. 2.
4. Mitipa	Eltimbo	c.40	Came with his father, (he is brother of no. 6).
5. Ndai	Eltimbo	c.40	Came with his father, who was a seminal brother of 6's father.
6. Kot (big-man)	Eltimbo	c.40	Came with his father. Married much later.
B 7. Kuri (big-man)	K. Ropkembo	c.60	Came with his brother and with no. 1. The brother later went back to Kitip.
8. Ndat	K. Ropkembo	40-45	Came later to join 7, after warfare stopped.
C 9. Ndimi	K. Kolkal	c.60	Came with 10 and 11, his brothers.
10. Ndonge	K. Kolkal	55+	Came with 9 and 11.
11. əndipi	K. Kolkal	55+	Came with 9 and 10. When his daughter committed suicide, he returned to the main territory.*
D 12. Engk (big-man)	K. Kolkal	45+	Came on basis of same links as 9, 10, and 11, along with 13.
13. Numndi	K. Kolkal	45+	Came with his seminal brother, 12.

E	14. Nukint (big-man)	K. Rulkembo	45+	Came with his father to live near 7.
F	15. Pøng	K. Kolkal	55+	Came with 9, 10, and 11.

TABLE 4(b): OCCUPANTS OF TIPUKA SETTLEMENTS WITHIN OLD KAWELKA TERRITORY

Location	Previously Occupied by	Incomer's ties with Kawelka
A (Mbitanui)	Kawelka Kundmbo	No. 1: sister's son No. 2: sister's husband No. 3: sister's husband's brother No. 1's son now has a Kundmbo wife.
A (Waimorong)	Kawelka Klammbo (Mandembo clan)	No. 5: sister's son of Kurupmbo, the other section in Mandembo. Nos. 4 and 6 shared this tie. No. 6 later married a Klammbo woman.
B (Rut)	Kawelka Kurupmbo (Mandembo clan)	No. 7: sister's husband, and also wife's brother to a different set of men. He later married a Kundmbo and a Membo wife as well.
C, D, F (Rukumrui, Aporong, Kokeiorong)	Kawelka Mandembo and Membo	Nos. 9 and 10: sister's sons of Membo. The others shared this tie. No. 9 later married a Kurupmbo wife. His two sons by her were actually brought up by the Kawelka. No. 10 married a Klammbo woman; No. 12 a Membo.

*The daughter was married, and wanted to invite her father and brothers over to a pig-cooking. The husband refused, and in protest she hanged herself; and this was given to me as the reason for the father moving back to his old place, although the exact connection between her suicide and his move was not explained. It is probable that he felt he had suffered ill-luck at his new place and that his ancestral ghosts wished him to return to his paternal territory.

by making fresh marriages with them. Many, also, particularly those
who are big-men, have become important exchange partners of men
in Kawelka Membo and Mandembo clans. Kuri eventually married
ten wives, two from his clan's minor enemies, Tipuka Kengeke, two
from Kurupmbo, one each from the other two Kawelka clans, and
two from the enemies of Kawelka Membo, Minembi Kimbo clan
(but note that these actually helped the Membo in one sequence of
fighting). These extensive affinal ties undoubtedly gave Kuri influence
in more than one local clan-group, and he is pictured nowadays as a
man who encouraged all the groups around to give up warfare and
expand their ceremonial exchange activities instead. His son, Pørwa,
told me that in the old days the father was *møi keap*, an indigenous
equivalent of Government officers who stopped fighting in the
Hagen area. Kuri's rise to pre-eminence as a big-man must in fact
have coincided with the Administration's imposition of peace from
1945 onwards; between 1933 and 1945 the Northern Melpa groups
knew about the 'white men' in Hagen but had not themselves been
brought under control. Valued pearl shells, obtained from the
Europeans, were reaching their area, however, and the increasing
numbers of these must have encouraged groups to elaborate their
exchange activities. It is interesting that Kuri achieved his position
specifically as a man who had ties with many groups rather than one
who had a strong local base and clansmen as his supporters; and that
he is spoken of as a leader in *moka* exchanges, not in warfare. His
rise, facilitated by the advent of Europeans, must have been paralleled
by the careers of many big-men in Hagen over the same period of
time. With Administration control, moreover, the new Kitepi
settlers were enabled to establish themselves firmly. Possibly, if
warfare (on a minor scale) between their own clan and the Kawelka
had continued, they would have been faced with harder choices of
allegiance and might have either 'become Kawelka' or returned to
their main area. One of them, Ok (Table 4 (a) no. A2), actually did
help the Kawelka against Kitepi-Oklembo, and his action was still
recognised with gratitude by the Kawelka in 1964-5.[6] He did not,
however, change his clan identity.

The factors allowing for the continued independence of the

Kitepi and Eltimbo settlers were thus: (1) warfare was stopped, (2) they were able to maintain links with the main body of their clansmen, who lived nearby, (3) their hosts valued them as exchange partners; in particular some of them became big-men and developed extensive networks of alliance with their hosts while improving their own status, and (4) they were able to draw the rest of their clansmen into exchanges with the Kawelka because of the already-existing ties of military alliance and intermarriage between Tipuka and Kawelka as tribes (particularly between Tipuka Kitepi plus Oklembo and Kawelka Membo plus Mandembo).

In addition to these factors, it is significant that part of the area they moved into lay close to Kawelka borders with the Tipuka Oklembo clan. Oklembo and Kawelka Mandembo were involved in fighting at this time, and both Membo and Mandembo men subsequently moved away from the borders into new areas. The Kitepi were thus relatively unhampered in establishing gardens in the area vacated, and also perhaps acted as a buffer between Kawelka and the Oklembo. Kitepi men even nowadays emphasise that their clan was never a principal enemy of Membo and Mandembo; the principal enemy was their pair-clan, Oklembo, while they themselves merely helped as allies. Such statements reflect the privileges granted the Kitepi by their Kawelka hosts.

The ultimate tenurial status of the Kitepi's land claims around their new settlements has not been (up till 1970) called in question by the Kawelka, and the intermingling of Kawelka and Tipuka settlements is incompatible with a concept of rigid boundaries such as seem to have been envisaged in land demarcation projects which were introduced by the Administration in the latter part of the 1960s. Difficulties will not arise unless abrupt changes occur: for example, if the land in question should acquire a high cash value. The same applies to pockets of Kawelka settlement within the Tipuka area, viz. Raporong (location G, Map 3).[7] The Kawelka Councillor, Ongka, has an exact knowledge of the original boundary between his own clan and the Oklembo, and in 1964-5, when there was a possibility of Kitepi men laying claim to forest timber for cutting and selling planks, he objected strongly, urging that no rights at all had been ceded over the forest areas above the new Kitepi settlements. The Kawelka recognise the secure use-rights of the Kitepi over gardens around their houses and that there is a new 'mark' in terms of land use between themselves and the Tipuka; but they do not recognise the Kitepi men's ultimate claims to the 'land'. As they say, *møi tininga, kongon Tipuka-nga,* 'the land is ours, the gardens belong to Tipuka'.

Finally, as I have mentioned, the Kitepi immigrants' situation was made easier by the withdrawal of Kawelka, particularly Mandembo men, from land near to the Oklembo border. I shall look at this process in further detail.

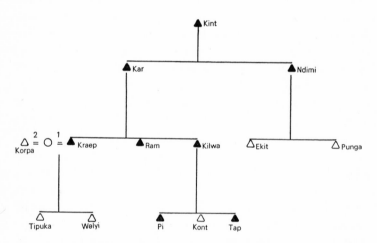

Figure 8. A Kawelka Kurupmbo lineage

At location F there was a settlement of Kawelka Kurupmbo men belonging to a single lineage as shown in Figure 8. The history of this small lineage is as follows:

Kint lived in the hills above D and was buried there.

Kar occupied F and died there.

Kraep and Ram left F and lived at a settlement further to the west, within the Kawelka area, called Maninge.

Kilwa also went to Maninge.

Kont subsequently went to his MZH, a Membo man, and has 'become a Membo'.

Tipuka and Wɔlyi went with their mother when she was re-married as a widow to another Kurupmbo man, and they have claims now both at G and at Maninge.

Ndimi's children, Ekit and Punga, were taken away by their mother to her natal clan and became affiliated to this.

As this history indicates, the whole lineage dispersed and there were no remaining claimants to the land at F. Pøng, the Kitepi immigrant, was thus able to settle in the old area where Kurupmbo men had lived, as their successor. He leaves uncultivated, however, particular pieces of land nearby, to which Klammbo men hold cultivation rights by previous tillage. The same kind of situation holds in other locations, for example D and E. The settlements there are Kitepi ones, but garden claims of Klammbo men are maintained within the locations. Again, some of the Klammbo men who had originally lived high in the forest at Okla dispersed to areas away from Kawelka territory, or moved into Kawelka-settlement-places further away from the Oklembo. Some went over the crest of the mountain into the Jimi Valley, living there with their affines, and have only recently returned, or have remained there for good.[8] Klammbo lineages were broken up and depleted by these moves, and this is reflected in the small size of the Klammbo as a group nowadays. Hence there was ample ground on which the Kitepi refugees could be accommodated.

Many factors, then, are involved in the history of Kitepi re-settlement within the Kawelka area. Among them is the factor given as part of a model situation at the beginning of the chapter: the Kitepi and their hosts were already in an alliance relationship before the immigration occurred, and in the interests of both sides this relationship has been preserved. Thus, of the two possibilities, their absorption into the Kawelka or their maintenance of a separate identity, it is the latter which has occurred. The material given in this and the previous two chapters has also, however, indicated that there has been an intake of individual non-agnatic members into Kawelka clans, as well as some degree of dispersal and break-up of

Kawelka lineages themselves. The next chapter will examine the composition of Kawelka clan-goups more exactly.

The main conclusion here is that both warfare and inter-group alliances in the past modified the exclusiveness of the Kawelka clans' occupation of their territories. Alliances enabled them to succeed on certain fronts against their enemies, so that they could expand their own settlement areas. This in turn enabled them to take in non-agnatic immigrants who became assimilated into the Kawelka groups, and to grant enclave territories to sub-groups of men among their Tipuka allies, who continued to retain their Tipuka identity, aided, perhaps, by the imposition of peace by the Australian Administration. The same fact of colonial peace both blocked the progress of Kawelka military expansion in one direction and gave them an outlet in another, for peace meant that they could safely begin to migrate back to their older territory in the Wahgi Valley. The Administration thus 'froze' one way in which territory and people were in the past redistributed, but opened out a second way, which the Kawelka were not slow to follow.

CHAPTER 5

AFFILIATION

In this chapter I turn back from examining the external inter-relations of clans and the effect that these have had, in the past, both on the exclusiveness of clan territories and on the affiliation of persons to clan groups, in order to look more closely at the details of con-temporary clan composition. It is clear that the contemporary situation is likely to reflect the past, and since what we are attempting to assess is the degree to which either patrifiliation or agnation is significant in determining clan composition, this in turn requires us to consider genealogical material over several generations. Before we can scrutinise the supposed empirical data in these terms, we are faced with definitional problems similar to those which I discussed at the beginning of chapter one. At issue there was the definition of 'descent' in general; here I am concerned with the term 'agnate'.

McArthur (1967:282) and Glasse (1969:134) have both pointed out that if one wishes to compare 'rates of agnation' in different societies, the term 'agnate' must itself be given an operational defini-tion. Barnes (1967), in dissecting Meggitt's thesis linking patrilineality to population pressure among the Mae-Enga, similarly urges that we must consider separately structure (in this context, the form of the genealogies in terms of which the Mae-Enga represent at least some of the segmentary levels within their main social groups), recruitment (the empirical processes whereby persons become affiliated to groups), and, finally, the pervasiveness of social attitudes (which, as he implies, may be rather difficult to assess). Barnes has also stressed that we must make a careful distinction between emic and etic categories here. In terms of the 'tasks of the anthropologist' which I set out in chapter one, there are two opposed possibilities. Either one can use an entirely etic set of constructs in discussing group membership, or one can set out emic categories, as recognised by people themselves, and describe the system, as it were, from 'inside' only, from the point of view of the actors. Ideally it is desirable to be able to do both of these things: the danger is that one may try to do both of them at once, to mix emic and etic criteria without perhaps realising that one is doing this (cf. Harris 1969:575 and Barnes 1967:40).

In chapter two some comparison was made of the emic genealogies and other idioms used by Melpa speakers to describe group segments and their inter-relations and the actual composition of some of the lineages within the Kawelka tribe. This showed that there is a disjunction between the agnatic models of structure which are employed and the mundane genealogical facts about lineage composition; and I suggested that the 'men's house group' idiom, providing an alternative model of structure to the descent idiom, helps to bridge over this disjunction. One implication of this treatment is that Hageners 'maintain' different kinds of genealogy and it is possible that the higher up the genealogies go from living persons the more mythological they become. The most relevant African parallel to the New Guinea Highlands here is perhaps the analysis of Bedouin genealogies made by Peters (1960), which Barnes recommends to Highlands ethnographers: 'The higher generations in pedigrees are fairly constant and constitute a description of what he [Peters] refers to as the "cultural past". The lower generations record ostensibly accurately who is the son of whom. In between is an "area of ambiguity", one or two generation levels where in effect there is argument about how the shifting pattern of relationships between taxa rising and falling in the hierarchy can be translated into genealogical terms.' This precise scheme may not be exactly repeated in any of the Highlands societies, although Barnes suggests that at least the two lower parts can be identified for the Mae-Enga. The general relevance, however, of Peters's argument to my problem of definition is that it draws attention to discontinuities in genealogical statements in terms of the contrast between emic and etic categories. The lowest level Peters identifies is one in which relationships are, at least ostensibly, etically stated, viz. 'who is the son of whom'. The highest level genealogies are unquestionably emic. In between there is an area of uncertainty in which etic facts are sorted and reassembled to form shifting emic statements.

The genealogies of the small lineages (the *tepam-kangemal* level in Melpa emic terms) which are given in chapter two are reasonably close to demographic fact, and can at least be employed to determine the succession of pater-child links over sequences of two or three generations. I am not asserting that I was told of all the marriages people made, all the children they had, or even of all the people who at one time belonged to the group, and even at this level a certain amount of re-ordering goes on in informants' statements. In some instances I was given an initial version of the relationships between men of a lineage, based on the kin term usages of its members, which was rather misleadingly agnatic in form. That is, the version was emic, and significant in emic terms. However, there was little resistance to my further inquiries, directed towards obtaining a more convincingly etic picture of the literal genealogical relationships between the lineage members. It is true that the etic facts tend to be transformed into emic facts over time, but, within certain generational levels, it is possible plausibly to establish what at least some of the etic facts are. For the Kawelka, I suggest that the generational levels within which etic facts can be obtained are the two generations above the level of currently-married men. Two generational steps up from these men often bring us to the apex of the currently-recognised *tepam-kangemal* or small lineage groupings. Beyond this level either no genealogical statements are proffered, or the supposed founders of lineages are described as sons of the myth-ological clan founder, or an intermediate emic level (as in the case of Kawelka Membo clan) is interpolated.

Salisbury (1956:4) has examined the problem of genealogies for the case of the Siane, in an interesting early article on 'unilineal descent groups' in the Highlands. He shows that a boy of about 18 in a particular lineage had a different view of the composition of his group from that of a man two generations higher up than himself. In his grandfather's generation the boy reduced the eight men listed by the older informant to three, and accordingly redistributed some of the sons of the five men omitted among these three. Nevertheless, both the boy and the older informant presented the same picture of the structure of the lineage, issuing at the level of their grandfathers in three separate lines, representing, it would seem, the idiom of the eldest, middle, and youngest brother which is important in ordering succession to positions of authority in the Siane lineage. For the Siane, then, it is clear that a considerable amount of 'emic distortion' occurs at the grandparental level of genealogies. In Hagen, however, there is no clear equivalent of the Siane system of succession to lineage authority, as I have pointed out in an earlier publication (Strathern, A.J. 1966:363-4). Although there is some tinkering with the top linkages of lineage genealogies when men wish to re-combine them to form new pairs, there is no systematic distortion and no entrenched effacing of facts from the genealogical record. It is thus possible, in most cases, to find out from a living man who his father's father was and where he is declared to have come from. It occasions slight embarrassment if one pushes to know whether the grandfather really came from within the group or was an outside immigrant, but, again, to judge by the fact that I have been told of immigrants at this generational level, the etic facts are recoverable: they are neither systematically eliminated, nor conveniently forgotten, although they are unlikely to be mentioned often by clansmen themselves, simply because they are largely irrelevant to contemporary affairs.

Now to apply these points to the definition of 'agnate'. With some effort, etic genealogies can be obtained over short runs of generations; above these levels there are no means of obtaining etic 'checks' on emic statements. The higher levels of genealogy can thus be assessed, in Barnes's terms, only as statements of structure. The lower levels, however, can be used as indices of recruitment processes. Instead of insisting, then, on a criterion of definition which would run across emic and etic stretches of genealogy and so confuse the two, I list as 'agnates' of Kawelka clans all those whose father's fathers, as far as I can tell, were accepted as group members, whether they came as immigrants or are themselves asserted to have been birth members of it. Thus, in the terms I shall use, an 'agnatic' member of the clan is a member of a lineal set of men whose membership of a particular group has been continuous over at least two generations. [2]

My reasons for not extending the definitional requirements beyond this level are related to Ryan's (1959:286) observation that 'when migrants establish themselves in a new clan-territory by virtue of their kin-relationship to a member of the agnatic core, and subsequent migrants attach themselves to the first lot without being related at all to the agnatic core ... it becomes useless to talk of clan-territory composition in terms of percentages of agnates and non-agnates, because the term agnatic is meaningful only when referred to a specific descent line.' My definition does not entirely escape Ryan's stricture in one sense, since I shall initially call non-agnates persons who accrete as clan-members via links with persons who are themselves not agnates, instead of distinguishing these by a special term. My definition of agnate, however, does refer to 'a specific descent line', and I am reluctant to extend the definition, since, as I have argued, above the level of the FF of contemporary adult men genealogies tend to change their character from literal accounts of lineage composition to charters which correspond to clan segmentation patterns; or else genealogical documentation disappears altogether, and we are left with a gap or only a presumed linkage between the FF and the putative clan founder. Since this chapter is concerned with empirical cumulative continuity in clan membership, I restrict my criteria to stretches of genealogy which can be expected approximately to record a historical situation. The rate of agnatic recruitment which I shall describe is thus one which is calculated over a span of only three generations of adult males.

There are two further definitional difficulties. Persons whose affiliation is changed from their patrifilial clan to another do not lose all components of their original clan identity. Even their children may be remembered to have an agnatic link with their father's patrifilial group. Clansmen of the original group remember them as 'persons of our group who have gone away and become members of another', and as long as the particular links are remembered the emigrants and their descendants must observe marriage prohibitions appropriate to their original patrifilial or agnatic status.[3] Thus men of a particular Kawelka clan, say Membo, who join another clan, whether among the Kawelka or a different tribe, are said to have 'become x' (the name of the clan being given), but they could not marry into Membo clan, nor could their children do so. Since this component of their original identity is maintained, they can in that sense be said to be 'still Membo'. On the other hand, they are not men who are resident on clan territory and act as 'Membo' persons in gardening, ceremonial exchanges and political alignments. In order to handle this difficulty, I distinguish between the clan-group, which comprises active group-members whose affiliation is expressed and maintained in a number of ways, and the clan-unit, which includes those members of the clan-group who are agnates and those remembered agnates of the clan who have become members of other clan-groups. Men whose clan-affiliation has been changed (and their sons) are thus members of one clan-unit and another clan-group.[4] The clan-unit, as I have defined it, does not include non-agnates of a group who have left it and joined another.

Since the process of losing and gaining members by mechanisms other than patrifiliation is a continuous one, as genealogies show, and since there is no strong pressure to remember agnates who left a clan-group several generations ago, it is likely that many persons who, if links were remembered, would be listed as belonging to the Kawelka clan-units have been omitted. This, however, cannot be remedied. In fact, in the clan-unit concept I am not concerned with a full account of literal genealogical connections but only with those which I was able to trace because Kawelka men mentioned them to me on specific questioning. Undoubtedly I missed some, so my estimate of persons lost to the Kawelka groups over the past few generations is bound to be conservative. Equally, it is likely that I have missed men who were incomers a few generations ago but left no children or have no living descendants belonging to the Kawelka clan-groups nowadays.

The second definitional problem is that of membership. This is a term which is likely to conjure up in one's mind a concept of a precise range of defined rights and obligations, perhaps backed by sanctions. We are possibly also apt to think of it in holistic either/or terms: either x is a member or he is not. For Hagen it is more appropriate to think of clan-group membership as defined by a number of factors, not all of which may be present to an equal extent in every case, and to recognise that in a small number of cases a man's affiliation may be uncertain, either in the sense that he keeps up a kind of dual affiliation or that his allegiance to a group is weak.

The factors which are important are:

(1) Co-residence, which is conducive to co-operation and participation in group affairs. Residence within a clan territory is not by itself a decisive indication of membership; there may be pockets of men living within a clan-group's territory who maintain membership of a different clan-group. Conversely, there are men accepted as members of a clan-group who live, temporarily or even semi-permanently, away from the clan's territorial areas. Co-residence and close association within the same settlement are more likely to imply that men sharing in this way belong to the same clan.

(2) Participation in *moka* exchanges. A man's chosen clan identity is publicly avowed when he contributes as a donor in a prestation to which clansmen are contributing, and dances and speaks as a member of the clan. Prestations take place only periodically, and clearly a man who is not co-resident with his group-mates can still affirm his allegiance to them at festival times. The Kawelka as a whole (see chapter two) are split between their Mbukl and Wahgi territories; when dances are held at either place, at least some Kawelka men from the other locality travel over to take part. (Nowadays travel is much facilitated by the existence of roads and the use of passenger-carrying trucks.)

(3) Land rights. Here it is important to distinguish between kinds of rights. It is a basic rule that one can be *pukl wuə* of a garden site only if one belongs to the clan-group whose men own the territory in which the site lies and if one has either cultivated the garden oneself, or has received the right to cultivate it from another group member, without valid disputants to one's claim. The *pukl wuə* of a garden can allocate planting and harvesting rights over parts of the garden to persons who do not belong to his clan-group. In particular his own wife has a right to be granted use of garden land by him, whereas in the case of other extra-clan categories of persons it is more a privilege which is involved. The husband remains *pukl wuə* of the ground, provided he is a member of the clan-

group which owns it. Land-use for subsistence has not (up to 1970) been a chronic issue of dispute in Hagen, so the question of whether a man is *pukl wuə* or not of ground he uses does not often arise.[5] For example, an uxorilocally resident husband cannot truly become *pukl wuə* of his wife's natal group's land, but he is likely to be granted use rights without difficulty.

(4) Contribution to payments other than *moka*, e.g. bridewealth. Persons outside the clan, e.g. matrilateral kin, often make some contribution to bridewealth payments for a clan member, but group members, particularly whoever is *in loco parentis* to the boy for whom a bride is being obtained, make the heaviest contributions and do so specifically under the rubric of their status as co-sub-clansmen or co-lineage members of the boy. Such payments can thus mark out a man's current membership of a lineage or sub-clan and hence of a clan.

Only adult men or boys close to marriage are likely to till gardens and hold *pukl wuə* rights over them, to make *moka* and contribute to bridewealth and other payments. Indeed, I restrict my tabulation of clan-group members to men and older boys who are active in group affairs. This raises the question of the rights and affiliation of women.[6]

Residence at marriage is expected to be virilocal, and in most cases it is patrivirilocal. The wife comes to live on her husband's land, bears children to his group, feeds and rears his pigs; but this does not mean that her own natal ties are extinguished. Wagner (1969:58) argues for the Daribi that 'in the case of a woman, marriage amounts to "recruitment" to the clan of her husband'.[7] In Hagen it is true that a woman goes to 'help' her husband's group, and she can be said to join his local settlement group and the wider clan-based community of which his settlement group is a part. In a sense, then, she is recruited as a member of a new local community, but she cannot be regarded as a member of her husband's clan-group in terms of all the factors outlined above. Moreover, she does not lose her natal clan membership or her effective ties with her natal family as a result of her marriage. Her position is different from that of the adult males of her natal clan-group and different again from that of natal male members of the group who have left it and joined another group. She can ask to retain planting rights over strips of garden previously allocated to her at her natal place; she encourages her husband to make *moka* payments to her kin; and she, with her husband, is likely to help with contributions towards bridewealth for her younger brothers. It is clear, then, in Barnes's phrase (1962:6) that she 'sustains an interest' in her natal group as well as in her husband's—indeed she also sustains an interest in the activities of her sisters, who are married into other clan-groups. Moreover, her basic group affiliation is not changed: although men may refer to the wives of their clansmen as *tininga amb mbø*, 'our women', or as 'the women of x', giving their own clan-group, the wives are actually always distinguished from *tininga amb kimunøl mbø*, 'our sisters', and are also known individually by their natal clan or tribal affiliation. This continuing affiliation of married women to their natal clans is in fact of great significance for the topic of clan-group composition, since, as we shall see, many 'non-agnates' are persons 'brought back' by their mothers to their mothers' brothers' settlements, on widowhood, separation, or divorce from their husbands, or, in the past, as refugees of war. Such 'returned sisters', like wives, belong to a local community and to a settlement-group, and in addition they are members of the clan whose men form the clan-group. I exclude them, however, from the clan-group itself in my tabulations, since in these I am interested in the affiliation of males.

It is clear that the ethnographic significance of terms such as 'affiliation' and 'membership' needs to be spelled out. Moreover, we need to put these and other terms into conceptual relationships with one another.

I begin with the notion of participation. A man associates himself with others by participating in a joint activity. He may do so from a special role and status position, or he may share such a position with other participants. Their role as joint participants may in fact be dominant over other role-relationships which they also have towards one another. In the Highlands, participation of this kind may be an important pragmatic criterion for obtaining membership of named groups, whose members carry out joint activities; but it may not be the only criterion, and by itself it may not be a sufficient criterion for membership. Furthermore, it need not even indicate that the person intends to be considered a member of the group. He may simply wish to help the group or some member of it. For example, he may be assisting a kinsman by contributing labour towards the building of a house, and he receives a reward of cooked food in the same way as the other housebuilders, some of whom may also belong to the house-owner's group. Here each group-member is in a sense acting as a point in an ego-centred set of people who are helping x to build his house. This role they share with other participants who do not belong to the same group. Although they may outnumber the other participants, supply more materials, and work longer, their group-membership can be said to be latent in this activity rather than strongly-expressed. On the other hand, there are likely to be other contexts which decisively symbolise group-membership: I have suggested for Hagen that participation in *moka* dances and speeches does this. These are activities in which group membership is overtly symbolised, and I refer to them as demonstrations of identity.

Association in task-groups thus need not imply affiliation to named, formal groups whose members may form the cores of these task-groups. We can distinguish associates from affiliates. Affiliation refers to the process or fact of acquiring membership. Recruitment refers to the action of persons in obtaining others as members of their groups. What is at stake in recruitment is some component or aspect of a person's identity, and in the present context we are dealing with basic group identity. The notion of identity also implies the idea of allegiance: this is the positive commitment of a person to his or her identity. (Of course the person may also be committed to other relationships as well.)

Some support for my introduction of the term identity here is given by Melpa linguistic usage. When a person's group membership is in process of changing, or has changed, people say 'he is becoming an x'. The question arises, how do the Melpa think of such a change, how do they symbolise identity? The verb used is *rarəm*, which appears also in the phrase *təpa rəndi wuə*, given in chapter one. It is found in three contexts, which seem to be semantically linked: (1) it can refer to the act of planting seeds or vines; (2) it can mean to put on, as of clothing; (3) it applies to a range of real or pretended existential changes. The semantic linkages are clearest between (2) and (3) here. For example, in myths a frog sometimes takes off its skin (i.e. *changes its clothing*) and 'turns into' a man; and in ordinary life a man who says *Kewa røklimb*, 'I will become like a foreigner', means in the first place that he will change out of his native clothing and put on shorts and shirt. He thus becomes like foreigners, especially Europeans, in dress, and the implication or wish is that he will become·like them in other respects also. Clearly, these two linked usages of the verb are appropriate also to changes of group identity; but it is the first meaning, of 'planting', which connects most clearly with other Melpa idioms relating to groups and their members. First, there is the fact that a group and its segments can be spoken of as *mbo tenda* and *mbo kat*, 'one stock and its offshoots'. The plant is rooted in the ground; in the same way each large group had its origin in a single place, the *kona wingndi*. Moreover, each individual Hagener refers to himself as an *mbo-wuə*, a 'planted man', that is, one who has an indigenous connection with his area, an autochthon. Again, the clan can be described as *pana-ru* 'garden trench'. The significance of saying that a person who changes identity 'plants' himself in his new area can now be seen. Essentially, he re-plants himself, he is like a plant transferred from one garden to another. In associating with his new group, he makes roots for himself (*pukl*). The difference between sisters' sons as immigrants and others is also now clear. Unlike others, the sister's son already has a 'root' with his mother's people, hence the metaphor which my informant Ongka made central to his explanation of the sister's son's position and which I quoted in chapter one. It is clear, also, that the sister's son has stronger roots than others, so that he is like 'a strong tree' rather than like parasites which attempt to put down new roots by growing as vines down the trunks of trees to which they have been transferred. The reason why the sister's son has a strong root in his mother's place is precisely that he was born from, and is thus 'rooted in' her. It is interesting to note here that one of the oblique terms for sexual intercourse is 'to plant a sweet-potato garden' (*okapana røkli*). The idea is that the man plants shoots in the woman like sweet-potato vines, pushing into and breaking the surface of (*mbo ronom*) his sex-partner as one breaks the surface of a garden to plant it. Conception is seen in this image as the planting of a shoot in a garden—an idea which parallels, though it does not mesh perfectly with, the concept of the clan as a division within a garden. More closely it echoes the statement that when a person changes group-membership he re-plants himself.

I would further suggest that in Hagen there is some pressure towards a man's maintaining only a single basic group identity, at least at a given time. Potentially he has access to more than one group; and in practical terms he is bound to be associated with more than one group anyway. If, however, he joins a group, there is pressure on him to 're-plant', permanently or otherwise. One wonders also to what extent such a suggestion would apply, or would be irrelevant to, other Highlands societies, in particular to the Huli with their apparent system of multiple parish membership (Glasse 1968).

THE KAWELKA CLANS

At the end of chapter four I stated that the Kawelka clan-groups had both gained and lost members through persons' changes of affiliation. It is likely, as I have mentioned, that assessment of members lost is more difficult than assessment of members gained, but in Table 5 I attempt to give an account of both processes over a period of three generations, going back no further than two generations above old men who were still living in 1964-5.

TABLE 5: CHANGES OF AFFILIATION INTO AND OUT OF KAWELKA CLAN-GROUPS

	Pre-1944				1944-1964			
	In		Out		In		Out	
	M	F	M	F	M	F	M	F
Kundmbo	21	3	10	2	14	—	14	2
Membo	44	11	9	2	32	2	16	4
Mandembo	11	2	21	4	20	3	30	4
	76	16	40	8	66	5	60	10

Total: 281 changes

The table includes persons, married or single, and their children where known, who moved by themselves or were taken by senior kinsfolk into residence with or away from Kawelka clan-groups and whose affiliation was subsequently altered. Wives of men incoming and outgoing and the mothers who brought back their children are not recorded, since it is changes of affiliation that the table is concerned with. We are thus dealing with changes of affiliation made by men and by their unmarried children. This helps to explain why there is a preponderance of males in the table. Within the 'in' columns, of course, it is probable that males are remembered better than females, since it is they who have sons that are now most likely to be members of contemporary Kawelka lineages.

The pre-1944 figures indicate more incoming than outgoing persons. This may be because outgoing members are remembered less well the further back one goes. On the other hand, Mandembo clan shows more outgoers than incomers for this period, and this certainly fits with my impression that Mandembo have been shrinking in numbers and territory whereas the other two clans have been expanding in both (cf. Bulmer 1960:228). Mandembo, in fact, shows a net loss of persons in both periods. The pattern, if it is genuine, would fit with occasional statements made by Kawelka men themselves. Ongka, the Klammbo leader, told me that his group was very small and its sub-divisions not very important, and that only he had taken in non-agnates and increased the numbers of men in his settlement-group. The then Local Government Councillor for Membo clan told me in 1964: 'Mandembo are a small group, but we Membo know how to bring back our sisters' sons to us.' And his Komiti (assistant), a young-middle-aged big-man,[8] told me the same, adding, however, that they had also lost men to other groups when they were defeated in warfare and forced to flee from the Wahgi: 'When we Kawelka were driven out we had to take refuge in various places with maternal kinsmen, and only some of us came down to Mbukl. We would have been bigger than the other tribes, but we have gone to swell the numbers of several groups, and so we ourselves are few.' It is evident, then, that men are well aware of the possible effects on group-strength of changes in affiliation by individual members, and that they link these changes predominantly to natal female members 'bringing back' children, and conversely natal (patrifilial) male members leaving to join their maternal kin.

Figures for contemporary Kawelka clan-groups are given in Table 6. They include only adult or near-adult males who were in 1964-5 active group-members. Here the definitions of 'near-adult' and 'active' cannot be precise. Table 6 (a) is the result of a more generous assessment of these factors, Table 6 (b) of a more rigid one. Table 6 (c) shows the categories of those included in 6 (a) but excluded from 6 (b). The second part of 6 (c) suggests strongly that non-agnates are more likely than agnates to be living away from their clan area as workers or to have an uncertain allegiance or affiliation to their clan-group. Whereas in the total population of the clan-groups agnates comprise 63 per cent and non-agnates 37 per cent of the whole, in the sub-population of males in 6 (c) (ii) only 39 per cent are agnates while 61 per cent are non-agnates; proportions which are the reverse of those in the total population. Interpretation of this point cannot immediately be given: it will be necessary to examine cases in more detail before we can say whether this 'shows' anything about the status or situation of non-agnates as such.[9]

These Kawelka figures show that agnates outnumber non-agnates, although there is variation between the different clan-groups in this respect. Barnes's suggestion, that there is a considerable degree of cumulative patrifiliation in the recruitment of persons to

TABLE 6: THE KAWELKA CLAN-GROUPS, FEBRUARY 1965

(a) INITIAL ACCOUNT

Clan	Total	Agnates	Non-Agnates	NA/Total* per cent
Kundmbo	80	54	26	33
Membo	109	53	56	51
Mandembo				
1. Kurupmbo	39	34	5	13
2. Klammbo	30	22	8	23
	258	163	95	37

*to nearest whole figure.

(b) 'STRICT' ACCOUNT

Clan	Total	Agnates	Non-Agnates	NA/Total per cent
Kundmbo	70	47	23	33
Membo	87	44	43	49
Mandembo				
1. Kurupmbo	31	27	4	13
2. Klammbo	22	18	4	18
	210	136	74	35

(c) PERSONS INCLUDED IN (a) BUT EXCLUDED IN (b)

(i) 25 males in 6(a) are omitted in 6(b) because they were either very old and inactive in 1964–5 or were rather young to be considered near-adult, thus:

Agnates		Non-Agnates	
Old	Young	Old	Young
3	15	2	5

(ii) 23 further males omitted in 6(b) belonged to the following categories:

	Agnates	Non-Agnates
Plantation workers and schoolboys, away from the clan area	3	6
'Marginal' men (with weak allegiance)	3	1
Inactive men with ambiguous clan-affiliation	3	6
Cripples	—	1
	9	14

Note: there are three doubtful cases of agnates in Membo clan. Doubt arises because I am not sure of the clan-group affiliation of their fathers' fathers.

clans in the Highlands, thus applies (Barnes 1962:6). It must be remembered that my term 'agnate' does not imply more than two or three generations of continuity in patrifilial recruitment, and that I am not using the de facto pattern of clan composition to indicate whether agnatic descent *dogmas* are important or not (cf. Reay 1967:14). Moreover, my initial category distinction of agnates/

non-agnates does not show the total rate of patrifiliation, since there are some non-agnates who are the sons of incomers to the clan-groups and who may well have been born on the territory of the clan-group to which they are now affiliated. One man, in fact, emphasised this point to me by saying that he belonged to the Kawelka because his navel-string had been buried at a particular settlement within Kawelka territory, i.e. he had been born at a Kawelka place. He was thus demonstrating that although he was not an agnate, he was nevertheless not an incomer either (compare the Mendi categories, Ryan 1959:265).

Many of the links which non-agnates have with other members of the groups into which they are incorporated belong to the *pam* (mother's brother-sister's son) complex of relationships. Sister's sons are one's *pamal* (plural form), and their children in turn can also be called *pamal*, although it is interesting and important that they can also be called 'children'. This latter usage, which I have mentioned in chapter one, clearly facilitates the assimilation of the children of sisters' sons into the kinship categories appropriate to those who belong to the same group.[10] Table 7 (a) shows the broad incidence of links between non-agnates and their hosts within the Kawelka clan-groups. For this Table I have used the ninety-five men in Table 6 (a) not the smaller number in 6 (b). A few men were cited as having double links, in which case I count each link separately. This procedure brings the number of links up to ninety-nine. Links within the *pam* complex amount to *c.* 63 per cent of the total. Persons with no known kin-link with their hosts are very few (*c.* 4 per cent, as I have presented the figures). These are persons who joined the group without being especially 'adopted'. I use the term 'adopted' to refer to the act of a man in taking over children, in the past usually refugees of war, to be his own children.[11] Kidnapped children are taken over similarly: in one case a man captured a woman during warfare and she brought her children with her as well. All the cases under 3 could be included under 5, except that those in 3 were inducted into a particular filial relationship with their host. For this latter reason they could in fact have been included under 2. Affinal links do not appear often.

TABLE 7: NON-AGNATES OF KAWELKA AND THEIR HOSTS

(a) BROAD INCIDENCE OF LINKS

Type of link	Incidence				
	Ku.	Me.	Kur.	Klam.	Totals
1. Within the *pam* complex	20	34	2	6	62
2. Classified as brother or son (apart from those in 1), i.e. WZH, WZch, matrilateral parallel cousins	2	5	2	—	9
3. Adopted or kidnapped where previously no tie, or child of person taken in this way	1	11	1	—	13
4. Affine	1	8	—	2	11
5. No known kin-link with hosts	2	2	—	—	4
	26	60	5	8	99

(b) CURRENT RESIDENCE OF INCOMERS

	Ku.	Me.	Kur.	Klam.
1. Incomer founded separate lineage and/or settlement	3	1	—	—
2. Incomer ± sons, or sons alone live with immediate hosts	11	41	2	5
3. Living with sub-clansmen of host	7	6	2	—
4. Living with clansmen of host (different sub-clan)	2	2	—	—
5. Living at mission village in clan area of host	—	2	—	—
6. Living with an affine within clan area of host	—	3	—	—
7. Living at place outside clan-area of host but still affiliated to his clan	—	1	—	—
8. Living away from clan of host and with diminished allegiance to it	3	4	1	3
	26	60	5	8

Note: this table, like 6(a), records links. A few Membo men had more than one link (i.e. more than one host) and are recorded twice here.

Ninety per cent of the links involved are immediate genealogical ones. That is, usually persons are taken in by their immediate rather than classificatory mother's brother, mother's sister's husband, affine, etc. This is a fact of some importance. It shows the significance of immediate kin-relationships, and it suggests that persons do not have an unlimited range of choice in deciding which group to affiliate themselves with. (In fact, it may not be they, but their mothers who made the critical choice, as we shall see later.)

Persons taken into a clan-group need not continue living with their host, although many do so. In fifty-nine instances out of the ninety-nine the incomer and/or his sons were continuing to live with their host (or with his sons, or with one of their other hosts) in 1964–5 (Table 7 (b)). In nineteen instances they were living with other clansmen of the host; once men gain membership of a clan they have some latitude in choosing with whom to associate within it. In a minority of cases men had now left the Kawelka clan-groups (eleven instances). Men who switch their clan-group allegiance frequently are likely to be 'rubbish-men', moving from one big-man to another; but not all of the men in these instances fall into that category. Some had returned to their patrifilial groups.[12]

Men who are now non-agnatic members of clan-groups have either been initially brought to the clan by another person or have themselves come and obtained membership; or they are the sons of persons who were in one of these two situations. If brought, they may have come with others, usually their siblings. As I have mentioned, the paradigmatic situation is that of a mother returning with her children to her natal group. In such a case it is the mother who initially decides what happens to her children; later, each son can individually make a choice whether to return to his father's or stay with his mother's clan.

Of the Kawelka non-agnates in 1964–5, thirty were born on Kawelka territory (in the case of two further men this is probably so but not certain) and were filiated to at least one parent who was a birth member of the Kawelka or had been accepted into one of the Kawelka clan-groups. These thirty can thus be regarded as birth members. Many are the sons, son's sons, or daughter's sons, of

Kawelka women. For most of them, there would be little question of their going to their patrifilial or agnatic clan-groups, since they would be brought up simply as Kawelka persons. For just over 30 per cent of the Kawelka non-agnates, then, their group-affiliation has probably been as unproblematic as that of the Kawelka agnates.

Table 8 gives some information on choices made which resulted in the present affiliation of Kawelka non-agnates. The table shows the prominence of cases in which a man's affiliation has been influenced by a choice made by his mother. Almost all of these are cases in which a woman has brought her children back to her natal clan, and those in 8 (b) all relate to periods of warfare, in which the mothers fled as refugees. At such a time their only hope of safety would be with their own brothers and father, provided these were not also threatened by warfare, so they were not exercising 'choice' among

TABLE 8: CHOICES RELEVANT TO THE AFFILIATION OF KAWELKA NON-AGNATES

(a) CASES WHERE ONLY ONE CURRENT NON-AGNATE IS INVOLVED

Situation		No. of men
Born in clan territory		5
Brought in by:	M	17
	FZH	1
	MB	2
	FZ	1
	MZS	1
Brought in by:	M + F	1
	M + M2ndH	1
Brought by joint decision of:	M + self	1
	WF + self	1
	ZH + self	1
	WZH + self	1
	Class. MB + self	1
Came by own decision		16
		50

Note: of these 50, 17 were originally brought along with siblings or other kin, now either dead or departed, while 33 were brought by themselves.

(b) CASES WHERE THE SITUATION OF A NUMBER OF CURRENT NON-AGNATES WAS INFLUENCED OR DETERMINED BY A SINGLE PRIOR 'CHOICE'

Situation		No. of men
Born in clan territory		25 + 2 uncertain*
Brought in by:	M	8
	FZ	1
	F	3
	MM	1
	Kidnapper	3
Brought in by:	M + M2ndH	1
Brought by joint decision of: MM, MF, and MZH†		1
Came by own decision		2
		45 + 2 = 47

(c) SUMMARY

Situation		No. of men
Born in clan territory		30 + 2 uncertain
Brought in by:	M	25
	FZH	1
	FZ	2
	F	3
	MB	2
	MZS	1
	MM	1
	Kidnapper	3
Brought in by:	M + F	1
	M + M2ndH	2
Brought by joint decision of: self + various kinsmen		5
	MM, MF, MZH	1
Came by own decision		18
		95 + 2 = 97

*The mother of these two men is said to have alternated in residence for a while between her natal and her husband's clan areas and then to have persuaded the husband to settle uxorilocally. I am uncertain whether her sons were born while she was 'alternating' or not.

†This young man's mother died and he was reared by his MM and MF, who later went to live with another daughter's husband.

a number of possibilities, but merely fleeing for their lives. In some cases the mothers will have had a choice whether to return to their husband's clan, after warfare was over, or not; in other cases, if the husband was dead and/or his clan defeated and scattered, a woman could be expected to remain with her natal kin, unless she was still fairly young and wished to remarry.

The relative infrequency of cases in which a mother's brother has himself taken initial action in fetching an orphaned or refugee sister's son is interesting. It is more often the mother who takes the initiative in bringing back her children to her brother. However, the accounts given to me may be slightly misleading. Since the sister is usually married away from her natal residence-group, it is she who has to make a move in order to return to it; but in some cases I have she may well have done so under persuasion from her own kin. I was sometimes told as a generalisation that big-men 'grease' their sisters to leave their husbands and return to them, bringing their children. The concept here is the reverse of the process which occurs in some societies with matrilineal lineages, in which a man tries to retain his own as well as his sister's children. Here we are told of big-men who try to retain their sisters' children as well as their own.

If the mother of a child dies while the child is still suckling, it may not be possible for the mother's brother to take on the child, as it will require a wet-nurse and no woman in the mother's brother's settlement may be able to supply milk (cf. Bulmer 1960:224). In such a case, a father's sister or even a grandmother of the child may be able to help: hence the isolated examples of men originally taken in by FZ and MM in Table 8.

In a few cases it is the father whom I have listed as making the choice relevant to a man's present affiliation. These are cases in which a father fled as a refugee or as a result of quarrels and took his children with him. Often the father fled to his own maternal kin, so that the son is now living with his father's mother's brother's people.

Finally, in eighteen cases the non-agnate came to his present group by his own decision (depending, of course, on the decision of his hosts to accept him). In most of the cases where children were brought by their mothers or taken care of by senior kin, the children were below ten years of age at the time when the move occurred. They would be likely to form an attachment to their hosts in the years while they were growing up, and this would make it more likely that they would stay when they became adults. In cases where the non-agnate himself made the initial decision to move, almost all of the men involved were over fifteen years old at the time of their moves; in a few cases, however, they were young boys, whose senior kin had been killed in fighting and who ran away to their mother's brother's clan as refugees. In one case, an older boy fled, carrying a younger brother on his back.

Most self-chosen moves, then, are made by adults or near-adults. This is almost a self-evident proposition, since only adults are likely to have the independence of action required for a change of residence or of affiliation from one clan-group to another; although, as has been pointed out, in a few cases boys who had lost their settlement-mates in warfare came independently as refugees to their maternal kin. Table 9 (a) gives a more detailed picture of the stages of life at

TABLE 9: STAGES IN LIFE AT WHICH RESIDENCE OR AFFILIATION CHANGES ARE MADE, AND REASONS GIVEN FOR MOVES

(a) STAGES

Move made	Set 1 Cases from among Kawelka non-agnates in 1964–5	Set 2 Larger number of cases, of persons living and dead
Before marriage	1	30
After marriage but before children were born	13	25
After children born	5	15
In middle-age (married men)	3	15
In middle-age to old age (married men)	1	12
Moves made by unmarried men (past the normal age of marriage)	2	4
	25	101

(b) REASONS GIVEN FOR 21 RESIDENCE-MOVES, TAKEN FROM SET 2 IN TABLE 9(a)

	No. of cases
Accompanied mother when she separated from her husband	1
Refugee of war	10
Orphaned	2
Moved to find pig-pasture	6
Moved to find good garden-land	1
Moved as a result of quarrels	2
Moved because of sickness and ill-luck, both interpreted as caused by angry ghosts	3
Uncertain case	1
	26

Note: 26 reasons are given for 21 moves—in a few cases more than one reason was cited.

which changes of residence and/or affiliation are made by men. It shows that moves may be made at any age, although an interestingly large number occurs after marriage, but before children are born. The table is constructed partly from the cases of non-agnatic members of the Kawelka clans in 1964-5, and partly from a larger number of cases of transfers of residence or affiliation on which I collected some material. I give figures on the current non-agnates and on the larger number of cases separately. Both sets of figures relate partly to the period when warfare was still being conducted. The larger set in fact contains many moves which were directly connected with warfare and the flight of refugees or their return to a previous place of residence after a period of exile. From this total set of 101 'moves', fifty-four can be dated as pre-1944 (when warfare was effectively stopped in the Northern Melpa area), and in forty-three of these I was told that persons moved 'because of warfare'. This importance attributed to warfare in causing changes of residence and affiliation fits with my argument in chapter four, that warfare had definite effects on settlement patterns. However, a difficulty is that informants very readily ascribe all cases which happened many years ago to 'warfare', without citing more specific details, and in some instances more complicated reasons may have been involved. At least, this is suggested by the pattern in cases where more details can be obtained (see Table 9 (b)). In these there are ten clear cases where persons moved as refugees of war, and a scatter of cases where persons moved for other reasons, either ecological or social. The importance of pigs is suggested by the fact that in six cases the desire to find good pig-pasture was given as a reason for moving. This, in fact, is the generalised reason given for the exodus from the Mbukl territories of Kawelka men who returned to the old Wahgi territory after peace was established. Hageners consider that pigs do well in fairly low-lying grassland-areas, where they find plenty of worms and grubs to eat. I cannot test their opinion objectively, but here all I am concerned with is their own 'cognised model' of the environment and its influence on residence-choices. Men who establish pig-houses in grassland-areas quite far from their clan-mates' settlements often have to expend much energy in walking from their new settlement to the main clan-territory and back, or else they withdraw for the duration of their residence from discussion and participation in clan affairs. Even a big-man may do this, in order to rear a large number of pigs which he can use in *moka* transactions later. His withdrawal does not necessarily mean he is alienated from his clan; it may simply mean he is building up his wealth in pigs for a future occasion when he will enhance his own and his clan's prestige by giving the pigs away in a public prestation. Nevertheless he loses a certain amount of his grasp of opinions and plans entertained by his group-mates. A solution which at least three important big-men of Mbukl had adopted to this problem was to set up more than one establishment. Each had his own men's house and a number of women's-cum-pig-houses at Mbukl, and in addition each kept one wife and a number of pigs in the Gumant river-Wahgi area. The men themselves commuted regularly between their two sets of households, and took part in political discussions at Mbukl whenever they wished to do so. One maintained that the arrangement had a further advantage: when exchange-partners pressed him to make *moka* to them at Mbukl and he was not ready to do so, he would travel over to his Wahgi settlement, which is more remote and awkward to visit, and take a holiday there. He thus saw the Wahgi as his country retreat. Setting up a wife by herself in a homestead can make for difficulties, of course: the wife might run away, or be short of help in caring for the pigs and gathering firewood, or in need of protection against visits by thieves or seducers. A big-man may depute one of his 'helpers', a man of lower status than himself, to look after his wife. Preferably the helper should be of his own lineage, for a close 'brother' can be trusted; or an 'incomer' to the clan who is attached to him rather as a client is attached to a patron. Arrangements are more secure when a number of a man's more closely-related clansmen set up homesteads together as colonisers of a single new locality area. The men can thus collectively keep an eye on the big-man's wife and herds while he himself is visiting the main clan territory or exchange partners in other clans. This arrangement had in 1964-5 been achieved by Nykint, an important big-man of the Kawelka Kurupmbo clan-section. In 1964 eight men lived at a single place in the Wahgi which he had taken the lead in colonising. At one time in the year they had ninety-six pigs, nearly twice the average of pigs per householder at Mbukl.[13] Nykint himself had twenty-one pigs there (as compared with the overall average of twelve per man), and in addition, unlike most of the others, he had another settlement place and further pigs at Mbukl itself. He commuted often, stopping off at night-time occasionally in the Kurupmbo settlement within Tipuka territory (location G, Map 3) on his way back from the Wahgi. Here he would pick up news before proceeding to his main place at the head of a ceremonial ground in Kurupmbo territory. For a big-man who aims also at being a leader it is most important to be 'on the scene' when discussions are held on *moka* plans, to direct them if he can, and perhaps to listen to and settle any disputes which may have arisen between his clan or clan-section 'brothers'. Since 1964, as I have mentioned earlier, the task of commuting has been made much easier for Nykint and other big-men who maintain dual settlements by the advent of passenger vehicles, heavy or light trucks which carry persons for hire.

Kawelka men are not unusual in making these moves of residence for ecological as well as social reasons. Warfare in the past generated a large number of migrations of groups from one territory to another, and since warfare has ended many groups which established themselves as enclaves under the protection of hosts have sent members back to their previous area or have colonised still further areas in search of more adequate garden-land or pig-grazing. Such moves to fresh areas or back to old ones both reflect and create divisions within clans, but they do not immediately or automatically lead to changes in clan-affiliation on the part of individuals. They do make it difficult for these men to co-operate on a daily basis with the group-mates who stay in their clan's main territory, and this can be a source of minor resentment. In one case a Kawelka man living at the Wahgi was said to be thinking of returning to Mbukl because his pigs were continually destroying his neighbours' gardens and getting him into trouble. His clansmen at Mbukl commented 'All right, let him come back, but if he does he had better settle down and work with us properly here instead of going off to the Wahgi and other places.'[14] The man in question was not a big-man, and it is recognised that big-men must spend a good deal of time visiting exchange-partners rather than 'working' at home. He was, rather, a 'walkabout man' who had lived in a number of places without giving his firm allegiance to any single local clan-group. He was a sister's son of the Kawelka Kurupmbo clan-section, and after his marriage he left his patrifilial clansmen to live with his mother's brother at the Kurupmbo colony in the Wahgi. After a while there he left to join men of his sub-sub-clan who were living in a Membo settlement-area, also in the Wahgi. These were not men with whom he had a close genealogical tie. Indeed his father's father, although not recorded as an incomer, cannot be linked by genealogy with any other Membo ancestors. There, in the second half of 1964, he fell ill, and decided that 'ghosts' (perhaps the ghost of his father) were plaguing him. Claiming that he was moving in order to escape the ghosts, he went down to the Baiyer Valley, many miles from the Wahgi, to live with his sister's husband. (His assumption probably was that Kawelka ghosts would not follow him outside their own territory. Cf. Meggitt 1965:171-2 on Mae-Enga ideas.) However, another reason for his move was his difficulties over his pigs' rooting in other people's gardens. It seems he appealed to other men of his sub-sub-clan at Mbukl to help him, perhaps asking to settle in their locality areas, but got little response. Their argument was that he should come and work with them and thus prove his value rather than simply asking for their help when he was in trouble. Meeting little sympathy among his group-mates, then, he began to make plans to move to his wife's natal place among the Epilke in the Baiyer Valley or even to extra-clan kin of his wife among the Ukini, a tribe at the far western end of the Northern Melpa area, and so right out of touch with his original clansmen. Within a few years, then, he had completed three residence moves, and was contemplating another, which would have involved him in removing his allegiance from the Kawelka and eventually changing his clan-affiliation.[15] His story demonstrates clearly both the contingent attitudes of persons towards clan-affiliation and the basic values underlying the attitudes. A man must make himself of some value to his group-mates if he wishes them to reciprocate by helping him. This is the pragmatic basis for men's generalisation that walkabout men who go from group to group are like women. Women also are not strong as true men are, they say. A strong man stays on his own ground and does not shift into positions of dependency in other men's households and settlements; whereas a woman goes to her husband's place and becomes a dependant there. 'Rubbish-men', who not only move from one place to another, but sometimes are directly subordinate to a big-man, and who 'are always bending down to enter some new man's house' are regarded as particularly weak. On the other hand, a bachelor who attaches himself to a big-man, works for him, and in return has a bridewealth payment raised on his behalf, may achieve a perfectly respectable status. The essential for him is that he should not switch his affiliation more than once or twice; if he does so, he becomes regarded as unreliable, and he does not build up enough 'credit' for his sponsors to reciprocate by obtaining a wife for him. As the case I have cited shows, any man, whether he is an 'agnate' or otherwise, may get himself into a spiral of decreasing status accompanied by frequent residence moves.

Equally, as the Kawelka's remarks suggest, one way for a man to extricate himself from such a spiral is to return to his original clan-group and build up his position by co-operating with others and taking part in ceremonial exchanges. All twenty-one of the men who made residence moves out of their clan territory and whose reasons for moving are given in Table 9(b) subsequently moved back into association with their clansmen again. Where a group is occupying more than one territory the situation of allegiance becomes ambivalent, however. Thus in the case I have cited the mover was criticised by Mbukl men for leaving their area, while the Kawelka men in the Wahgi no doubt approved of his initial action in joining them. The situation can be worse when a man leaves his immediate brothers or other settlement-mates against their will. One case of this happening relates to the small Tipuka Eltimbo group at Mbukl— a group which is particularly 'short of men' and in danger of being absorbed by larger host clans. As with the Kawelka, the Mbukl contingent of this group has been depleted by the migration of some of its men to the Gumant River/Wahgi area. In April 1966 a friend wrote to me about the death of an old Eltimbo man I had known at Mbukl:[16]

> A Tipuka Eltimbo man has died. The reason why he became sick was that his two brothers had left him at Raporong [the name of his small settlement-place] and had gone to the Gumant river. He was 'strong' and determined not to go with them. He was cross with his brothers and forbade them to go also. Later, however, he himself took one of his sows and went off to Raemb [at the Gumant]. His own dead father was angry at this. 'At first you did not want to go to Raemb, why are you going now?' the father's ghost said, and made him sick. He said 'All right, I'll kill a pig as a sacrifice for you'. He built a sacrificial hut and said to his father's ghost 'You eat the pork and stay inside the sacrificial hut' [in Melpa called 'spirit men's house'] adding 'Now I shall go and become baptised'. He said to his companions 'I'm not very sick, it's just that my back is sore, I'll lie down a bit'. As he said this, he died. Usually men die in their sleep; this man's manner of dying was different.

The implications of this story are that the subject became *popokl* (angry and frustrated) because his brothers left him. Frustration led to sickness, sent in pity for him by his dead father. The sickness was a mark of protest and a way of requesting his brothers, one of whom was a big-man and had formerly built his own small ceremonial ground at Mbukl, to return. Later he too left his paternal place, whereupon his father's pity turned to anger. He sacrificed to his father, but the ghost itself was now *popokl* and killed him.

This is the interpretation which I think a Melpa-speaker would give of the story. A psychological interpretation of imputed ghost attacks of this kind seems possible,[17] but here I wish to stress only that the fear of ghosts can work two ways: some men, as in a case I cited earlier, may leave their natal place in order to escape the attentions of a ghost; others may feel that if they do so their father's ghost will make them sick and hence they either do not move or return, after moving, when they next become ill. If a man's father has himself died away from his clan place, his son is faced with a more severe choice: to return to his clansmen he must abandon the area where his father was buried and which his ghost is likely to frequent.[18]

Ritual 'sanctions' of this kind often work only *post hoc*. The attribution of sickness to ghostly action can occur only if a person becomes sick. As we have seen, many persons do change their residence and/or their clan-affiliation, although those who do this too often are likely to be disparaged as rubbish-men. One choice which is also likely to be looked on askance is that of taking up uxorilocal residence at marriage; but there are ambivalent attitudes to this.

Hagen male dogma argues that men are strong and women weak, hence women should move into virilocal residence at marriage, and work and bear children for their husbands. But men also recognise that in fact some women are not weak but strong, in the sense that they insist on their husbands' coming into residence with them at their natal place. Such action moreover, suits a clan-group, or a settlement-group, or big-men, who feel short of supporters and helpers. While a group which has lost men in this way may deplore the situation, a group which has gained men (and, potentially, their children) may welcome it, provided it suits their needs (cf. Barnes 1962:7; Reay 1967:13-14).

Table 9(a) records 126 moves of residence/affiliation between clan territories and clans. Of these 20 per cent were moves of a man into uxorilocal residence. The current incidence of uxorilocality in the Kawelka clans in 1964-5 was much lower than this. Only nine men out of 210 (see Table 6(b)), or *c.* 4.3 per cent, were living uxorilocally on Kawelka territory.[19] The larger number of cases of moves, however, yields enough material to tabulate at least some aspects of the situation of uxorilocal men (Table 10).

UXORILOCALITY, RESIDENCE, AND AFFILIATION

To begin with, the blanket term 'uxorilocal residence' may be somewhat misleading. Residence with a wife's people may be temporary or permanent, self-chosen, or imposed; the husband may have another settlement of his own or not, and he may be more, or less, dependent on and incorporated into the wife's settlement and clan. A polygynist who allows one of his wives to live at her natal place and visits her there from time to time should not be regarded as 'uxorilocal' at all. And wives who live at their natal place away from their husbands' own settlement but maintain conjugal relations have clearly not 'pulled' their husbands into residence with them in the way that Hageners refer to when discussing uxorilocality. These are wives who are residentially separated from their husbands but not necessarily estranged from them. Although they have not 'pulled' their husbands, they have been 'strong' by refusing to go to live at their husband's place; and their choice can affect the affiliation of their children. In one case at least the younger children of a woman separated in this way from her husband have definitely become members of her own natal clan; in another the situation is not so clear-cut, for the mother is of Tipuka Eltimbo clan and her husband of Tipuka Kitepi. As we have seen earlier, the Eltimbo are partially incorporated into Kitepi clan, so the issue of the children's affiliation is less sharply-posed than would be the case if the clans involved were enemies or allies-cum-rivals.[20]

In all but four of thirty cases of uxorilocality which I extracted from Table 9 (a) the husband lived within the territory of the clan to which his wife was affiliated and with her brothers and/or father in a single settlement or locality area. The exceptions were: 1) a man who at first shared houses with his wife's brother at Mbukl. The brother then left for the Wahgi territory, so the husband had the houses to himself; 2) two men who have made 'wrong marriages' by taking wives from their mother's clan,[21] and have gone to live with their close matrilateral rather than their close affinal kin within the wife's general clan territory; 3) a man who re-married the widow of a sub-clansman and came to live in the previous husband's place which was situated in the clan territory of his classificatory mother's brother. This last is a tortuous example, and I omit it from the tables.

The number of cases is not large but is perhaps sufficient to show that there is much variability. In many cases, Table 10(a), the husband is not closely incorporated into his affine's settlement but has his own homestead. Several different reasons are given, both by the husband and his own or his wife's consanguineal kin, for the choice of uxorilocal residence: in only four cases was I simply told that the man was 'pulled' by his wife and her kin. In other cases advantages of the arrangement for the husband, given his difficulties as a refugee or as a result of quarrels, were stressed. Whether

TABLE 10: THE SITUATIONS OF UXORILOCALLY RESIDENT MEN AND THEIR CHILDREN

(a) RESIDENCE

Situation	No. of cases
Husband shares both men's house and women's house with affines	1
Husband shares women's house, but has own men's house	
(a) his wife has a separate section of the house	1
(b) his wife shares with another woman	3
Husband shares house of some kind, not certain of exact situation	3
Husband lives in separate homestead but same locality-area	14
Husband lives in same sub-clan area as affines	3
Husband lives in area of wife's clan only	4
	29

(b) REASONS*

Situation	No. of cases
Came as helper of big-man or companion of other man	3
Came as refugee or from a dwindling group	5 + 2 uncertain cases
Afraid of sickness in his natal clan area	2
Came because of quarrels in previous group	3
Came in search of good land or pig-pasture	5
Previously resident in clan area and married within it	6
'Pulled' by wife and her kin	4
	30

(c) DEGREE OF PERMANENCE

	No. of cases
Temporary co-residence with wife's people	7
Apparently permanent (man is still alive)	13
Permanent	9
	29

(d) STAGE IN LIFE AT WHICH UXORILOCALITY IS TAKEN UP

	No. of cases
Before birth of first child	22
After birth of first child but probably before middle-age	4
In middle-age	2
When old	1
	29

*In one man's case, two reasons were given, both listed.

Note: 'permanent' refers to cases in which the husband has now died after living all his married life uxorilocally.

the man stays permanently with his wife's people or not depends on his initial situation of choice (for example, whether his own kin survive or not) and correspondingly on his degree of dependence on his hosts. (One measure of this can be seen in Table 10(e),

(e) SITUATION OF GARDEN CLAIMS

	No. of cases
All gardens at wife's place	19
Divided between wife's place and place of natal clan	9
All at natal clan-place	1
	29

(f) AFFILIATION OF CHILDREN (IN CASES WHERE RESIDENCE IS PERMANENT OR APPARENTLY PERMANENT— cf. 10(c))

	Where uxorilocality is apparently permanent	Where permanent
Children definitely affiliated to mother's clan	—	8
Situation uncertain, but children likely to affiliate with mother's clan	—	1
Situation undecided, children all still young	5	—
No children yet born	1	—
Asserted that children will affiliate with father's clan	7	—
	13	9

Note: the table refers to currently cultivated gardens and to gardens in recent fallow. Uxorilocal men may have old fallow claims or claims on gardens once worked by their fathers at their own natal place in addition to the gardens they are actually making at their wife's place.

although a man who makes almost all of his gardens at his wife's place does not *ipso facto* relinquish his right to make gardens at his own natal place.)[22] As can be seen from Table 10 (d) most uxorilocal men move to the wife's place early on in their marriage, before children are born. It is at this time that a wife is least likely to accept residence away from her own home; and a husband may agree to accompany her in residence at her place, expecting to remove her later—in which he may or may not be successful. A big-man who takes in an uxorilocal son-in-law (see 10(b)) may himself urge the son-in-law to join his settlement and become his helper, especially if he himself has no grown-up sons to help him with garden work. Finally, Table 10(f) shows clearly that in cases of permanent uxorilocality the children are likely to join their mother's clan-group; in those cases where the husband was still alive and it was unsure whether he would continue to stay at his wife's place, the situation of his children's clan-membership was undecided. In a single case of temporary uxorilocality (not listed in 10(f) the man's son later affiliated himself to his maternal clan, when his family was disrupted by warfare.

The children's affiliation depends, then, on (1) the attitude of the father and of his own clan-group, (2) the attitude of the mother's kin and their wider clan-group, and (3) the children's own subsequent choice when they grow up. They are most likely to affiliate with their mother's clan if the father was 'pulled' into uxorilocal residence and remained permanently at his wife's place. Of the four cases in Table 10(a) where the man is said to have been 'pulled' by his wife, in three the husbands are still alive. All are mild, complaisant men, unimportant in *moka* exchanges, while the wife of at least one of them is headstrong. In the fourth case the wife's sub-clansmen gleefully claim that they persuaded the husband to stay with good food and kindness while threatening to retain their sister if he tried to remove her to his natal place. They say they did so explicitly to keep their sister's children and so to strengthen the sub-clan. A similar threat may be involved in one of the three contemporary cases, in which the wife has previously been divorced. Among the reasons advanced for her first marriage's breakdown was the suggestion that her father and brothers had 'greased' her to return to them—a stock suggestion, in fact, but one which may have weighed in the second husband's mind when he agreed to go to live at her place. Further factors involved here were: the husband himself is quite unimportant, the wife's natal place is not far from his own, in fact it is one of the Tipuka settlements within previous Kawelka territory; and her kin have other connections with the husband's own clan-section.

An issue which might be expected to have some bearing on uxorilocal residence and on the affiliation of children is the question of whether bridewealth is paid or not. However, no simple statement can be made about this. In all cases of first marriages agreed to by a girl's parents some bridewealth is paid. No specific subcategory of payment within the bridewealth is said to secure the husband's rights *in genetricem* over his wife, although there is a category which refers to his rights of sexual access to her. Nevertheless the whole bridewealth is said in a general way to compensate the parents for the loss of their daughter, and implicit in this notion is the assumption that she is expected to bear children for her husband's group. Bridewealth is also seen as giving a husband the right to remove his wife. But all these rights are contingent on circumstances. If the husband chooses to go to his wife's place, even if he has paid bridewealth, he can do so, provided her kin accept him. His children can affiliate with her clan, provided he or his kinsmen do not effectively protest against this. The payment of bridewealth thus does not automatically secure children's affiliation. We cannot set up a neat model in which marriage with bridewealth issues in virilocality and patrifilial recruitment, while marriage without it implies uxorilocality and matrifilial recruitment.

That this is so is shown precisely by some complications surrounding the case of the husband resident at the place of his previously divorced wife. He had arguments with his wife's father over the bridewealth he had paid. Claiming that two pigs were outstanding from the bridewealth, the father-in-law called him an 'ashes man' (rubbish-man), seized his wrist, and told him no longer to share a men's house with him. The husband then went to live in his wife's house within the same settlement. I did not see this dispute, but heard about it from a man of the same clan-section as the husband, who commented that they (the clan-section mates) had told the husband not to go to his wife's place, where he would be a *kintmant* ('servant') of her people, for it was wrong to do so after he had paid bridewealth for her. 'All this he knew, and yet he carried on living there, despite the fact that they are always quarrelling over the amount of the bridewealth.' After his own father's death, the man was helped by an outstanding big-man of his clan-section to raise bridewealth and pay it. Then there was a disagreement over the amount to be paid, and the big-man removed some of the shells and pigs which formed part of the payment, and gave them to another exchange-partner. The trans-actors in the marriage have been upset (*popokl*) ever since then, and the matter is hard to sort out because the big-man has since died. The husband himself had hard words with his big-man sponsor and as a result said he would go off and live at his wife's place. But his father-in-law was not satisfied and complained continually that the wife was bearing children 'for nothing', i.e. without proper bridewealth having been given. The informant explained here that when a good bridewealth payment is made, it goes 'down' into the feelings of the bride's parents, and when she has children they help to make the children grow and have a 'good skin'; otherwise they neglect their grandchildren and later, when they are dead, send them sickness.

In this case, then, the father-in-law's demand for adequate bridewealth was not influenced by the uxorilocal residence of his son-in-law. Wife-givers may become upset at what they claim is a failure to pay for sexual rights even if they are gaining the son-in-law as a settlement mate. What determines their attitude is their own situation. In the case I have cited, the father-in-law is not a big-man and he has grown-up sons of his own. He has no special need for his son-in-law's help in work, and the son-in-law is not a valuable exchange partner. The case contrasts strongly with one I cited earlier, in which a man's affines gave him special treatment in order to persuade him to stay with them and to obtain his children as members of their sub-clan. In the earlier case, the affines were occupying an expanded territory and felt they were short of men.[23]

The aggrieved father-in-law did not threaten to claim his daughter's children, but he did claim that proper payment should be made for them. Rhetorical assertions made in the course of disputes may not be conducive to interpretation in terms of clear rules of legitimacy, filiation, and affiliation, but I shall attempt to state the general assumptions on which such assertions are based and which do provide the groundwork for discussions about bridewealth and children's affiliation.

Bridewealth gives the husband exclusive rights of sexual access to his wife; and, as is mentioned in chapter one, several acts of intercourse are considered necessary to 'make' a child. Hence the man who has paid bridewealth is usually the presumptive genitor, and the child has a single recognised father who is also married to the mother. This is the normative and statistically preponderant situation. However, if a woman leaves her husband and goes to live with another man, and after a year or so bears a child, the situation becomes slightly awry. Her new partner is now presumed to be the child's genitor and so the child is considered to be physically filiated to him. Further, the *de facto* conjugal situation of the parents is recognised by the woman's kin. What usually follows is an attempt to regularise the situation by making the new husband-father give some bridewealth and/or some payment for the child which has been born to his de facto wife's kin. The previous husband now tries to recover the outstanding amounts from the bridewealth which he himself paid, again from the wife's kin. Even if he does not succeed in doing so, he is unlikely to be able to claim his ex-wife's children by her new husband. These are filiated to the new husband by the presumed fact of his paternity, and he, in turn, must recognise his paternity by making payments to the mother's kin. Further, as already remarked, he must make these payments even if he is residing at his own father's place. The subsequent affiliation of his children will depend on a range of factors, as we have seen, and in the next chapter I shall look at situations of choice in more detail.

In conclusion, even with the minimal definition of 'agnate' that I have adopted, it is still the case that 35 per cent of the men who in 1964–5 were full members of Kawelka clan-groups were non-agnates (Table 6(b)). However, just over 30 per cent of these were born on Kawelka territory and had at least one Kawelka parent, so that they both had a tie of filiation with the tribe and could claim a local connection with it from birth. Most of the non-agnates had an immediate kin-tie with other clan-group members, and links within the *pam* complex (mother's brother-sister's son and cross-cousin relationships) amounted to about 63 per cent of the total. Table 8(a) shows that where only one current non-agnate is involved, most commonly he was either brought in by his mother or came by his own decision, often to his mother's people. In cases where clusters of men were involved, at least twenty-five of the men had been born in the clan territory, while another nine had been brought by their mothers. In the past, mothers were sometimes forced to flee to their own kin when their husbands' clans were defeated in warfare; nowadays they are either persuaded to return by brothers who are keen to gain a following or themselves leave after disagreements with their husbands. The position of sister's sons is relatively secure in their mother's brother's group, and is both recognised as a possibility in the regular terms relating to the affiliation-status of members (the 'man-bearing'/'woman-bearing' pair of terms) and buttressed by ideological idioms which state that they have 'roots' in their mother's group as a tree has roots in its own land. In most cases where a mother brings her children back to her natal kin she is widowed, divorced, or separated from her husband; but in a few cases the husband may join her in uxoripatri-local residence. This mode of residence is looked on with a certain amount of disfavour by men, since it tends to imply that the wife, contrary to Hagen male expectations, is 'stronger' than her husband.[24] In practice, however, it may be the wife's father, as a big-man, who encourages the husband to settle with him. The affiliation of the children in such a marriage is left open: neither the husband's payment of bridewealth nor the children's residence at their mother's place is held automatically to ensure that the children 'belong' to either parent's group. The situation rather opens out a choice for the children which otherwise they would not have. Choice is also open to the children of a 'returned' widow or divorcée mother, but there is in these cases a stronger expectation that they will stay with their mother's group.

CHAPTER 6

CHOICES

In any analysis of group membership in Highlands societies the question of degrees of choice in affiliation deserves to be carefully investigated. One of the early characterisations of Highlands societies in general, cited by Langness (1964:162), was that they appear to allow for considerable freedom with respect to social relations. Attempting to sum the situation up, anthropologists ventured that these societies could thus be described as 'structurally flexible' (Brown 1962, quoted by Langness). The contrast perhaps implied here is with societies which are describable as 'structurally rigid'; but to make it effectively meaningful one would have to define further the concept of rigidity. It could apply, for example, to the degree to which conformity with certain norms and rules is usually enforced in a society, or, slightly differently, to the degree to which an individual can choose between a number of courses of action in accordance with alternative norms and rules. Without going into this conceptual problem more closely, we can put its relevance to the present inquiry quite simply: what ranges of alternatives are available to people, under what circumstances, and how are they used? Theoretically the most rigid situation is that in which a person's group-affiliation is fully ascribed to him at his birth and in which neither he nor others can change any component of his affiliation by voluntary action subsequently. The person's total social position (which would include his group-affiliation) would be so much the more rigid if, for example, he was not free to choose his friends, his wife and hence his affines, the kind of use he should make of his

extra-group kinship ties, and so on. Leach (1962:133) lays it down
that 'in all viable systems there must be an area where the individual
is free to make choices', and he adds, 'so as to manipulate the system
to his own advantage' (he could have said 'bypass the system' to
cover a further range of cases). Leach does not back this proposition
up by any anthropological theory, but offers it as a common-sense
proposition—although his reference to the 'viability' of systems
suggests the need for a theory to underpin this common-sense viewpoint. In any case, we can accept it heuristically as a text for looking
into areas of choice in group-affiliation. In empirical terms, what we
are looking at is a number of acts of choice made by individuals.
To understand their choices we must know something of the
framework of compulsions, opportunities, and advantages within
which they act and to follow the outcomes of choices we must look
at the statistical patterns which result from them. The first section
of this chapter looks at patterns of intermarriage between the
Kawelka and groups around them, explaining that since the
strongest alternative regularly available to a person is to join his
mother's group, if he does not affiliate with his father's, rates of
intermarriage between groups are bound to be linked in some way
with rates of 'transference' of persons between them. A favourable
attitude to the incorporation of sisters' sons on the part of mothers'
brothers' people partly issues from the fact of inter-group alliances,
for immigrants from an allied group are less 'strangers' and hence,
from the point of view of their hosts, easier to trust and to take into
the community. The second and third sections of the chapter
examine case-material and figures on changes in group-affiliation
more closely; and the fourth, after a further excursus on choice,
summarises conclusions.

THE CONCOMITANTS OF ALLIANCE

At the beginning of chapter four I outlined a model which
described some features of Hagen society, and in the rest of the
chapter I noted that close alliances between groups have allowed
a certain amount of sharing of territory between them. Hence one
finds enclaves of men living with host groups, to which they are

tied by extensive exchange partnerships. Affinal and matrilateral ties are important as lines of communication for such partnerships, so one expects to find that allied groups are fairly closely intermarried. Since also, as we have seen in the previous chapter, a considerable proportion of the non-agnatic members of the Kawelka clan groups are either sisters' sons or descendants of these, it is clear that rates of intermarriage should indirectly affect what may be termed rates of interchange of persons. The reasoning here is that the more marriages there are between groups the greater the likelihood that, as a result of widowhood, divorce, separation, or uxorilocal residence, there will be a flow of sisters' sons from group to group. Widowhood and the other factors are thus intervening variables in the hypothesis, and its plausibility depends, in the first place, on these factors operating constantly in relations between allied as well as enemy groups. It is quite possible that they do not operate in this way, and unfortunately I have not tested for this. However, even if, to take the most likely possibility, divorce were more rare in marriages between allies, it would still be true that the natal kinsfolk of women would be more willing to accept their children and themselves back, since the children's patri-identity would lie with a relatively friendly rather than a traditionally hostile group. Hence, even with infrequent divorce, there would be a high chance of sisters' sons joining their mothers' groups in cases where divorce had occurred.

To assess the hypothesis we must know something of the actual rates of intermarriage between the Kawelka and other groups. Marriage rules in Hagen ensure a certain degree of dispersal of affinal ties. Once a marriage has taken place between two 'men's house groups' (*manga rapa*, sub-divisions of a clan) and children have been born of the marriage, there can be no further intermarriage between the two *rapa* for from three to five generations, depending on how long the connections between the *rapa* are remembered (cf. Strauss and Tischner 1962:98). The implications of this rule have to be established separately for every clan, since there is some ambiguity about which levels of segmentation are to be taken as relevant for the calculation of prohibitions. This in turn is connected with the ambiguous status of the men's house subdivisions in certain clans, for example in Klammbo clan-section whose divisions are 'only small men's houses' and function more as sub-sub-clans than as sub-clans. To give a hypothetical instance, a man may not marry his sub-clan sister's husband's 'sister', where some degree of classificatory relationship is implied by 'sister'. Some informants would say that the rule applies to sub-sub-clan 'sisters', others that lineage 'sisters' are meant. Each informant sees the rules from the point of view of his own position within his particular group and draws on cases he knows of in order to predict the situation for others. At least two factors are involved in producing variability in ideas about application of rules to the small segments of a clan. First, there is the influence of size. Where a group is large and deeply segmented, its lineages may be treated for intermarriage purposes as are sub-sub-clans in smaller groups. Second, where, for purposes of alliance, men wish to reduplicate marriages between their groups they may declare that small segments are separate *rapa*, which previously or in other contexts had been treated as a single *rapa*. Hence it would be no easy matter to estimate the theoretically 'possible' number of marriages between two clans in order to compare this with the actual number of marriages made. One would need to know the clans' transactions and relations between their segments in detail to do this. Moreover, in making actual estimates, one could not start from a *tabula rasa*. Instead, one would have to take into account the existing network of marriages and kin relationships resulting from past marriages and see how these were interpreted as constituting bars to further specific marriages, and also how these bars were occasionally overcome when it was desired to contract further marriages. Given a premium set on the constant renewal of affinal ties between allied groups, it would not be in a clan's interest to exhaust its intermarriage possibilities with another clan by making too many marriages with it in a single generation. Instead, it would be expedient to make a few marriages in each generation. The creation of new sub-sub-clan divisions over a number of generations would facilitate this process of alliance-renewal.

Unfortunately, I cannot establish the marriage possibilities between the Kawelka and their neighbours in such detail. I can only suggest some broad patterns of preference, based on the gross likelihood of inter-marriage possibilities. Table 11 gives the incidence of wife-taking by Kawelka men over two generations (thirteen marriages in which the wife's clan was not ascertained are omitted).

TABLE 11: THE INCIDENCE OF WIFE-TAKING FROM OTHER GROUPS BY KAWELKA MEN OVER TWO GENERATIONS

(a) SENIOR GENERATION (SOME MEN NOW DEAD)

Wives from	No. of wives			
	Mandembo	Membo	Kundmbo	Totals
A Within Kawelka	14	12	11	37
B Neighbours (Tipuka, Minembi, Klamakae, Kombukla)	44	48	45	137
C_1 Kope and Kumndi, towards Mt Hagen	1	1	13	15
C_2 Tribes near to the Gumant river	0	6	1	7
D Tribes in Central Melpa area near to Hagen township	0	4	2	6
E North Wahgi tribes (Wəlyi, Kendipi, Roklaka)	7	1	2	10
F Baiyer Valley tribes	3	3	4	10
G Jimi Valley tribes	7	3	0	10
H Outside Hagen (Banz, Goroka)	0	0	0	0
	76	78	78	232

Note: Membo men married six women from Gumant tribes, but five of these were women living as refugees with the Tipuka Eltimbo group who were neighbours of the Kawelka; so that these marriages could as meaningfully have been included under category B.

The table does not give a full picture of intermarriage rates, since it does not record wives given to other groups. There is some preference for exchange marriages between allied groups, so that the total rate of intermarriage with the Tipuka and Klamakae tribes in category B may be higher than the rate of wife-taking may suggest. The rate of wife-taking by Kawelka men from neighbouring

(b) JUNIOR GENERATION

	Mandembo	Membo	Kundmbo	Totals
A	8	9	3	20
B	20	31	30	81
C_1	1	3	4	8
C_2	1	1	1	3
D	3	13	3	19
E	2	1	0	3
F	1	4	2	7
G	2	3	0	5
H	0	1	0	1
	38	66	43	147

Note: Membo have taken many wives (13) from category D in the junior generation. Most of the wives are from Ndika clans whose men are neighbours of Membo men in their re-colonised Wahgi settlements. Hence these marriages could also be plausibly included under B.

tribes is clearly high. Table 12 refines the picture given in Table 11 by distinguishing the Kawelka's traditional enemies from their allies; and this table can in turn be refined by considering alliance patterns of Kundmbo clan separately from those of the Membo-Mandembo pair of clans. By itself Table 12(a) would suggest that although more wives are taken from allies (plus minor enemies), the number taken from major enemy groups is still rather high, certainly by comparison with numbers of wives taken from tribes further afield. Table 12(b), however, shows that it is Kundmbo clan which has taken a large number of wives from supposedly major enemy groups. The Kundmbo pattern practically reverses that for the other two clans, in fact, and closer inspection of the figures and of Kundmbo's alliances shows that the Kundmbo have intermarried mainly with groups among the Minembi and Kombukla with which they do have either traditional military alliances or recently developed exchange partnerships. Table 12(c) indicates part of the pattern. The greatest number of Minembi wives is taken from Kimbo clan, which was the special military ally of the Kundmbo in the past. The figures are suggestive, but unfortunately I cannot demonstrate the preference patterns conclusively, since I do not

TABLE 12: WIFE TAKING FROM TRADITIONAL ALLIES AND ENEMIES

(a) DETAILED ACCOUNT

Wives taken from	Mand.		Me.		Kund.	
	Sen.	Jun.	Sen.	Jun.	Sen.	Jun.
Allies or minor enemies (Tipuka, Klamakae)	39	15	36	18	13	11
Major enemies (Minembi, Kombukla)	5	5	12	13	32	19
	44	20	48	31	45	30

Wives from allies, etc.:	132
Wives from major enemies:	86

(b) SUMMARY

Wives from	Me.-Mand.	Kund.
Tipuka, Klamakae	108	15
Minembi, Kombukla	35	51
	143	66

(c) KUNDMBO WIFE-TAKING

Wives from:

Minembi:	Kimbo clan (military allies)	14
	Engambo (now exchange partners)	5
	Yelipi (now exchange partners)	3
	Mimke (neighbours of Engambo and Yelipi)	5
	Komonkae + Ruprupkae	3
	Nambakae	1
	Papeke (some exchange partners)	1
Kombukla main section:	Andakomone (3 clans)	5
	Andakelkam (2 clans) (now exchange partners)	14

Note: the figures in Tables 10 and 11 expand and correct those in Strathern, A. J. and A. M. 1969, Tables 7 and 8.

know exactly how the marriage rules apply to these clans. To obtain these, it would be necessary to discover not only the names of all the small *rapa* in the Minembi clans but also exactly how their wife-taking and wife-giving relations are ordered with respect to each *rapa* in Kundmbo clan. The number of *rapa* cannot simply be predicted for a particular clan from the overall numbers of persons in each clan either, since in some cases a shrunken clan has preserved its previous segmentation pattern into a number of *rapa*, and its *rapa* may still function as they did before in marriage alliances, although each comprises fewer members than previously and it may not be feasible for them to act independently in ceremonial exchange activities.

On the other hand, the direction of the figures is clear enough for certain gross contrasts to appear. Thus, according to Administration census figures, there were 1,248 persons in 1962 within the Anda-komone section of Kombukla tribe. (These figures include in-married wives and exclude out-married, non-co-resident sisters, but this need not affect the present argument.) By contrast, the Anda-kelkam section numbered only 203. It is extremely likely that the number of relevant *rapa* divisions is far greater in the Andakomone than in the Andakelkam section (since the contrast in their total populations is so great); yet, as Table 12(c) shows, Kundmbo men have taken more than twice as many wives from the section whose men either are or at one time were their neighbours—the Andakelkam—than from the larger, but more remote and unfriendly Andakomone section. It is true that Kundmbo also fought against Andakelkam section; but the fighting was followed, as I have noted in chapter four, by a new series of marriages with one of the Andakelkam clans to re-establish friendly relations. The marriages with the other clan of this section date mainly from the time before the Kundmbo drove its men out and took over their territory.

Again, there is an obvious contrast between the single wife taken from the Papeke clan, who numbered 593 in 1962, and the fourteen wives from Kimbo, who numbered only 383 persons. Papeke and Kundmbo were fighting at the time when Kundmbo and Kimbo joined together as allies to oppose the Kombukla Andakelkam and obtain more land for Kundmbo men to settle in, away from the borders of other Minembi clans. Hostility to Papeke and military alliance with Kimbo are thus well-established facts. Neither of these two Minembi clans (Papeke and Kimbo) is a shrunken group which has suffered massive defeats in warfare, so I conclude that their segmentation patterns are likely to be similar, and that there are more Papeke than Kimbo *rapa*. The preference for taking Kimbo wives is thus a real one when compared with wife-taking from Papeke. But it would be much harder to show that there is a preference for taking Kimbo wives by comparison with taking wives from Mimke clan. The Mimke are a much smaller group (126 persons in 1962) than Kimbo: almost exactly one third of Kimbo in size. And the number of wives taken by Kundmbo men from Mimke is also about one third of the number taken from Kimbo. Yet the Mimke are not so strongly allied at a group level with the Kundmbo as Kimbo are, although they were not direct enemies[1] of Kimbo in warfare. At this micro-level it is unlikely that wife-taking will rigidly follow inter-group alliances, since marriage arrangements are partly an individual affair, and men can have exchange partnerships outside the main sequences of exchange in which their clans are involved.

In accounting for intermarriage patterns, then, it is best to take each Kawelka clan separately and show whether its men have taken most wives from a single ally, or a pair of allies, or a spread of clans. Thus, from its four neighbouring tribes Membo clan has taken 25.5 per cent of its wives from Tipuka tribe, 12.6 per cent from Klamakae, 14.7 per cent from Minembi, and 2.8 per cent from Kombukla.[2] Mandembo show an even higher preference for taking Tipuka wives (41 per cent, forty-three wives out of a total of 105 considered). High intermarriage rates with Tipuka tribe are thus established for these two clan-groups, and this fits with the pairing of Tipuka and Kawelka as allies. Moreover, it is fair to compare the figures for Tipuka wife-taking directly with those for wives taken from the Minembi, since these two tribes are comparable in size, number of exogamous groups and segmentation pattern: in fact the Minembi are rather more numerous than the Tipuka.[3] Membo takes 14.7 per cent, Mandembo 5.7 per cent of its wives from Minembi, an average of 10.2 per cent for the two clans; whereas the average

for the two in relation to the Tipuka is 33.25 per cent. More detailed
analysis again would show a concentration of Mandembo marriages
with their special allies, the Kitepi-Oklembo pair of clans in Tipuka
tribe, and with the Yelipi clan of Minembi tribe, which was
alienated from the rest of the Minembi and survived through a
grant of land from the Tipuka and through establishing friendships
with the Kawelka.

Direct comparison of wife-taking from the Minembi, say, and
from the Klamakae would, however, be misleading. The Klamakae
are a small tribe (241 persons in 1962) divided into only two exogamous groups, and the number of their *rapa* must be much smaller
than that for the Minembi. Hence it is that Membo, who themselves
exceed the total population of Klamakae tribe, have taken only
12.6 per cent of their wives from Klamakae.

Such complications in the assessment of revealed preferences in
intermarriage patterns should warn us against attempting to
establish too direct a correlation between gross rates of wife-taking,
alliance (whether newly-established or traditional) and rates of
interchange of personnel between clan-groups. A few points,
however, can be made.

First, I have argued earlier (chapter four) that only friendly clans
are likely in the past to have granted refuge to large numbers of
each other's men as a result of warfare. 'Friendliness' was not a
simple matter, either, for allies might on occasion be ranged against
each other as minor enemies and this could lead to embarrassing
choices for refugees, dependent on the one group but traditionally
identified with the other. The imposition of colonial peace since
1944 has altered the situation: till recently it increased the prospects
of friendship between refugees and hosts, but since the potential
cash value of land has become known, possibilities of discord over
land ownership have emerged.

Second, it is important to distinguish between inter-group and
inter-individual relations. Here again the abolition of warfare has
modified the situation. In the past an individual affine or mother's
brother might welcome a man as a visitor or refugee, but if the man
came from a major enemy group he would be in danger of attack

from his host's group-mates. The likelihood of attack would be lessened if he were a sister's son of the group; and further lessened, if he came to give his allegiance to his maternal clan rather than simply visiting it. Nowadays men are less likely to worry about the danger of losing their lives through visiting kin, but there is always the possibility that someone might put poison in their food, and they are often wary while visiting in a major enemy area. All this means that there is still a preference for marrying into and associating with relatively friendly groups, and for switching one's residence or affiliation to such a group if one does so in adulthood. (Switches resulting from actions of one's mother during one's childhood cannot be looked at in the same way.) Similarly, a group is much more likely to trust an incomer if he comes from an allied clan, or at least not from a major enemy clan: he may, of course, be from outside the local ambit of inter-group amity and enmity.

Third, since warfare has been stopped, there have been attempts to alter the earlier framework of major enemy relationships, by paying extra wergild for deaths and thus extending exchange relations to ex-enemies. To the extent that these attempts have been successful, they have eased tensions which in the past inhibited residence-moves between the territories of enemy groups.[4]

Fourth, it must be reiterated that relations even between allies are not, and never were, simply friendly. There is always some rivalry and antagonism between them too. Persons who switch their affiliation to their original group's ally may find that their own group objects to the loss of men. Two generations up from senior men today a Kawelka Kundmbo man married a Kimbo woman and went into uxorilocal residence with her at her father's place. From him there descends a flourishing expanded lineage of Kimbo men with many polygynists and two or three major big-men, known collectively as the 'born of the woman' (amb-nt-mei) rapa in Kimbo Tipukmbo clan-section. The Kundmbo see this lineage as descended from their man, rather than the Kimbo woman, and continue to be angry at this loss of their 'grease'. I was told by a Kundmbo Komiti that in 1963 they had gone down to the Kimbo government census-point and courted for five days to have the men of this lineage come over to them. They returned, without gaining their point, and starving, for they had been given very little food while the dispute was in progress.[5] In another case between the two clans, a Kundmbo big-man sponsored the marriage of a sister's son, who had joined him in his settlement as an orphan, the marriage being with a Kimbo girl. The girl would not stay and returned to her father's place. The Kundmbo at once entered a long and contentious series of courts to recover the bridewealth paid for the girl. The big-man had also taken in another sister's son, along with his mother, who belonged by patrifiliation to the Kimbo; and the Kundmbo declared that if they did not succeed in recovering their bridewealth they would make sure that the Kimbo boy would not return to his father but would stay and affiliate himself with them.[6]

These cases remind us of the complications which surround actual disputes over affiliation changes, and in the second part of the chapter I shall turn more explicitly to the situations of choice in which actors find themselves. Table 13 shows the incidence of residence-moves, whether these resulted in affiliation-changes or not, between the Kawelka and other tribes and between clans of the Kawelka themselves. The purpose of the table is to enable us to compare these residence-moves with the patterns of intermarriage shown in Tables 11 and 12.

The instances of moves are drawn from the same set of cases relating to both pre- and post-1944 as in Table 5. Within Kawelka each move counts twice, once as 'to' and once as 'from' a Kawelka group. A few men made more than one move, and each move is counted. The letters after each tribe's name refer to its location, in terms of the scheme given in Table 10. Expectably, the total of moves with Tipuka and Klamakae outnumbers that of moves with

---

Notes to Table 13:
1. *Moves with Klamakae include some men who were originally of Maplke but joined Klamakae before they moved to Kawelka territory.*
2. *Moves with Kope include 5 into or out of an area at the Gumant river shared by the Kope with other tribes—a 'resettlement area', in fact, where men have migrated since warfare stopped in order to exploit pig-pasture.*
3. *The category 'other' includes cases where details of an incomer's tribe are not known; and some men who had moved to work as 'cargo-boys' at a plantation and had stayed permanently away from Kawelka territory up till 1964-5.*

TABLE 13: RESIDENCE AND AFFILIATION CHANGES BETWEEN THE KAWELKA AND OTHER TRIBES AND BETWEEN KAWELKA CLANS OVER TWO TO THREE GENERATIONS

Moves between Kawelka and:	Me.	Mand.	Me.+ Mand.	Kund.	Totals
Kawelka (A)	15	14	29	3	32
Tipuka (B)	21	23	44	6	50
Klamakae (B)	22	2	24	—	24
Minembi (B)	5	3	8	13	21
Kope (C_1)	2	—	2	9	11
Kombukla (B)	1	5	6	3	9
Roklaka (E)	—	—	—	6	6
Kendipi (E)	—	4	4	—	4
Rəmndi (C_2)	—	4	4	—	4
Ndika (D)	—	1	1	3	4
Nengka and Mile (slopes of Mt Hagen)	—	—	—	4	4
Palke (G)	—	3	3	—	3
Lkalke (C_2)	3	—	3	—	3
Wəlyi (E)	2	1	3	—	3
Keme (D)	—	1	1	1	2
Kimke (C_2)	—	—	—	2	2
Epilke (F)	2	—	2	—	2
Maplke (G)	—	1	1	—	1
Pøndi (F)	—	1	1	—	1
Penambe (D)	—	—	—	1	1
Andakapkae (F)	1	—	1	—	1
Ukini (F)	1	—	1	—	1
Kiklpukla (C_2)	—	—	—	1	1
Weimbke (D)	—	—	—	1	1
Nønda (D)	—	—	—	1	1
Ndilika (C_2)	—	—	—	1	1
Other cases	1	2	3	—	3
	76	65	141	55	196

Column header note: "To and from:" spans Me., Mand., Me.+Mand., Kund.

Kombukla and Minembi, and sixteen out of the thirty moves with the latter involve Kundmbo clansmen only. The figures show a broad fit with my discussion of alliance and intermarriage. They reveal also the special relationship between Membo clan and the Klamakae. Only 12.6 per cent of Membo's wives have been taken from Klamakae, but, as we have seen in chapter four, there has been extensive residence sharing between the Kawelka clan and Klamakae following the initial expansion of the Membo into what was before Klamakae territory. Here is a case, then, where the rate of wife-taking is not a reliable index to the degree of residence interchange between two clans.

CASES: MEN

Earlier, I have said (chapter five) that in order to understand patterns of affiliation and residence we must look, where possible, at the attitudes and situations of all the parties involved. Analysing switch of residence and/or affiliation, then, we can pay attention to the attitudes and situation of (1) the host and his group, (2) the in-comer, and (3) the incomer's ex-settlement and/or group mates. It is evident that a number of combinations of attitude and a number of outcomes are possible. For a man to obtain permanent residence and perhaps affiliation with a new group he must gain the acceptance of both host and group, whereas a temporary change may require only the immediate host's agreement. In all cases the host himself must, of course, accept the incomer. He may do so because he thereby gains some particular advantage, or simply because he feels obligated by some special tie with the incomer. Here the two facts that incomers often join big-men, indeed are solicited to come by them, and that incomer and host are often related as sister's son and mother's brother, are highly significant. Big-men can gain special advantages from increasing the number of their close settlement-mates and supporters; and they can recruit such supporters by appealing to values inherent in the mother's brother-sister's son relationship. To an incomer the value of exploiting this tie rather than another is also great: he has ready-made claims on his mother's people which he does not have with any other group apart (normally) from that of his own father. Men do join their affines or other kin also, but if they do so, either choice has been restricted or further factors of preference or advantage have entered to outweigh the value of going to their maternal kin. Finally, there is the question of the incomer's choice in moving from his original place or leaving his original group at all. He may not have had any option, for example if his group-mates expelled him or if his group were destroyed or dispersed in warfare. Or he may have moved in order to maximise some value, such as the exploitation of pig-pasture, or to minimise some annoyance or escape from an unpleasant situation, e.g. to avoid sickness which he interprets as due to ghostly attacks or to remove himself from clansmen with whom he has quarrelled.

In addition to considering contexts in which choices are actually made it is important to know how the concept of choice is seen by Highlanders themselves. The notion of choice depends on perception of a set of possibilities and implies some preferential ranking between these, that is, some motivation for making one option rather than another. Melpa speakers are as pragmatic as the Highlanders in general are often said to be in citing prudential reasons for their actions—'I did this to avoid being killed, to escape a ghost, to find good gardens for growing coffee, so that my skin would be good,' and so on. They also make categorical statements about moral norms— 'it is bad to hit your brothers, it is good to give generously,' etc. All these kinds of prescription provide frameworks in which choices are generally made and evaluated. Speculation about motives as reasons for a choice of action on the part of someone else is, however, rather rigorously avoided. It is possible to ask 'why' questions, but the assumption is that unless a person's reasons were made public they are his own business or the business of his own small group if one does not belong to this. The regular word for 'why' translates literally as 'what—it having done' and the locus for the action of 'having done' here is the person's *noman*. *Noman* may be glossed as 'social consciousness'. The *noman* is spoken of as inside a person's chest, set against his windpipe. If the two are 'straight' (*kwun*) in relation to each other, the person's intentions are correct, that is, in accordance with ordinary norms and expectations; if the *noman* is set crookedly against the windpipe, intentions go astray, are 'wrong' (*klawa*). Further, the intentions at the top of the *noman* may be fixed while underneath they may be shifting and multiple. A person decides to do something when a single intention emerges and 'comes up' (*okla onom*) into the top of the *noman*, but the point which Hageners are quick to add is that the *noman* lies inside a person and cannot be seen—hence one cannot tell why (i.e. the *noman* having done what) the person does something. One can ask what he had heard or what he said before he did the action and can conjecture the state of his *noman* from this, but one cannot be sure. Regularly, it is conjectured that an untoward action results from *popokl*, frustration or anger, coming into or being made in the *noman* (*noman popokl enem*), particularly if the person becomes sick.

It can be seen that an insistence on the relative inscrutability of motives fits with a notion of individual privacy. If a person changes residence he is not likely to be questioned closely on his reasons. His hosts will say, perhaps to the anthropologist especially, 'He is here for no reason' (*we omba morom*), or 'He is here with us because he is our sister's son' (*elim-nga pamal-kin omba pep morom*), the first answer blocking inquiry completely and the second stressing that he has a right to be where he is whatever his reasons. In addition, Hageners ascribe autonomy to the *noman*. 'He did it with his *noman*', they often say, meaning 'That was what he wanted to do', and with the implication that it would have been inappropriate to stop him. If one prevents another from carrying out an action, he may become *popokl* and quickly find some form of sickness (Strathern, A. M. 1968); and this belief helps to give some sanctions to individual autonomy of action. In turn this evaluation of autonomy helps to provide a favourable climate for persons changing their group affiliation; although the notion of autonomy itself is not of much value in explaining how, why and when these changes are actually made: to understand these points we have to look directly at case material, starting with a summary of the territorial consequences of warfare in the past, and then considering individual cases.

Particular cases of dispersal through warfare have been mentioned in chapters two and four. Territorial displacement could result from engagements in both major and minor warfare, but only in the former was a group likely to be decimated and driven out or dispersed totally and permanently. That the destruction of groups as territory-holding political units has occurred in the past is shown by the fact that in probing the histories of men's affiliation to groups, one discovers immigrants who by patrifiliation had belonged to clans or tribes which are nowadays extinct as corporate entities or survive only as enclaves incorporated into host groups. Occasionally, two refugee groups may coalesce: when the Tipuka living at Ep (see chapter four) were attacked by the Kombukla, Eltimbo men managed to flee northwards to the Mbukl area, where they established themselves along with other Tipuka men. About the same time men of another tribe, the Lkalke (or Klalke) fled in the same direction, and these joined with the Eltimbo, helping to make up their numbers which had been depleted in the fighting. Their original identity as Lkalke men is now almost forgotten. Occasionally they are referred to as 'Temboka' men, i.e. men whose origins lie far south of Mbukl in the Nebilyer Valley. The Tipuka and Kawelka histories provide examples also of clans which were wiped out in warfare. Thus Ongka, in his account, mentioned the Køwulmbo, Kumømbmbo, and Akelembo clans of Kawelka, and others told me of the Kurungapei clan, all now extinct; and the Tipuka clans which did not survive the Kombukla attack at Ep were Oumbo, Rongemb, and Apke, all forming part of a major section of Tipuka tribe.

Accounts of this kind raise questions which are relevant to the whole topic of the migration and expansion of Highlands populations. If it is the case that major warfare was more destructive of life than minor, and resulted in greater upheavals of population, one can ask 'Why did major warfare break out?' Hints in informants' own descriptions, much truncated and mythologised as these may be, suggest that groups were most likely to be attacked by a large combination of enemies when they themselves had become overbearing and were a threat, not just to one, but to a number of their neighbours. They would then be cut down to size, or driven out and forced to become refugees or to colonise a further area. Provided there were empty areas to colonise, and that these offered the same ecological advantages as areas already occupied, there would always be a considerable incentive to choose colonisation; and so migration would be a continuous process of expansion into unoccupied ecological niches.

Whether one can also posit that the incidence and effects of warfare were directly linked with population density seems more difficult to decide. Did warfare mean that populations were more or less evenly spread in relation to available ecological resources?[7] One mechanism which might be posited would be as follows: groups with a high population density would initiate warfare and gain new territory, thus spacing themselves more widely than before. However, success in warfare might depend simply on the total number of men who could be mustered, and groups with a high population density would not necessarily be those with the largest numbers of men. (In an instance mentioned by Rappaport on the Maring, the Kauwasi people are spoken of as the 'largest of the Maring local populations' as well as one which 'may well have been pressing the populational limits of their territory'—so here both factors were found together—Rappaport 1967:152.) The most successful groups could, then, be ones which expanded in territory as well as in numbers, and retained their political unity, rather in the manner which Sahlins (1961) posited for the segmentary lineage systems of the Nuer and Tiv. These expanding groups would press on weaker neighbours, penning them into small territories, so that some of the smaller groups might have the highest population densities. The small groups would then have to face continual encroachment and final extinction, or their men might actually join and become incorporated into the expanding groups; or they would disperse elsewhere or colonise a new area. The total effect would be to reduce the incidence of pockets of high-density occupation of this kind. Once taken in by an expanding group, men could join various settlements within the larger territory of their hosts, and thus space themselves out. The process of expansion by a single large group would be slowed down both by the development of internal dissensions within it and by combinations of its neighbours against it. As Meggitt has pointed out in outlining a similar model of processes among the Mae-Enga, a successful group would build up its population and eventually have to attack again, to gain more territory; and this time it might be defeated and its spiralling success halted or reversed (Meggitt 1967:32).

It is clear that parts of this model can be applied to the warfare-history of the Kawelka and surrounding groups. Thus, both Membo and Kundmbo clans increased their territory by driving out weaker groups to their west, and Membo, at least, subsequently took some of their Klamakae ex-enemies in as refugees. Their success was achieved, however, not simply by their own strength and numbers, but through alliances which they had with other neighbouring groups. Without these, Membo and Kundmbo might not have been able to expand at all. A full analysis of the dynamics of success and defeat in Hagen warfare must, then, take alliances into account.

Again, it would be tempting to suggest that destructive major warfare breaks out when population pressure builds up, and parts of the Kawelka origin story might be interpreted in this way. Were the Kawelka pressing on other populations when they were attacked and driven out to the relatively-unoccupied Mbukl area?, We cannot be sure of this; at least we cannot be sure that genuine subsistence-pressure rather than simply 'expansion-pressure' was involved.

At any rate, it is clear from the above discussion that there were many circumstances in which men were forced to abandon their territory and flee, and territory was not always left unused by the victors. Refugees thus either had to found a new territory or become absorbed in other groups. They might scatter initially and later be called together by a big-man who had obtained an enclave territory for them from kinsmen; or they might remain scattered and their descendants would eventually lose their original identity. The imposition of peace by the Australian Administration at first froze all the processes of defeat, enclavement, dispersal, and so on, and has subsequently enabled groups to recover their identity and to send migrants back to portions of their original territories. It has also made it easier for individual men who fled to return to group–mates in cases where only some lineages of a group were broken up and dispersed, while the rest retained their hold on the group's territory.

Hageners speak of clans as solidary groups of men, 'brothers', who co-operate in exchange and warfare. But they also recognise that quarrels arise between clansmen, and result in the expulsion of weaker by stronger parties or in the more-or-less voluntary departure of men who are angry at an insult or an unsatisfactory settlement of a dispute.

Within clan-groups it is expected that men will not poison one another or seduce one another's wives; but both events are held occasionally to occur. An accusation of the latter can be met simply by payment of a fine; the former is more serious, and occurs less often. Further, while supposed adulterers are often dominant men, who have a high status in their clan-group, accusations of poisoning seem to fall on weak men who lack strong support-groups of lineage mates.[8] Classically open to such accusations is the 'little man' who is a helper or servant (*kintmant*) of a big-man and who perhaps comes originally from another clan. When his big-man patron dies, the big-man's clansmen may suspect that the 'little man' has been hired to kill him by enemies and has mixed poison with his food or drink. Cases of expulsion of individuals are:

1.*[9] A man, originally of the Keme tribe (in the Central Melpa area), lived in the Baiyer Valley. He was the son of a Kawelka Kurupmbo woman, and during an epidemic of sickness at his home he came to live with his mother's people. He lived in the settlement of a Kurupmbo major big-man and was helped to marry a wife. However, when the big-man died, he was accused of poisoning him, and fled for his life. He went further north, to the Jimi Valley, where a daughter of his was married to a man of the Palke tribe. There he was again accused of a poisoning and he was hunted in the Jimi forests and killed.

In this story the important factors are the high status of the Keme man's host, and his own helplessness when faced with accusations of poisoning. His position was probably worsened by the fact that he had earlier been living with Minembi clansmen, major enemies of his host group. This is perhaps why suspicion of poisoning was fixed on him; but undoubtedly his weakness against attack was also a factor.

I collected no cases in which adultery with a clansman's wife was followed by expulsion. Adultery within the clan can occur in a number of contexts:

(1) In struggles between different clan-sections, as acts of aggression against the other side. In one fight between two sections of a clan which broke out at a distribution of pork[10], some men wielded cudgels against one another while others took to raping wives belonging to men of the opposite section. The two sections were at odds over past fights and thefts, and the rapings were seen simply as part of a series of hostilities between them.[11]

(2) Adultery is sometimes committed by a dominant man with the wife of a rival. In one such case in April 1965 a young big-man seduced the wife of another prominent young man in a sub-clan paired with his own. He paid $10, a pig, and a pearl-shell in compensation.

(3) A few 'rubbish-men' who are permanent bachelors have a history of waylaying wives of their clansmen and raping them. If they have a big-man as their patron, they will not be punished for this, beyond an occasional beating. Clansmen commenting on one such case pointed out that rubbish-men are likely to be frustrated: 'He is a rubbish-man and we never raised any bridewealth for him, so he is frustrated (*popokl*) and rapes the women.' The man in question was old by 1964; he was an agnate and had two married brothers. He lived, not with these two, but with a major big-man of their sub-clan.

(4) Occasionally, rather than adultery being followed by expulsion, it seems that raping a man's wife or wives was used as an aggressive act to drive him out of the clan.

2.* Two men, both non-agnates of their clan, used to live near each other. One is an accepted big-man, brought to the clan by his mother's mother when a young child after his mother's death—it is said that his grandmother suckled him. His father was killed in warfare, and when he grew up his grandmother told him that his mother had prophesised that he would fall sick if he returned to his father's place. So he stayed at his mother's brother's place, to which the grandmother took him, and his uncle obtained his first wife for him. He became a big-man and married five wives in all. His neighbour was also brought to the clan as a child, by his mother on the death of the father, and became an *amb-nt-mei* member. He too married five wives in all, but eventually lost all but one of them through divorce or death. It is possible that at one stage he was a rival of the big-man. Disputes between them arose over the organisation of a *moka* exchange payment. Partners of the big-man (from his original agnatic clan, which borders the group to which he belongs) gave him some pearl shells. The big-man suggested to his supporters that they should cook some pigs and present them to his exchange partners in return for the shells, after which he would distribute the shells themselves. His neighbour contributed a pig, but the big-man refused to give him a shell. He raised a quarrel over this, after which, some of his ex-clansmen claim, 'We all turned on him, stole his bananas and pigs, and raped his wives, and in rage he left us.' Other informants did not mention the rapings here, but it is quite possible they took place. Clearly, at any rate, the big-man had more support behind him than his neighbour, and it was the latter who withdrew.[12]

3.* In case 2 the big-man cheated and his victim left the clan; in another case a man tried to cheat the same big-man but was likewise ousted. He persuaded a daughter of his to leave her first husband so that he could send her in marriage elsewhere. The husband's kin then came and demanded return of the outstanding bridewealth. However, the father had dissipated this, and he was saved by the big-man, who intervened and paid up for him. Later, when the daughter was remarried, the father hid the new bridewealth and did not pay his debt to the big-man. The latter discovered this, became furious and drove him out, apparently by a display of anger. Here, then, the big-man appears to have worsted a clansman simply by dominance behaviour, perhaps backed up by threats. It should be emphasised that big-men were not invariably able to dominate others in this way: whether they could do so depended on their own forcefulness and that of their opponents.[13] Yet it is likely that big-men at least attempt to dominate others more often than others attempt to dominate them, and that when a man is driven out by a single other man the victor is a man of higher status than the one expelled.

There is also the situation of voluntary departure after quarrels. Cases of this kind in fact shade into those of expulsion already discussed. The linking feature is often that the person moves because he is upset (*popokl*) at some supposed mistreatment. His clan-mates may specifically have provoked him, and are at the least unlikely to ask him to stay. Since he is *popokl*, he is likely to declare that he is moving residence in order to alter his affiliation as well; but he may change his mind later.

The first case shows a close similarity in one feature to case 2 above, where a man's wife is seduced by his clan-mates.

4. In September 1965 I was present at a court dispute in which an old man and his eldest son complained that their clansmen were making it impossible for them to live on clan territory. The old man claimed that clansmen had broken a fence around one of his gardens and allowed pigs into it and had stolen ripe coffee-berries from his trees. He protested that he was no *wuə eta* (refugee living in dependency on others), but a true clansman on his own land. When his group was defeated in warfare he had come to a new territory carrying the younger generation of clansmen in his arms, and why were they ungrateful now? His elder son argued that he made *moka* along with his clansmen and had helped to raise bridewealth for some of them. He had given £15 also to a clansman and wanted the money back, but had been refused. Worse, the clansmen had come and seduced his wife, they were all putting their penises into her, and this was the cause of the court, and the reason why he had taken his wife off to her own natal place. The younger son had also left his clan-territory and gone to live with his maternal kin in a neighbouring friendly clan, and now he declared that he would not pay tax with his father's people but with his new hosts. The Local Government Councillor listened to these complaints and suggested that the two brothers could decide for themselves what to do, but the old man and his wife should be allowed to stay on clan ground in peace. Commenting on this case, a Komiti (Councillor's adjutant) of the clan which had taken in the younger son, said that the latter would be welcome with them, he was on his own ground as their sister's son. He revealed that the elder son had been accused of stealing his clansmen's pigs and had denied it but that his wife, under interrogation, had revealed that he was guilty. He was sent to jail and while he was away four of his clansmen had had intercourse with his wife. The Komiti mentioned that the wife was known as a sexual adventuress, pictured as falling backwards and asking for intercourse whenever she met a

man alone. No compensation for adultery had been paid to her husband, and this was partly why he was upset: his claims over his wife were not being recognised. The old man had also left his homestead and recently joined his younger son: the door of his men's house had been torn off and a cooking drum removed. The clansman whose pigs had allegedly been stolen by the elder son was harvesting the old man's coffee; and other clansmen with supposed grievances against the family had stolen sugar-cane from their garden and broken its fence.

A younger man of the Komiti's clan was less welcoming towards the younger son and his old father than the Komiti himself. He declared that the son was a well-known thief and layabout and if he gave trouble they would throw him out.

This case, then, is very close to ones in which a person is specifically driven away by his clansmen. Quite why the clansmen had turned against this family was not clear to me. My impression was that advantage was taken of them because they were men of relatively low status, not physically powerful or socially influential, and they had become embroiled in a number of disputes. They were able to find hosts in groups with which they had ties, but not to obtain recompense for the wrongs they declared had been done to them. Moreover, the future security of at least the younger son was challenged by a man of his new host's group: he would have to behave or else. As we have seen, the same standard had already been applied by the son's own patrifilial clansmen—indeed, they had already demonstrated their aggression—so we cannot argue that his position would be less secure with his maternal than with his paternal kin.[14]

A man who is upset only with his immediate brothers or father may have the alternative of moving into association with another clansman rather than moving away from his patrifilial clan altogether.

5. The youngest of a set of four brothers was unmarried in 1964, although he was well past the usual age of marriage. The eldest brother was old and deaf, and lived uxorilocally away from his clan, and the next had also spent many years away from his clansmen and was known as a redoubtable pig-thief and seducer of women when he was young. In old age he had reformed, become baptised as a

Christian, and returned to his clan area. The third brother had two wives and was respected as a minor big-man who 'makes exchanges but does not speak', i.e. holds no sway as a leader. The youngest brother worked on plantations away from Hagen during his adolescence, and on his return he gave a number of pearl shells and cash to the third brother (who was obviously his best prospect for investment). Unfortunately, the latter did not reciprocate by raising a bridewealth payment and obtaining a wife for him. In *popokl* the younger brother went off to live with a sub-clansman in a different settlement. When a dispute arose between him and the second eldest brother he refused to enter into discussion and simply put a match to the cane wall of his brother's house in an attempt to burn it down.[15]

Here, then, the grievance was against a set of brothers only. Moreover, the younger brother was not insulted or threatened in any way. In cases where a man's pride is more deeply involved, he is more likely to leave his clan altogether.

6.* Three brothers were brought up by their maternal kin after their father had died. The eldest launched himself with the aid of his immediate and a classificatory mother's brother and of his sister's husband, all of whom have since become major big-men. He and the sister's husband, both big-men by this time, recolonised part of the old Wahgi territory of the Kawelka after 1944. The youngest brother stayed at Mbukl, but the middle one joined the eldest. Now, however, the eldest brother criticised him for not making *moka* with his pigs, why was he raising them at all? In anger the middle brother retorted that he preferred to keep his pigs until they were big, whereas others made *moka* quickly but with inferior pigs. His ability and willingness to contribute to *moka* and to maintain prestige in competition with his elder brother had been impugned, and he left, saying he would withdraw his support entirely. He joined a big-man of the Ndika tribe, husband of a woman of his sub-sub-clan, and no longer associated with the Kawelka in their enterprises. (By 1970, however, his anger had softened, and he was again helping his clansmen in *moka*.)

The next case shows that disagreements over *moka* can lead to considerable passion being displayed. The protagonist in this case left his clan in high dudgeon, but after a number of months he returned.

7. A is a young man with two wives. In 1964 he was elected Local Government Councillor of his clan. After his father's death his mother had been re-married by a major big-man of the same sub-clan, and A is regarded as in some sense the big-man's son. In October 1965 the big-man was leading his sub-clan mates in making a *moka* prestation of pigs to an important exchange partner married to one of A's sisters by the same mother. A was thus the immediate wife's brother of the exchange partner. He seems to have had difficulty in obtaining the pigs he had promised to contribute, and on the day when his sub-clan mates were actually marshalling their pigs for the final ceremony of transfer he was still negotiating at the place of one of his affines for some pigs to be given him so that he could use them in the *moka*. His sub-clansmen made wry comments at his absence from their ceremonial ground. One said 'It's like when a mushroom ripens early and is rotten before the one beside it is ripe' (i.e. A would be ready to make *moka* only when it was too late). Another added 'Yes, A is the one who eats all the legs of pork' (sent as initiatory gifts for *moka*—i.e. he eats the initiatory gifts but doesn't make returns). One of A's wives now brought up two pigs, and later the other wife brought one also. There were cries that it didn't matter if A himself had gone, his wives had come with the pigs. A sub-clansman's wife urged that they should talk kindly so that the two wives would not be upset; and a wife of the leading big-man commented that one of the pigs brought was a good one. The ceremony of transfer now proceeded. The pigs were lined up, tied to a row of stakes down the centre of the ceremonial ground, and sub-clansmen made speeches. A rival exchange partner from a different clan staged an interjection, complaining that they had not given to him, and big-men of other sub-clans in the donors' clan rose to answer him. The recipient partner examined his pigs with a view to distributing them to further partners and between his two wives. He began this at 3.20 p.m. At 3.30 p.m. a sub-clansman arrived with the news that A did not want his pigs to be given away. He was upset as his wives' relatives and a clansman had all failed to help him with pigs, and he had eaten a

cordyline-leaf, the *mi* (mystical divination substance, here used to mark a solemn oath) of his tribe, to register his anger and to forbid the transfer of his pigs. One of the sub-clansmen who had commented before shouted out that they were all helping A by giving to his sister, so what was the argument about? The new arrival said that A was threatening to go to his mother's place, leaving the place where his father was buried, if they gave his pigs away, and that they must hold them till the evening when he would return. Sub-clansmen remarked disbelievingly 'Surely he can't mean it'. At this juncture A arrived from the bottom end of the ceremonial ground. He was wailing and shouting, and stamping the ground. 'I had eight pigs ready in my house', he cried, 'but you have made *moka* without me. I'll never see you men again, I won't stay here! If that man (referring to his step-father, the sub-clan leader and big-man) has money, or pearl shells or pigs, then so have I! I'll never make *moka* with you men again. Whenever you made it before, I helped you, but I'll not help you again. Are my wives widows that they've brought the pigs here themselves, without me?' He turned to men of the opposite section of his clan and said he was not upset with them, only with his own sub-clansmen, then continued: 'It was I who cooked pigs and gave them to my sister's husband before, she's my sister, not theirs, it was my 'root' [i.e. relationship], why have they left me out?' He had a cordyline leaf with him and at this point chewed it again, swearing he would not stay. 'I'll take my pigs back', he went on, 'I'm not *popokl* with all of you, only with those two (naming his step-father and the second most forceful man in the sub-clan). I'm holding this cordyline and swearing by the *mi*, they have said I'm a rubbish-man. It was the same when they made *moka* before, they put me to shame then too. Show this cordyline to both of them, look, I'm eating it still! Are they saying only they can give away pigs and shells and pay out bridewealth?' Men of the opposite section in the clan interjected feebly at several points, telling A not to eat the cordyline in this way (because, if a man subsequently breaks his oath, the *mi* substance may kill him). Seeing that the pigs were being led away, he shouted 'You're not to take them off! They're going to take them away even though I said no!' The protagonists in the *moka* acted as if unmoved, while A strode up and down among them but made no actual attempt to fight or hold on to his pigs. His sister helped her husband. A went off to some distance and shouted for his pigs, while the step-father engaged in a private discussion with the other exchange partner who had come to witness the occasion. That evening I mentioned the incident to the recipient partner. He simply smiled and said 'A is not a big-man, he had promised me eight pigs, he was angry and ashamed because he had not been given more time.' A himself made good his threat to leave his clan, and he also took off all his European-style clothes (shirt and shorts) and resigned his position as Local Government Councillor. He lived with his mother's kin, at a settlement a few miles away from his clan area, for several months. However, by 1969, he had returned and was living closer to his step-father's place than before, and the earlier quarrel was not mentioned. Although I cannot demonstrate this, my interpretation of this sequence of events is that the step-son actually realised his inferiority to the big-man, his step-father, and after trying to gain sympathy by demonstrating his rage and then by leaving his clan area, he finally admitted that he was dependent on the step-father for support in exchange relationships and returned. The original reasons why the *moka* was not delayed to help him were two: first, a baptismal ceremony was impending and the aim was to schedule the *moka* before this; and, second, the recipient was pressing on the donors as he was ambitious to stage a *moka* of his own within the same month. Quite what was thought about A's dangerous action in swearing by his tribe's *mi* and then returning to his clan I do not know.[16]

Most of these cases of departure after quarrels, then, involve both pride and relative power within the clan. The two situations in which men are most likely to leave their clan with assertions that they will withdraw support from it and change their allegiance are when they have been worsted by a big-man and when they are angry with clansmen for failing to recognise their claims. As case 8 shows, the two situations may be found together.

Not all residence moves are made as a result of quarrels. Sometimes men move for ecological reasons, as I have stated earlier (chapter five). One account which I have suggests that the moves made by Kawelka men back to the Wahgi were prompted initially by at least a feeling of land-shortage, as well as the aim of finding a better place for pig-keeping. The account was given in 1964 by a big-man Komiti of Membo clan, Kont, who was not one of those that took part in the migration.

> Councillor Nggoimba forbade anyone to plant on his ground at Tiyapana [a settlement area which is just outside the present accepted boundaries of Kawelka occupation]. The river Piling is a boundary between the Klamakae and the Kawelka, but Nggoimba tried to claim Tiyapana.[17] The Klamakae won the court case, so Nggoimba next tried to live at Rokle, Pat, and then at əm [further hillside settlements within Kawelka territory], but he felt the ground was not good enough. There were too many men and the ground was insufficient for them. Onombe, Nggoimba's father, had lived in the Wahgi and fled down to Mbukl, so Nggoimba now decided to go back to his father's place. This was his own ground, and now he is firmly established there, and since then many other Membo men have joined him. At first some of the men went to Kuning Tip, but then they saw that the ground at Kenta and Mapa was good and went there. There is a division among us Kawelka now, just as there was before in the old days: they are Kuma Kawelka and we are Kopon Kawelka. At first we thought that they would bring their fat pigs down to us, but this is not so. We won't go to live up at Kuma and they won't come down to us at Mbakla.

Kont regretted the loss of men to his own clan, the Membo, for a majority of the migrants to the Wahgi have been Membo men. (In 1964-5, of forty-six men belonging to the Kawelka clan-groups who were living in the Wahgi, thirty-one came from Membo clan.) He pointed out that the move was prompted by the search for garden-land, and he implied that relations between Nggoimba and the Klamakae were not very amicable. It seems that Nggoimba claimed gardens for himself instead of agreeing to share with Klamakae men as other Membo men had done. Kont also commented that the Kuma Kawelka, although remaining members of the Kawelka tribe, had contracted new alliance relationships with their neighbours among the Ndika, by intermarriage and by prestations of pork and shells in *moka*. Here we see a new process at work: the formation of a separate community of men, still linked by affiliation to their fellow-clansmen at Mbukl, but giving their allegiance more to activities linking them to each other and to their new neighbours. However, space is probably insufficient for the Membo men in the Wahgi to expand further. By late 1969 there was conflict with a Ndika leader over the use of land for house-building, and the Administration decided to freeze the situation by forbidding further Kawelka men to leave Mbukl and come to the Wahgi.[18]

Recent migrations by men of the Minembi Yelipi clan at Mbukl partly parallel, and partly differ from those of the Kawelka. As in the case of the latter, they have been made explicitly in search of ground. The Yelipi were driven out by other Minembi clans from their previous territory and were granted a new one by kinsmen in a Tipuka clan. Their new area is steep, surrounded by forest remnants, and probably subject to rapid run-off of water and to soil erosion. Moreover, since their defeat the Yelipi have never (up to 1969) quite managed to re-establish themselves as a strong group. After a less than entirely successful *moka* festival held in late 1964, a number of Yelipi men decided to re-migrate, down to the Baiyer Valley (i.e. to an area only 3,500-4,000 feet above sea level, from their present territory which ranges from *c*.5,500 to almost 7,000 feet). Their aim was to set up coffee gardens and earn cash, i.e. to opt out of the nexus of traditional prestige economics in which they had been unsuccessful and try a new mode of life. Unlike the Kawelka, they did not this time obtain a new territory for themselves. Instead they went individually to extra-clan cognatic kin and affines distributed among the Minembi, Klamakae, and Kombukla groups. The attraction of their new settlement area is that it is fertile and will grow good coffee (nearby is a flourishing European coffee plantation); the difficulty is that the bulk of their clan-mates still live in the main territory, and if they wish to continue co-operating with them they must regularly commute, travelling the six or seven miles' distance between the two settlement areas. It is not impossible for them to do this.[19] They could even theoretically maintain gardens in both areas, and those of them who are polygynists could divide their wives between the two also. For the ordinary men, with one wife and no strong political ambitions, it is much more likely that they will gradually take less and less part in clan discussions and tend more and more to identify with the groups of their hosts. However, it must be emphasised that the option of reverting to their main clan territory will remain open to them; and in 1969 there was no talk that they had ceased to be Yelipi and were becoming members of other clans. The example of the Kawelka settlement at location G (Map 3) indicates that, provided a settlement is not too far from the main territory, its members can retain their major identification with their clan; although to live in an enclave settlement is to realise that its members continually have to balance their allegiances and identification with their hosts against those they have with their original clan. Indeed certain previous members of G have moved back into the main Kawelka territory; and the one who has indicated determination to stay is under pressure to pay taxes with his hosts and not with the Kawelka, as a symbolic act of allegiance to them. He had also built a trade-store on the hosts' land and gained an income from this which was to some extent resented by the land-owners. My impression of the situation in 1969 was that most of the tension had arisen recently, since cash and tree crops had entered the economy, and that tension was held in balance by the stated rule that so long as members of G contributed to the enterprises of their hosts and remained friendly, they would neither be ejected nor required fully to change their clan identity.[20] One could add, as for the case of Tipuka enclaves in Kawelka territory, that the overall alliance between the two tribes is important as a framework for containing and permitting enclave arrangements. Returning to the Yelipi migrations, we may notice that their Minembi tribesmen allowed them in as settlers partly because they were 'all of one name'. Perhaps this fact of belonging to a single tribe will enable the Yelipi immigrants and their hosts to co-operate without coalescing. More crucially, perhaps, the Baiyer is probably underpopulated: its ground is fertile, but it is hot, there are dangers from death-adders which infest garden-edges, and men reputedly contract sicknesses there more than on the hillside settlements at 6,000 feet and above. Hence there is room for immigrants in search of land, provided they are willing to pay the costs of exposure to sickness and isolation from their clansmen. Similar costs must be met when men migrate to new settlement areas in the Wahgi and Jimi Valleys.[21]

Big-men, in the acceptance of newcomers as in other contexts, are entrepreneurs, that is, men who exploit some aspect of a situation and take certain risks in order to extract gains. The risks involved are:

(1) that if one accepts incomers into one's settlement their subsistence needs may be beyond what one can eventually allow for. In Hagen, so long as land shortage is not a general problem, this risk is not a very great one.

(2) the incomer may prove of uncertain allegiance and may accept bribes from outside groups to poison his host. Even nowadays, big-men feel this is a true risk and many declare they have avoided taking in non-agnates altogether because of it. This does not debar them from accreting to themselves patrifilial clan-members as helpers. Two factors help to guard against the risk if one actually does accept incomers. First, one can accept only immediate kin, preferably sister's children, with whom there is a strong sentimental tie. Second, one can take in men from relatively friendly, rather than major enemy, clans. Another safeguard is to recruit sisters' children when they are still young, before they have gained a sense of allegiance to their own patrifilial group. They are then also less likely to leave their maternal kin when they grow up.

Two contrasting examples of acceptance of incomers follow.

8. ǝndipi was an old man by 1964, but was acknowledged to have been one of the foremost big-men in *moka*-making within Membo clan for the past twenty years. At *moka* in which he is involved as a donor or recipient his pigs are often placed on the first stakes at the head of the ceremonial ground, and this is a mark that he is *wuǝ nyim mumuk*, 'a big-man who holds the head of the *moka*'. His father, an Lkalke man, died when he was about five years old, and his mother re-married a big-man of Kawelka Membo clan. As a young man, he fought against the Minembi and Klamakae, and now he lives in one of the new Membo settlements, Pitim, very close to his ex-enemies. He has, however, in the classic manner of the successful big-man, established friendships with them. He uses Klamakae land for some of his gardens, and pays its owners handsomely with presents of cooked pork; and he gives pig-*moka* to an important Minembi big-man who lives nearby. In the vicinity of

his settlement he has gathered around him various people, including Kora, a sister's only son. The sister would not stay with her husband, and brought Kora and a daughter back to ɔndipi's place when both were very young. Kora grew up thinking of ɔndipi as his father and only realised this was not so when he was adolescent. ɔndipi sent the daughter in marriage to a Minembi neighbour, of the same group as his big-man exchange partner; and when his own eldest son died, he allowed Kora to inherit the widow. Kora's original patrifilial kinsmen, of a Tipuka clan, came and asked him to return to them when he was grown up, but he preferred to stay with his mother's brother, who had brought him up. Kitpi is the youngest of a set of four brothers among the Kawelka Kurupmbo. ɔndipi accepted him as a son-in-law, but stipulated that he should come and live in uxorilocal residence and 'help' him. Kitpi is a quiet man, and he agreed to this arrangement. ɔndipi asked him to come after his eldest son, Ruin, had died, and he felt he needed workers to make up for his loss. Kitpi is not spoken of as a Membo man, but it is possible that his children will become Membo if he continues to live uxori-locally after ɔndipi's death. Ruk and Raema are also Kurupmbo men by patrifiliation, and, unlike Kitpi, they maintain their allegiance to their paternal clan by participation in *moka*. Their father is still alive, whereas Kitpi's died when he was young, and this is a significant factor. The father is an ex-polygynist and their mother felt she was not well cared for among the wives of his settlement, so she returned to her brother ɔndipi, taking Ruk and Raema with her. In 1964 the two lived in a separate settlement near to ɔndipi's, and made all their gardens on his land. However their father had made the major contributions to their bridewealth payments. In domestic affairs they help both their mother's brother and their father; in political terms their affiliation is with Kurupmbo.[22] Kukili is the son of a woman of ɔndipi's sub-sub-clan, and was associated before with two Lkalke men who came to live with ɔndipi. ɔndipi helped Kukili to obtain a wife, and Kukili has since remained at his settlement. Kngal also is a sister's son of ɔndipi, and his father is still alive. In 1964 he was adolescent. His mother brought him and his sister on a visit and has stayed ever since. When Kngal was married, ɔndipi made a bid for retention of his allegiance by bearing the major part of the cost of his bridewealth; but the father participated in the arrangements also. The father's place is some ten miles away from əndipi's. In 1964 Kngal had not yet decided whether to live with his mother's brother as a married man or to go back to his father; but in 1970 he was still with the Membo.

əndipi's own surviving sons were not of marriageable age in 1964. He had five wives and ten children in all, and his brother Raklpa also had ten children. It is clear that help with agricultural work from co-resident kin must have been valuable to both men, and Kora and Kukili, as well as Ruk and Raema, were grown up and able to work long before most of əndipi's own children. As he is in a pioneer settlement area and has access to fertile gardens beyond his clan's boundaries, əndipi has been able to provide ground for his non-agnatic supporters as well as for his own wives. His expanded work-force and fertile land are undoubtedly the economic base for his success as a big-man. It is noticeable that he has himself helped to bring up some of his non-agnatic adherents. An alternative pattern is shown by the case of Ai, a major big-man of Kundmbo clan.

9. Ai's father used to live in the Wahgi area and belonged to a division of the Kawelka now defunct, the Kurungapei (based previously at Kuk). At the exodus from the Wahgi territory he joined a matrilateral parallel cousin at Mbukl, and obtained with his help a wife who had previously been married to a Kundmbo man. Ai was brought up at Mbukl and involved in fighting against the Kombukla. With the success of the Kundmbo in these engagements, Ai moved into the new frontier area, and thus had ample access to land—here his action resembles that of əndipi in case 8. He established two different settlements near to each other, with one wife and some adherents in one, himself and further associates in the other. In 1964 there were several persons living in these settlements, in addition to Ai and his own three wives and children. Rop is a man of Ai's clan section. After a sub-clan mate of his died, he obtained the widow, who is a sister of one of Ai's wives. This brought him into a potentially close relationship with Ai and he moved to join him in his settlement. He is in no way a helper or 'servant' of Ai, but does associate with

him in *moka*. Puri, Rop's married son, is married to a daughter of Membo əndipi (case 8), and this gives Ai an exchange link with the Membo big-man. There is also an agnate of the lineage to which Ai is connected by his father's matrilateral ties. He has no wife, nor was one ever obtained for him, although two of his brothers are senior married clansmen, one with two married sons of his own. He is dependent for food on one of Ai's wives, and in return makes gardens and does domestic tasks.[23] He was already an old man by 1964. Young men of the clan-group sometimes declared he was *wuə wulya*, 'a man without sense', and this was why no one had ever raised bridewealth for him.[24] Koi was a non-agnate of the clan-group, but was born in its territory: his father was an uxorilocal immigrant who came as a war-refugee. On the father's death Koi separated from his brother after a quarrel, abandoned his land claims and went to join Ai. With Ai's help he obtained four wives in succession, but each one left him and in 1964 he was again a bachelor, dependent on a wife of Ai for food. Although a bachelor, he was not regarded as a rubbish-man and he did take part in *moka* along with Ai. His clansmen could only speculate on the reasons why he could not retain his wives. (Koi was killed in an accident in 1966.) Opa is the middle brother of a set of three; the other two in 1964 had migrated to the Wahgi area, joining relatives of the Kope tribe. The father is dead. Opa is a sister's son of the neighbouring Kombukla tribesmen. The eldest brother was helped to marry by the mother's second husband, who is also now dead. Opa was over the usual age of marriage by 1964, while the youngest brother was just adolescent. Ai became Opa's patron, although with his own sons growing up he was chary of spending bridewealth on Opa's behalf. Late in 1964 Opa himself managed to obtain rights of re-marriage over the widow of a Kombukla man who disliked her new husband within the Kombukla group itself (the latter was old and lame, while the woman was still in her early thirties). As a cross-cousin of the first husband Opa had some claims over the woman, but there were complications, since the Kombukla men wanted to retain her. A court-case was held, at which Ai represented Opa, at the same time trying not to offend his Kombukla exchange partners. The case was not settled quickly.

Eventually the woman herself died, and Opa was again left without a marital partner.[25] Nendipa was a bachelor between twenty-five and thirty years old in 1964, who belonged to the opposite clan-section from Ai and had joined him specifically in the hope of obtaining help with bridewealth. Earlier he had lived with another big-man, Roltinga, but Roltinga did not help him to obtain a wife, so he moved over to try out Ai. Nendipa's father is dead and he has no brothers; his father's brother is alive but is himself a widower with no resources. There is a major big-man of Nendipa's own sub-clan, Ndamba, but Ndamba already has two helpers, both now ageing and wifeless, and has no incentive to take on Nendipa as well, particularly since four of his own sons are now (1969) grown up and married. Ndamba's sons commented that Nendipa's only chance was to stay with Ai, work for him, and hope that eventually he would be 'sorry' and obtain a wife for him.[26] Nendipa's case shows clearly that (1) men may join big-men specifically in the hope of gaining a wife in return for work; (2) a man needs an immediate sponsor: if his father and brothers are dead, whether he is an agnate or not, he may have difficulty in raising bridewealth; and (3) big-men do not necessarily respond to the hopes of bachelors whom they take in. Whether they do so depends on their own needs for helpers, and also, probably, on affective ties, which are powerful only if the big-man has brought up an incomer from an early age. A consideration here is the fact that bridewealth is high (see chapter seven). It is both hard for a bachelor to raise the requisite amount by himself and unlikely that a big-man will do so unless he has already gained benefits, or can expect to gain benefits by this action. In addition to men of his own clan whom Ai has taken into his two settlements, he has granted residence and land-use rights to a sister's husband, Akel, of Minembi Engambo clan, and his two married sons. These have not asked for incorporation into Kundmbo clan, and it is said that when Akel dies his sons will return to their patrifilial place and the land will revert to Ai. This is probable enough, for the sons make *moka* as Engambo men and other sons of Akel in fact live on the main Engambo territory. The value of Akel to Ai is that he and Akel are vigorous exchange partners, and as Akel lives on Ai's ground he is unlikely to default on his payments. The scale of Ai's investment in Akel can be seen from the fact that in 1964 he had given Akel thirty pigs in *moka* and the latter was preparing to make returns.

The main contrast between the actions of Ai and əndipi lies, then, in the fact that most of əndipi's settlement mates are sisters' sons who were brought back to him by their mothers when young; whereas Ai's are men who came to him as already-established clansmen when they were adult. The contrast, in fact, reveals that big-men can create close supporters and associates for themselves by exploiting either extra-clan or intra-clan ties, or combinations of both. Further examples could be given to show ranges of variation: some big-men have no incomers in their settlements at all; others allow incomers to join them; others, who specifically need help with work, actively recruit them with promises and material aid. As I have mentioned earlier, each specific arrangement carries with it some implication of mutual benefit, but it is in a big-man's interest to see that he does not disburse wealth in marriage payments on behalf of an incomer unless he needs the incomer and can be fairly sure of his allegiance. The costs of nurturing sisters' sons may be high, but the prospects of obtaining their allegiance are good, depending to some extent on whether their close patrifilial kin are alive or not; whereas the initial costs of obtaining an adult helper are low, but his allegiance may be uncertain. The best situation for the big-man is one in which a helper has little choice but to continue working for, and associating himself with, him. Then he may put the helper further in his debt by obtaining a wife for him. A bachelor who, like Nendipa in case 9, has already tried other big-men of his clan and has neither received help from them nor agreed to stay with them for long, is in a weak position, and his clansmen were probably right in their assessment of his chances of obtaining a wife. When a true father raises bride-wealth for his son, this is done within a context of implied reciprocity; but the father is much less likely to demand specific service from his son than is a big-man from his client. Or, to put it another way, a client may have to spend long enough at his big-man patron's place to become like a son to him.

It can thus be seen that big-men do not necessarily make clan

composition less patrifilial than it might otherwise have been, since
they may gather patrifilial clansmen rather than incomers to themselves as clients and supporters. Nevertheless, a considerable proportion of the non-agnates in the Kawelka clan-groups in 1964 were
either protégés of big-men or the sons of protégés (see Table 14 (a)
and (b)). Forty out of the ninety-five non-agnates in the clan-groups
(as per Table 6(a), chapter five), or 42.6 per cent, were either directly
taken in by big-men or were sons of men taken in by big-men, and
a further nineteen, or 20.1 per cent, were taken in by a big-man's
seminal brother (or again were sons of such men). Big-men number
only $c.11.3$ per cent of the Kawelka men (cf. *The rope of moka*,
chapter nine, Table 26, p.200), so the proportions of non-agnates
whom they have sponsored are certainly greater than those expectable by chance.

The Kundmbo figures differ from those for the Membo. Among
the latter, forty-one of the fifty-six non-agnates have been associa-

TABLE 14: NUMBERS OF NON-AGNATES IN KAWELKA
CLAN-GROUPS WHO WERE TAKEN IN BY BIG-MEN

(a) STATUS OF HOSTS

| | No. of men in clans | | | |
	Membo	Kundmbo	Mandembo	Totals
A_1 Taken in by major big-man; or son of person so taken in	15	2	5	22
A_2 Taken in by seminal brother of major big-man; or son, etc.	3	0	3	6
B_1 Taken in by minor big-man; or son, etc.	13	4	1	18
B_2 As A_2, in case of minor big-man	11	2	0	13
C Not taken in by big-man or by brother of big-man	14	18	4	36
	56	26	13	95

(b) DETAILED ACCOUNT

Sponsoring big-men	Men taken in on relationship of types:	
	A_1 and B_1	A_2 and B_2
1. Membo clan		
*Ndat	1	0
Waema	7	2
Ɔndipi	7	1
*Pokl	3	4
*Ndong	6	0
Rui	2	2
*Klønt	1	1
*Kindi	0	2
Ndip	0	2
Kont	1	0
2. Kundmbo clan		
Roltinga	4	0
*Køngi	1	1
*Kum	0	1
*Munumb	1	0
3. Mandembo clan		
Ongka	4	1
Nykint	1	2
El	1	0

Note: *means now dead.

(c) RELATIONSHIP OF INCOMER TO HOST IN CASES WHERE HOST WAS NOT A BIG-MAN

	No. of men
Sister's sons (+ their sons who are now clan-group members)	18
Wife's brothers (+ their sons, etc.)	9
Wife's father or daughter's husband	2
Daughter's son (+ his sons, etc.)	3
Wife's son by previous husband	1
Incomer with no special link (+ his sons, etc.)	2
Brother of uxorilocal husband	1
	36

ted with big-men, whereas in Kundmbo clan only eight out of twenty-six are in this position. As we have seen in cases 8 and 9, Membo ǝndipi has taken in many non-agnates: he and another major big-man, Waema, account for seventeen of the forty-one non-agnates who live with big-men in Membo clan; whereas Kundmbo big-men have rather tended to draw on patrifilial clansmen as supporters and helpers. At this level, factors of chance do make a difference. Kundmbo Ai had only one sister,[27] who in fact did return to him, bringing her husband and two of his sons, but these, as we have seen (case 9) have not become incorporated into Kundmbo clan-group. Another big-man, Mør, was himself an orphan and has no sisters; and a fourth, Ndamba, has two sisters, both married to big-men who have managed to retain them.

CASES: MOTHERS AND CHILDREN

Although in the preceding section I have largely been concerned with the choices and situation of men, it has been clear, particularly from case 8, that the choices of women are important also. Indeed case 8 suggests that it may often be sisters who wish to 'return' to their brothers rather than brothers who actively persuade the sisters to come to them.

The circumstances in which children may be brought to and eventually become affiliated with their mother's clan-group are:

(1) Uxorilocal residence, discussed earlier (chapter five). Its incidence is low: between 4 and 5 per cent of men living on Kawelka clan-territory in 1964–5 were uxorilocal husbands. Only in cases where the husband remains till his death at his wife's natal place are his children very likely to affiliate with their mother's group.

(2) Complete orphanhood: on the death of both parents maternal kin may fetch and care for children.

(3) Widowhood. On the death of her husband a woman sometimes succeeds in removing herself and her children to her natal place. If she does not remarry, her children are likely to join her clan.

(4) Separation. The wife is not divorced from her husband, but lives at her brothers' place, and she may obtain custody of her children, particularly if her husband should predecease her.

(5) Divorce. Unlike separation, divorce entails negotiations over return

of unexchanged portions of a woman's bridewealth. Arguments over the custody and eventual allegiance of her children are likely to arise during these negotiations.

Initially, it is important to note that between 80 and 90 per cent of divorces occur before children are born (Strathern, A.J. and A.M. 1969:153), so that problems of affiliation do not arise. In the remaining cases, children are likely to be young, and if so the mother removes them. Later, if the husband and his clansmen wish to recover the children, they can ask them to return; however, not only is this a matter for the children's own choice, but the husband should indemnify his ex-wife's kin for their 'work' in bringing up his children if he wishes to take them back to his own group.

Again, most widows either remain with their husband's clan but do not re-marry, or re-marry a man of the same clan. Usually, closely-related clansmen of the first husband claim her and her children if she agrees to re-marry, and no new bridewealth has to be paid to her kin to mark this arrangement. Instead the new husband simply pays a pig to his clan-mates which they cook and consume as a sign of relinquishing their own potential claims over the widow and as a sacrifice to the shade of the first husband. If he wishes to make *moka* with her kin, the new husband may also make courtesy gifts to them.

Of 150 widows in a sample drawn both from the Kawelka and from a Central Melpa tribe, the Elti, seventy-seven remained, unmarried, with their husband's clan, forty-nine were re-married within it, eighteen had returned to their natal homes and remained unmarried, and six had re-married (with new bridewealth) outside the first husband's clan. That is, only 12 per cent had returned to their natal place and stayed there (Strathern, A.J. and A.M. 1969:149).

Separation is not very common either; although a quarter of the Kawelka polygynists in 1964-5 were separated from at least one wife, and it is wives of polygynists who most often take up this arrangement, because they feel less in competition with co-wives when they live at their own place away from the others and can explicitly direct their pigs into exchanges with their brothers.

We are dealing, then, with categories of events, each of which

constitutes only a small percentage of the total set of outcomes generated by the marriage relationship. Taken together, however, these
variations from the norm of patrilocality and patri-affiliation do have
a noticeable effect on clan-group composition, as we have seen in
earlier chapters and tables. It is necessary to consider these categories—orphanhood, widowhood, separation—in more detail and
with some individual cases.

The cases of residence and affiliation changes to and from Kawelka
tribe over the past two or three generations which I collected as a
supplement to material on the current clan-groups of the tribe
included eight instances where a child or a set of siblings was left
completely orphaned, and another five where the father was still
alive but the mother had died and the children were very small.
This was out of a total of about 180 cases.

In two of these cases the children were kidnapped during warfare
and brought up by the kidnapper as if they were his own children.
The female children kidnapped in this way were later married to
men of the kidnapper's own clan. In the other cases the children
were fetched and cared for by: mother's mother, mother's sister's
son, father's sister, father's sister's husband (each one case), and
mother's brother (two cases). There are probably other cases, which
did not appear in my sample as it was concerned with movements
into and out of association with clan-groups, in which orphan
children are cared for by father's brother's wives or by father's
co-wives, but there is no strongly-held norm that this should be the
situation. Instead it is expected that extra-clan, especially maternal,
kin may step in on these occasions. When children are young they
are likely to be taken on visits to their mother's people, treated
kindly, and given small birds, opossums, and tree-grubs as delicacies
to eat. Perhaps they thus learn to associate their mother's brother's
settlement with food-giving, whereas in their own clan area women
other than their immediate mother are unlikely to offer them food
or to treat them with particular solicitude. Possibly for this reason
children themselves are happier to go with extra-clan kin than to
become attached to a settlement within their own clan territory
where they had known no special kindness before. However, it is

equally possible that in the cases I have the effective reasons were either simply that the children were very small and no wet-nurse could be found for them within their father's clan-community, or that not only their parents but all the members of their father's settlement group had been killed or dispersed and only extra-clan kin could possibly have saved them.

Most widows, as we have seen, stay with their husband's clan-group. Old women, with grown-up sons, who are widowed are unlikely to re-marry or to return to their own natal places. Instead they stay, as mothers and grandmothers, in their married sons' settlements. Two factors probably increase the number of widows who are still re-marriageable on the deaths of their husbands. The first is that girls are usually rather younger than their husbands (when the marriage is a first marriage for both partners). The difference in age, however, amounts to only a few years in these cases. Second, the age difference may be greater in cases where the husband is a polygynist and marries a number of wives over a period of years. Roltinga, a Kawelka Kundmbo big-man about forty-five years old, was planning in 1965 to marry a girl who had come to his settlement and was probably thirty years younger than himself; and his action was not regarded as unusual. The results of arrangements like this are clear. First, the jealousy which exists between co-wives can be accentuated, for the new wife has an advantage in sexual attractiveness over the established wives but lacks their status, expertise, and long-standing relationship with the husband. It is not surprising to find that a quarter of the Kawelka polygynists have one wife who lives separated from them, usually at her natal place. Further, the junior wives, less established perhaps at their husband's place, are the ones most likely to have young children and also to be themselves re-marriageable when the polygynist husband dies. Circumstances of this kind are found only when the husband was a major big-man. Many 'polygynists' are in fact duogynists only, and married their two wives within a few years of each other, so that large discrepancies between the ages of their children by each wife do not arise. It may be worth noting here, incidentally, that big-men are not uniformly successful in leaving behind them large numbers of sons who themselves become prominent in clan affairs. One might expect that a major big-man, who usually has more wives than other men, would be most successful in this respect, since he would have the best chance of producing a son or sons who would take after him. However, this likelihood is partly counteracted by the facts that one or more of his wives may separate from him and that on his death other wives may leave and take children away with them. Thus, even if he produces sons genetically capable of emulating him, these do not always succeed him in his own clan.

In the set of 180 cases there were twenty-nine in which the father had died and the mother removed her children, and sixteen in which a wife separated herself in residence from her husband and took her children with her. (These were cases divided almost equally between pre- and post-1944.) In fourteen of this total of forty-five cases the woman re-married (outside her first husband's clan), in all but two instances taking her children to her new husband's place. In the two exceptional instances the woman actually left the children by her first marriage with her own natal clan-kin and went to her new husband without them. What is particularly surprising about one of these cases is that the woman's child, a son, was still suckling when she left him. The boy was taken in by his MFBSS (i.e. a member of his mother's lineage) whose wife suckled him and brought him up as if he were her own son—although his original matri- and patrifiliation are still remembered. The case was told to me with some embarrassment, since a mother should not leave her children in this way. The mother's motive in this case was said by her kinsfolk to be fear that her new husband's sub-clansmen would poison her son, as a child belonging by original patrifiliation to an enemy group (she thought the new husband's group had in fact poisoned her first husband, jealous of the fact that he was a big-man); hence she left the son with her own agnates, to keep him safe. In the other case I was given no reason for the mother's action; her son was suckled by his married elder sister, whom he grew up to regard as his mother. At his marriage in 1964 the sister provided fifteen out of twenty pigs for his bridewealth, while his true mother and her husband, who did not turn up for the occasion, sent only $10 as part of the $100 which formed the cash part of the payment. It was said they were too ashamed to come.

Only three of the sixteen separated women subsequently became divorced and re-married: separation, in fact, does not preclude the continuing exercise of conjugal rights, and should not be looked on as a regular first step towards divorce. On the other hand, even if the woman does not re-marry, the question of her children's eventual affiliation is raised, for they are likely to have been brought up at their mother's rather than their father's place. The other eleven cases of re-marriage outside the first husband's clan relate to widows.

It can be seen that a majority (thirty-one) of the women in the set of forty-five cases in fact did not re-marry but stayed at their own natal, and usually patrifilial,[28] place, with their children. It must be noted, however, that it is acceptable for a separated wife to leave her children behind at her husband's place, to be cared for by a co-wife, if the co-wife will agree to this arrangement. Such cases are rare, and result from a separated wife's plan to re-marry elsewhere. Significantly, in one instance where this happened the woman later returned from another marriage to her first husband's settlement, and re-claimed her children. She herself said she did this out of jealousy, to prevent her co-wife from claiming part of the bridewealth payments for her daughters. The first husband is a major big-man, and he later obtained large payments for the daughters.

A woman may be widowed at any stage of life. We might expect that, if she is still quite young and has small children, her husband's clan-mates would wish to retain her, and in the majority of cases they do so.[29] In the set of 180 cases, as we have seen, there were twenty-nine in which widowed women brought their children back to their natal groups, and in eighteen of these twenty-nine cases the widows did not re-marry. In five instances of the eighteen the widow was probably still capable of bearing children; in nine she was probably past the menopause; and in four the details are uncertain. The figures are too small for firm conclusions to be drawn, but they show that widows who return to their kin are not always old women: we are not dealing with a situation in which old women go back to their own kin and younger ones do not. Indeed, I have already mentioned that older women with grown-up sons are likely to stay with these rather than returning to their own natal place, the more so if their immediate parents and perhaps brothers have themselves died. In the same set of cases there were thirteen separated wives who removed children to their natal place and did not re-marry. Nine of these were not yet at the menopause (probably) and only two were past it. Separation, then, can occur before a woman is old; in fact, it is most likely to do so. We are not dealing with a pattern of terminal separation.

Since it is not possible to find clear 'developmental cycle' reasons for women's choices of returning to their own kin on widowhood or separation, we must look at individual cases in more detail to see some of the motives which can be involved.[30] However, investigation of motives is notoriously difficult. In many of the cases the women were dead before 1964 and I could not ask them directly. Often informants simply conjecture what the woman's motives were likely to have been or state that 'she returned to her brothers', as if to point out that her sibling tie was obviously a sufficient reason for her actions. It seems best to group reasons into general categories rather than attempting to tabulate them, since the information is less than full.

The first kind of reason relates to pre-1944: temporary or permanent hostilities between the wife's and her husband's clan. A woman's loyalties are distributed uneasily between her natal and her affinal kin, and this was so in the past also. I was told that a wife's anger at her husband's group for killing her clansmen might cause her to leave the husband and to take her children with her, partly in order to replace men of her natal clan who had been killed. Or, on her husband's death she would take the opportunity of refusing to remarry within the husband's clan, and would secretly remove her children. Then, ensconced in the safety of her own clan area, she would refuse to return, and her clansmen would decline to return any of the bridewealth paid for her. An additional motive on the wife's part might be a (sometimes realistic) fear that she would be accused of poisoning her husband and that his clansmen would kill her for this. All these points help to suggest that there were penalties attached, for both sexes, to marriage into a major enemy group, and thus to explain why such marriages were not favoured.

A story underlines the dangers of marrying a wife of a major enemy group. It dates to pre-1944 and was told to me by Kawelka informants:

10.* A man of Kawelka Mandembo clan was married to a woman of Minembi Papeke, traditional major enemies of the Kawelka clans. She had borne him a son, but had taken the child on an extended visit to her own clansmen's territory a few miles away. She sent word to the husband that she was willing to return if he would meet her at a point near to her clan's area and escort her back. She had alerted her brothers, and as her husband came through the woods to meet her they closed in and killed him. They cut his body open, filled it with stones, and left it in the bed of a shallow river which runs near the Papeke border. Some men of Minembi Engambo clan, sisters' sons of Kawelka Mandembo, found and recognised the body and lugged it an hour's distance to a point not far from Mandembo territory, shouting out what had happened. Mandembo men came and buried it. The wife, who may have entered into a liaison earlier and wished to be rid of her husband, then married an Engambo man. Her son by the Kawelka father grew up with the Engambo and was himself later killed fighting for them.

In contemporary marriages, personal disagreements are most likely to arise between co-wives, and to centre on jealousy over sexual relations, the use of pigs in *moka* exchanges, and the allocation of garden strips. Men with more than three or four wives find it hard to keep the peace between them and to provide adequately for their demands. Many big-men have lost more wives than they have managed to retain and in old age may be left with only one. Polygynists try to separate their wives in one way or another, to lessen the chances of conflict between them: each has her individual claims on the husband. This separation in turn emphasises the unity of the sets of mothers and children in a polygynist's settlement as against their overall unity as children of a single man—a fact which is reflected in the idiom by which separate sub-clans in a clan are spoken of as the sons of the different wives of a polygynist father. Each wife tries to ensure also that her husband gives most wealth in *moka* gifts to her kin rather than to a co-wife's kin; and each introduces her children to their own matrilateral kinsfolk—there is no special tie with the natal kin of a father's co-wife who is not also one's mother, despite the fact that the same kin-terms can be applied to these as to immediate maternal kin. Here we see matrilateral ties distinguishing sets of siblings in the manner posited by Fortes in his concept of complementary filiation (cf. Fortes 1953).

It is important to see the effects of matrifiliation as operating in the context of alliance relations and marriage rules. Marriage rules ensure that each set of siblings is provided with maternal kin different from those of other sets of siblings within their lineage. At the same time the relative concentration of marriages with allied clans allows the men of these clans to speak of themselves in general as related by mother's brother-sister's son-cross cousin ties (*apa-pel*). For a woman married into a distant clan with which new alliance relations are beginning it is important also that more than one marriage should be contracted between her clan and her husband's clan. She prefers to have clan sisters married into different segments of her affinal clan, so that she can visit them easily. This preference of women is explicitly recognised by men and helps to ensure that wherever there is alliance (i.e. for *moka* exchanges) there is also a certain degree of reduplication of marriages.

The interests of brothers may not always, however, coincide with the wishes of their sisters. Marriages are important vehicles of exchange relations, and on occasion a woman's brother wishes to maintain exchanges with her husband while she herself wants to break up the marriage.[31] In this situation the brothers angrily question their sister and make it plain that they wish her to stay with the husband; yet they are unlikely to turn her away if she insists on leaving the husband and coming back to them. They may fear, especially nowadays when social contacts are much wider through the advent of roads and transport, that she will run away altogether to a new husband if they refuse to accept her back.

A woman's loyalties are situational, and more uncertainly divided between her natal and her affinal kin than are those of men. If her husband fails to pay a debt to her brother, she sides with the brother and may even remove her children from the husband in a fit of anger; but if the brother refuses to give her (i.e. herself and her husband) wealth in *moka*, she disputes this with him and sides with her husband.

There is no regular linking of one sister with a brother inside sibling sets, but when a sister 'brings back' children, whether as a widow or as a separated wife, she usually chooses a particular brother to whom she attaches herself and her children. As cases suggest, she is more likely to choose a brother who is a big-man; and big-men in turn are more likely to welcome returning sisters than other men, provided they do not feel that in gaining the sister and her children they have lost too valuable an affinal exchange partner. Further factors can come into play: a sister may prefer to go to the brother with whom she and her husband had previously kept up most active exchange relations; and she may have to go to the brother who has most garden-land to spare for her. Brothers often, but not invariably (see chapter three), share a single settlement, and their sister may maintain an association with them all, although she may regard herself as being especially cared for by one of them. The big-man Əndipi, for example (case 8), shares a settlement-place with his patrilateral brother Raklpa, but his co-resident sisters are always spoken of as returning to him rather than to Raklpa.

Some further cases will show the complications that can arise out of the removal of children to their mother's brother's places. I also include a case of orphanhood—no. 16— in which the children themselves went to their mother's sister's husband.

11. In this case the wife was driven away from her husband's place by the jealous attacks of her co-wife, but she did not ask for a divorce. She stayed at her home and bore children by the husband, who came on visits; and this arrangement was still enduring in 1964-9. When her eldest daughter was married, her husband took part, but much of the bridewealth went to her brothers and parents. She, however, clearly felt that her husband still had a duty to look after her. In 1965 she lodged a complaint with local Councillors to the effect that her husband had neglected her while she had to stay in a mission hospital at Kotna with her youngest son, who had been

severely burnt in a house-fire. Her father and brothers took the same opportunity to claim certain debts from the husband, and he paid these next day, on the public understanding that his wife would now bring her children and come to live with him. However, she did not do so, and indeed by 1970 had begun an affair with a new man. Her brothers, apparently annoyed at this behaviour in a middle-aged woman, drove her out, and she went to her new friend as a wife. The previous husband's bridewealth does not seem to have been returned. The new husband paid a small bridewealth, received by her father only, while her brothers claimed her adolescent daughter and young son; her two older daughters have both been married for some time.

The first husband in this case seems to have lost out entirely. Yet there seems to be no reason for his quiescence apart from his own peaceful and undomineering personality. No big-man of his clan has taken up the case on his behalf. He is, incidentally, a non-agnate of his clan; but this would in no way debar him from vigorous action if he felt inclined to protest.

12. A Minembi Yelipi man married a Papeke girl, and when he gave the bridewealth for her he promised her mother an extra pig; but he failed actually to hand it over. Later he was involved in a fracas within his own clan and was jailed. He was sent to the far end of the Baiyer Valley to help build a new Administration police post. He was there for two years, and during this time he befriended girls of the local Ukini tribe. On his return from jail he at once prepared bridewealth and married an Ukini girl. The pig he had promised to his first mother-in-law he now gave instead to his second. When he was jailed, the first wife had been pregnant, and she had gone back to live with her parents. She bore a son who by 1964 was weaned and about three years old. After her husband's return and second marriage she declined to go back to him, and eventually it became suspected that a man of the neighbouring Mimke clan was approaching her and her parents with offers of marriage should she divorce the first husband. The husband took up court over this issue, aided by his clansmen and his Local Government Councillor, and demanded that his wife and child return to him. But he was met by his

wife's people with the reminder that he had defaulted on his promise to pay the pig and an assertion that he had neglected his child by not visiting and bringing food for it. If he wanted the child back, they said, he must pay them for all the food they had given it. Eventually the husband won his charge against the Mimke man for enticing his wife and extracted a fine of two pigs which the Yelipi men who had supported him in the court cooked and ate together. But he did not gain the return of his wife. It was clear that he would himself have to pay up compensation if he wished to recover her and his child as well; and as his action in marrying a second wife had displeased the first, it was doubtful whether she would agree to go back to him at all.[32]

This case illustrates the importance of *nurturing*. A mother gives breast milk to her child: her kin should be paid for this. If her kin bring up her child, they gain rights over it which can be liquidated only by payment. The next case contains an example of such a payment.

13.* Minembi Papeke and Yelipi form a 'pair' of allied clans; but the alliance between them was broken by fighting, in which the Yelipi were ejected from their previous territory and re-settled on land given to them by Tipuka Kengeke clansmen. In the fighting the Papeke mother's brother of two Yelipi boys was killed. The boys' father and mother took them to live with the Papeke in protest against this action of the Yelipi in killing their relative. The father died, and his two sons were brought up along with their matrilateral cross-cousins. The cousins eventually paid part of the bridewealth for their wives. Later, after 1944 when warfare was stopped, there were moves to pay compensation for the killings between Papeke and Yelipi, and the two young men, who had been reared by the former and whose father had belonged to the latter, acted as go-betweens in the negotiations over these payments. This brought them back into contact with their patrifilial clansmen, and at last they decided to return to the Yelipi. This was less difficult for themselves, as adult men, than for the two sons of one of them, who had been born on Papeke territory and whose mother's bridewealth had been paid by the Papeke also. The Papeke required indemnification for their payments and their nurturing. A Yelipi big-man, keen to gather supporters, stepped in and paid up a number of pigs and shells for the two sons, and thus gained them and their father and his brother as settlement-mates. The sons have since stayed with the big-man; while the two senior men, now both old, have moved yet again and alternate in residence between the Baiyer Valley and the big-man's place.

In this case a large payment was required, for the boy's father's maternal kin had a very strong claim on them: they had brought up the father himself, had raised bridewealth for him, and had also helped to rear the sons. Moreover, they were the more likely to require nurturing payments as they and the Yelipi were not on the best of terms. If patrifilial clansmen recover children but do not make payments for their upbringing, the children's maternal kin will make trouble. In the past men would threaten to fight over this issue.

14.* A sister of a Membo big-man was married first to a Klamakae tribesman. From this marriage she brought back one son to her clan while the younger son stayed with his father. She remarried a man of Tipuka Kengeke clan, bore two children to him, then again separated from him and took both children away with her. They were brought up by her brother. When the eldest child, a daughter, was ready to be married, the Kengeke men came and requested her return. The Membo agreed to this, thinking that they were to be given a share of the bridewealth in recognition of their having reared the girl. But this was not done. In revenge, Membo men waylaid the bridal party bearing gifts of pork to the Kengeke and snatched the meat for themselves. The Kengeke followed with sticks, ready for a brawl, while the affines-to-be called the marriage off. A Membo leader told the Kengeke when they arrived at Mbukl that he had plenty of Kawelka men at his back if they wanted to fight; and they returned to their own territory without doing much. The Membo handed all the children back to them but took no part in raising bridewealth for the boys when they came of age, since they had been given no share in the bridewealth received for the daughter.

Here, then, the maternal kin themselves agreed to return the children of their sister to their patrifilial kin, but on the assumption that they would receive pay; when cheated of this they took revenge, offered to fight, and took no further interest in the children. The individual kin relationships here were clearly affected by the claims of the rivalrous, minor-enemy clans to which the children were linked. Such clans demand calculated reciprocity in their relations, and if positive reciprocity is not upheld, negative reciprocity takes its place.

Children themselves, especially boys, have a strong say in their affiliation, from the time when they are adolescent, and, as we have seen in case 13, men may eventually, as adults, decide to rejoin their father's people. The next case parallels case 13 also, in that a big-man plays a crucial part in recovering a strayed agnate.

15.* About 1944 a Kawelka Kundmbo man and his wife both died, supposedly of poisoning. The two had four living children, two girls and two boys. The father's only true brother failed to take the orphans in (when I asked Kundmbo men why this happened I was told briefly 'He was a fool'). The eldest child, a girl, took the other three off to their mother's sister's husband's place among the Nengka tribe, who live on the slopes of Mount Hagen. Their mother's brother had also died, so they could not go to his place. In time the two girls were married, and the Nengka men took all the bridewealth for them. The next eldest child, a boy, had gone to work as a contract-labourer on the coast, and the Nengka married off his sisters while he was away, without keeping a share in their bridewealth for him. On his return he used his wages both to raise part of a bridewealth for himself and as a basis for investments by means of which, he claimed, he repaid all the Nengka contributors to the bridewealth payment within a year. His younger brother had already been told that he was 'not a Nengka' and ought to go home, and he had returned to the Kundmbo in adolescence. He himself remained, but his wife left him and he was a bachelor again. He decided to visit his agnates, the Kundmbo, when they were holding a festival, and at this a minor big-man gave him two pearl shells and a cooked pig. He returned again at the funeral of a Kundmbo big-man in 1963; and in July 1964 he came back to be a Kundmbo man, and this time was granted land by the father's brother who had neglected him as a child. Nevertheless, his allegiance to the Kundmbo was not fixed: after 1964 he returned once or twice to the Nengka, and it was not clear where he would eventually settle. He went to work on the coast again, where he apparently became deaf and developed a speech defect. In 1970 he was back with the Nengka as a bachelor with few prospects.

This case shows a number of interesting features. First, one of the children took the initiative in removing herself and the rest to extra-clan kinsfolk. Second, the children's position at their mother's sister's husband's place was clearly not so strong as it would have been if they had been taken by their mother to her brother, or the mother's sister had been married into a nearby, friendly clan and not a distant one. A mother's brother's clansmen would have been unlikely to cheat their sister's son of part of the bridewealth for his sisters, and even less likely to tell him to leave and return to his patrifilial place. Third, there is the action of the big-man—apparently not followed, in this case, by his gaining the returned agnate as a supporter. Finally, despite the Nengka's relative ungenerosity to him, the young man had still not decided to throw his lot in fully with the Kundmbo by 1965, and by 1970 he had returned to the Nengka area.

These cases indicate the varieties of circumstances which surround the question of the affiliation of persons to clan-groups whenever there is some alteration from the simple, and statistically preponderant, situation of patrifilial recruitment. Most importantly, they point to the crucial significance of upbringing: those who bring up a child have strong claims on its affiliation. These claims may be annulled by a special payment, and may be weakened if the persons involved are not the children's mother's brothers' clansmen; and when children grow up, they may decide to return to their original patrifilial clansmen. However, the claims of those who bring up a child are strong.[33] With the claims go responsibilities. If a mother's brother takes on a boy as a potential member of his clan-group, he also takes on a responsibility for obtaining a wife for him. One can see the advantage to a mother's brother of rearing sisters' daughters as well as their sons, for the daughters will bring in bridewealth, which can be used to pay for their brothers' wives. As children approach adulthood and the question of their marriage is raised, it becomes important for their affiliation to be settled also, although the last case (no. 16) shows that it is not always settled finally at this time. It is a considerable help if a boy has an immediate sponsor who will act as the major negotiator for his marriage. Usually his father fills this role, perhaps aided by a big-man if he is not one himself; but if the boy is with matrifilial kin his mother's brother takes on the task. In the next chapter I shall examine the 'life-chances' of men who join clans other than their patrifilial one, to see whether they are likely to be men of lower status than others or not.

The aim of this chapter has been to concentrate on situations of choice. In the long-standing debate between anthropologists on the definition of descent and on similarities and divergences between non-unilineal and unilineal descent groups, the issue of whether or not there is choice over affiliation has been given prominent billing. Unilineal protagonists (e.g. Leach 1962) have argued that non-unilineal systems automatically allow a degree of choice whereas unilineal systems in theory do not: in these group membership is determined from birth by reference either to the father or the mother, depending on whether descent is reckoned patrilineally or matrilineally. The fact that in practice apparently unilineal systems often do allow for a degree of optation, either on the part of those who are recruiting members or on the part of those recruited, is not permitted to interfere with this initially neat typological distinction. They have further argued that, since in the one kind of system there is choice, and in the other there is not, in non-unilineal systems groups cannot be bounded by descent alone: other principles, such as residential choice, must come into play. Leach (1962:132) goes further still, and states that 'not only is it the case that membership derives from choice rather than from descent but the membership itself is at all times ambiguous'.

Schneider (1965:60-3, 67, 75) has heaped scorn on these views, shrewdly arguing that the condition of choice does not necessarily make group-membership ambiguous; in fact, if persons are required to make *a* choice, then this condition must clearly reduce any ambiguity of that kind. He stresses also, a trifle more obscurely, that 'it is a misplaced definition, so far as the analysis of structure is concerned, to discriminate two structures in terms of individual choice', because 'we are concerned with the question "how is this system structured?" not with the question "given this structure, how can a man pick his way through it?"' (p.67). This second point is rather hard to follow. If the unilinealists, in their concept of descent, are concerned specifically with the structuring of choice, it seems a little unfair to tell them that they cannot be legitimately concerned with this since 'structure' has nothing to do with choice. All depends on the definition of structure and on what it is that is being structured. If one sets out to study the structuring of choice, it is quite clear that in terms of a theoretical, if oversimplified, model the unilinealists are correct in arguing that non-unilineal descent, conceived of as a principle relating to group-membership, automatically does open out possibilities of multiple affiliation. The interest lies in determining how these possibilities are realised, and ordered, in ethnographic fact.[34]

A solution to part of this confrontation between Chicago and Cambridge academics has emanated from Yale. Scheffler, perhaps as a result of his work among the Choiseulese people in the British Solomons, formulated a distinction between cultural constructs and transactional processes. The term descent should be used to translate certain ideas or concepts which people have of genealogical links between themselves and ancestors: a descent-construct is thus a formulation of a set of links of this kind. 'Agnatic' and 'cognatic' constructs are examples of such sets. Having identified what a people's constructs are we can go on to see how these are used in the transactional processes of social life, what rights they confer on individuals, whether they determine group or category membership, whether they are used as symbols of group identity. This approach, instead of starting out with an alleged difference between the ways in which agnatic and cognatic descent operate and an accompanying typology of unilineal and non-unilineal systems, directs attention first to understanding and translating what the people themselves say, and second to following how they use their constructs in social activity. It implies, also, that a range of constructs may be found in a single society, with an associated range of uses—precisely what Scheffler himself found among the Choiseulese (Scheffler 1964a, 1965, 1966).[35]

Applying Scheffler's distinction to the Fortes-Leach-Schneider debate, we can see that it breaks up the portmanteau concepts of descent and structure which these theorists appear to be wielding as weapons of argument. Instead of regarding descent as both a translation term and an analytical concept relating to the definition of membership in bounded corporations, we give it a neutral, general definition, and employ it as a translation term only, which does not commit us in any way to propositions about 'social structure'. And it suggests that we should also look separately at what the structure of a people's constructs is and at the way in which these are utilised to determine a distribution of rights in their social life.

Scheffler thus does away with the argument about whether descent should be used only for a principle determining membership in corporate unilineal groups. His conclusion does not, however, immediately imply anything about the more substantive issue of whether cognatic descent groups operate in the same way as unilineal ones; nor does it imply that the specific generalisations which have been made (e.g. by Fortes 1953) about corporate lineages are invalid. It merely gives us freedom to talk about cognatic as well as patrilineal and matrilineal descent. It is interesting to see that Fortes, in his book on *Kinship and the social order* (1969) refers appreciatively to the work of Scheffler (p.254); and in his collection of essays, *Time and social structure*, he notes that recent field researches in New Guinea by Meggitt, Paula Brown, and Langness (and others) 'have shown how "dogmas of descent" may be used to identify segments of tribal structure, recruitment to which is, in fact, based on a variety of filiative and affinal kinship credentials' (1970:123). Thus Fortes, while approving of Barnes's (1962) distinction between filiation and descent, indicates that he thinks descent dogmas are of some significance in New Guinea Highlands societies—perhaps rather more so than Barnes allowed in his 1962 article (cf. also Kaberry 1967).

Scheffler's distinctions, it should be noted, are purely conceptual ones. He is not arguing, as I have mentioned, against lineage theory, nor is he attempting to suggest that the problem of choice in affiliation is an unreal one. His own analysis of Choiseulese society shows a clear concern with establishing how agnatic and cognatic descent-constructs are actually used. Keesing (e.g. 1970) has similarly demonstrated the use to which different kinds of descent construct are put by the Kwaio of Malaita.

The models of Choiseulese and Kwaio society which Scheffler and Keesing have produced are, however, to judge by the ethnographic material so far available, unlikely to apply directly to most of the New Guinea Highlands societies, although they illuminate the material on the Huli of the Southern Highlands (Glasse 1968:esp. pp.23-35). It is rather Scheffler's main distinction which is applicable. In his terms, while the Highlanders definitely have descent-constructs, these do not themselves appear to be used as a significant grid (except perhaps among the Huli) for determining regular processes of affiliation to groups. Instead they are employed as symbols of group identity, exclusiveness and inclusiveness, and continuity. Their use in this way inevitably leads to some conceptual difficulties, since it is by cumulative recruitment of succeeding generations that the continuity of groups is actually preserved. For Hagen I have argued that there is some accommodation between the descent constructs and the rules and facts of recruitment, such that, while descent-constructs are usually promulgated in an agnatic form, concepts of cognatic kinship are also used and are applied both to determine kinship between non-agnatic cognates, who are supposed to share the blood of an original ancestress, and as symbols for what is shared by members of the main formal social groups. Thus both individual cognatic kin and co-clansmen can be described as 'one blood people'. It is significant, then, that there are alternatives not only in the sphere of recruitment but also in the ideology which refers to groups as a whole.

The empirical question to which we return is how much choice is there and how is it ordered? In earlier chapters I have argued that Melpa concepts of affiliation indicate two things. First, affiliation may be either through one's father or one's mother. No tracing of descent-strings is involved; proper filiation is enough. Because clan groups are localised and patrivirilocality is a normative form of residence, patrifiliation is the regular primary way of obtaining group membership. But equally, because of the processes of divorce, separation, widowhood, uxorilocal residence, and because of disturbances brought about in the past by warfare and currently by inter-individual disputes, men sometimes become affiliated to other groups, predominantly to those of their mothers, where they are recognised as *amb-nt-mei* members and their sons become *wuə-nt-mei*.

The particular conclusions which I should like to pick out from the case-material and place alongside this last generalisation are: (1) since there is some preference for close intermarriage between allied groups, transfers of persons between these groups are also rather frequent; (2) the reason for this is that the group with which one has the strongest secondary claims, capable of being activated whether or not one is able to make good primary claims on one's father's clan, is one's immediate mother's clan;[36] (3) many cases of non-patrifilial recruitment result from a mother's action in removing her children to her own natal place, notably on divorce or separation from her husband; (4) other cases result from moves made by boys or men of their own choice, as a result of orphanhood, in the past of disturbances caused by warfare, or of quarrels with their patrifilial kin which produce 'frustrated anger' (*popokl*) in them. Further moves result from a desire to find good gardens or pasture-land for pigs. Moves of residence and changes of affiliation need not be permanent. Choices are not 'once and for all'. However, there is some stress on the idea of giving one's loyalty and stable support to a sponsor and his group, and those who fail in this respect lose status. A few men maintain a kind of dual affiliation, residing as dependants now in one group, now in the other, but these are likely to be classed as 'rubbish-men', who 'eat fragments of other people's food' (*røng pund nongk anderemen*).[37]

This last point brings us to the topic which I shall examine in the next chapter: the relative status of agnates and non-agnates within clan groups.

CHAPTER 7

STATUS

In discussing clan-group composition in the Highlands, anthropologists have sometimes argued that non-agnates, although under particular circumstances admitted into these groups, tend to be of lower social status than agnatic members. Thus Ryan (1959:269, 1969:170) states that non-agnates in Mendi clans make fewer marriages than agnates, tend to marry only once, to have only one wife at a time, to pay less for their wives, to pay a bigger proportion of bridewealth themselves, and to be helped by a narrower range of kin. They are handicapped also 'in their ability to contribute to other important intergroup payments' (1969:170). Ryan particularly comments on this since the Mendi themselves deny that this is so; or at least, to be perhaps more exact, they deny that non-agnates are 'discriminated against in any way' (ibid.). His explanation is that many non-agnates were originally refugees 'whose clans had been dispersed in warfare,' so that 'one would expect to find them suffering some social disadvantage' (ibid.). He stresses that non-agnates are likely to be accepted by their hosts, but that they are subject to disabilities arising from the 'disruptive circumstances' which originally led to their migration and change of affiliation (1959:269). Looking at the figures which Ryan gives, one finds that, out of fifty-seven non-agnates in one clan territory, thirty-one were original immigrants and the rest their children (presumably not all yet adult) born after the fathers' changed residence. Eleven of the thirty-one had come as a result of warfare in their patri-clan's territory and a further eleven were the children of widows who had returned to their natal clan on their husbands' deaths. A further eight had moved 'for reasons connected with land'. Finally, one man was simply said to be on an extended visit (Ryan 1959:265). Ryan further explains (p.266) that there is a considerable preference for migrating to one's mother's natal clan territory. The Mendi prefer also to marry into friendly, rather than enemy clans, and men can cultivate land at their mother's natal place as well as at their father's. Non-agnates do not have to make irrevocable choices of allegiance in order to gain land claims.

In order to assess Ryan's general explanation of why non-agnates are at a disadvantage, we should need to know whether the thirty-one immigrants whom he cites all came from clans which had been dispersed or at least badly disrupted in warfare; or whether, if this were not so, their own relations with their patrifilial clans had nevertheless been broken off. We should need to know also whether men who came, or were brought, to their maternal kin were as likely, *ceteris paribus*, to be disadvantaged as men who went to other connections, and whether the children of the original immigrants were also likely to suffer from disabilities, although their claims to affiliation in the new clan would be clear and the circumstances of their upbringing would be undisturbed. As it stands, the hypothesis would seem to apply most forcibly only to the eleven (of the thirty-one original immigrants) who came specifically as refugees.

Ryan's discussion implies that land rights are not a problem for immigrants, since shortage of land is not marked in Mendi. Their disadvantage must lie rather in the field of social relationships which can be used for raising and exchanging wealth. They may, for example, have lost either actual wealth or useful exchange partners as a result of warfare, and perhaps find it difficult to build up wealth again. In coming to maternal kin they possibly lose touch with their own agnates, although Ryan's description of the choices which may remain open to the sons of such men implies that ties with patri-kin are not always foregone in this way.

Meggitt (1965:ch.3) examines the question of the status of non-agnates closely for the Mae-Enga. The Mae appear to suffer land-shortage, and certainly calculations about land seem to permeate their attitudes to the intake of non-agnates. Meggitt's account shows clearly that while individual men may wish to recruit outsiders as supporters or simply as successors when they have no sons of their own, their group-mates are constantly on the watch against the possibility that incomers may need too much land, or may not give their full allegiance to their host's clan, or may even form an enclave within it and later try to break off and claim part of the clan's territory for their original agnatic group. Only if a clan is declining dangerously in numbers and cannot defend its territory or maintain its status will its men gladly receive immigrants. Given that land is a central issue, Meggitt concludes, after examining a range of data, that agnates in clan-parish groups tend to be older and wealthier, to work less hard, and to possess more wives than non-agnates. 'Because they can demonstrate putative agnation, they control wealth and authority in the parish and can deny non-agnates equal access to these goods.' How do they manage this? They 'withhold security of land tenure from outsiders', since 'anybody who lacks assured land rights is unable to plan ahead and successfully manipulate political relationships' (1965:44). On the other hand, it appears that some of the non-agnates, at least, do stay with their hosts (because they have no feasible alternatives?) and their sons form the category which Meggitt isolates as quasi-agnates of the clan. This term represents a distinction made by the Enga themselves. It can be seen that whereas Ryan includes the sons of immigrants in the non-agnate category, and apparently finds that even so non-agnates (thus defined) suffer socio-economic disadvantages, Meggitt includes his quasi-agnates with agnates in his assessments of status, wealth, work, marriage, and so on, and finds that only the first-generation immigrants—the non-agnatic, 'attached' members of the clan-parish as he defines his terms—are at a disadvantage. For example, Meggitt gives a table (1965:40) estimating the economic status of married Mae men (perhaps the men of a single Mae parish). We find from it that sixteen of sixty-four agnates (25 per cent) were wealthy, two of four quasi-agnates (50 per cent), and none out of seventeen non-agnates. The seventeen non-agnates and the rest of the men in the other two categories are listed as ordinary men.[1] Had the quasi-agnates been combined with the non-agnates, about 11 per cent of the non-agnates so defined would have been wealthy men.

One reason why Mae non-agnates turn out to be of lower status than others is that on the whole they are younger men, whose affiliation, perhaps, is not fixed, and Meggitt suggests that there is a drift of non-agnates back to their patrifilial clans after they marry, 'in order to take up land in which they have unqualified rights and not merely qualified privileges' (1965:38-9). This in turn suggests that options do remain open to these immigrants for a while, and that they may return to their patrifilial clan and achieve good status there. Perhaps, then, some of the numerous bachelor non-agnates whom Meggitt lists (p.41) were not men well above the normal age of marriage who would be likely to remain of low status, but young men about to decide whether to return to their agnates or not.

That many do return seems implied by the much smaller numbers of quasi-agnates than non-agnates in the Tables. Further case-history material could perhaps illuminate the situation of non-agnates among the Mae, explaining why some stay and others leave, but the general picture is clear: land rights are crucial, and men are concerned with security of land tenure. Although wealth may not be precisely based on simple production criteria (cf. Strathern, A. J. 1969a), security of tenure is regarded as important. While quasi-agnates appear to have that security, non-agnates do not. Meggitt argues that this security is based on 'agnation' (once again including the quasi-agnates).

In Hagen (up to 1970) the situation over land in general resembles that among the Mendi (as they were in the 1950s). Hence we do not find land emerging as a focus for calculation, dispute, subterfuge, and rhetorical insistence on rules so much as among the Mae. It is necessary, then, to examine material comparable to that which Ryan gives, and to consider whether one can show that immigrants are economically handicapped by a lack of supporters and exchange partners or not.

The first complication which has to be taken into account is the imposition of peace by the Administration. Ryan (1969:170) refers to Vicedom and Tischner's earlier work on the Hagen area in support of his point that many non-agnates were refugees and that refugees were at a disadvantage.[2] The specific point which Vicedom makes is that refugees fleeing for their lives might have to 'buy their way' into a clan-area by making presentations of valuables to their hosts after they had settled. They might become the *eta* or workmen of the host big-men, and it would be some years before they recovered their own wealth and status. Vicedom distinguishes the *eta* from those he calls slaves, and says they have higher status than the latter. Their big-man host gives them gardens and breeding-pigs, and in return they help him with his work and support him in warfare (Vicedom and Tischner 1943-8, vol.2:47-8). The picture here is similar to that which Watson gives of Matoto's actions in taking in a whole group of men defeated in warfare (see chapter four; also Watson 1967). Similarly, big-men took in individual refugees, usually kinsmen, and these too worked for them (Vicedom and Tischner, op.cit.:48).

If this picture is approximately correct, and if a similar situation applied among the Mendi, it seems clear that the closer in time to the pre-colonial period that the anthropologist works, the more he is likely to find immigrants heavily dependent on hosts and perhaps inferior in status to other ordinary men in their clans of residence. Ryan worked among the Mendi between 1954 and 1956, only four or five years after the Administration set up a station in the area, so that he was studying clan groups whose composition still largely reflected pre-contact conditions. The ending of warfare might be expected to have a number of results: first, of course, no further groups would be forced dramatically to break up and disperse or seek refuge en bloc with a host group. Second, groups previously dispersed might eventually return to their old areas or colonise new ones. Third, with an influx of wealth, brought by Europeans, it might be possible for a man previously disadvantaged to obtain wealth and improve his status and exchange partnerships. Fourth, individual refugees dependent on big-men might find it safer, easier, and more attractive now to return to their own clan-areas or to move on to other big-men if their current hosts were not helping them to obtain wives. All these changes would take some time to make their impact; but it is clear that my own field-work, conducted some twenty years after warfare had been stopped in the Northern Melpa area, was carried out in a situation considerably more affected by change than was Ryan's. Thus it would be unrealistic to make comparisons too directly between Mendi clan-groups in 1954 and Hagen clan-groups in 1964. In particular, we should not be surprised to find that non-agnates suffered less of a disadvantage among the Kawelka in the 1960s than among the Mendi people in the 1950s.

This consideration does not apply with the same force to Meggitt's material, since the major factor among the Mae would appear to be an awareness of land-shortage. Since the ending of warfare, Mae population density has probably increased, and the position of non-agnates may have become worse rather than better. Possibly young men short of land claims have migrated out to plantation work elsewhere and thus relieved the situation to some extent.

I have suggested in chapter six that an incomer to a clan-group requires a sponsor. Children who go, or are taken, to a mother's brother have such a sponsor ready-made, provided he is still alive when they come of age. A sponsor is needed not only to grant garden land but, most crucially, to contribute the nucleus of a marriage payment for a boy to obtain contributions from other men. Without a wife a young man cannot begin seriously to rear pigs and involve himself in the ceremonial exchange system which is still the road to high status within clan-groups. If men are of low status, then, this is closely connected with their inability to obtain, or retain, a wife.

The best guarantee for a boy that a wife will be obtained for him before he is much more than twenty years old lies in his immediate father and mother being alive and active at the time when he comes of age. It is better still for him if his father is a major big-man, of course, with more access to wealth than ordinary men. In addition, analysis of actual bridewealth payments shows that clansmen, and particularly lineage kinsmen contribute heavily (87 per cent of the total bridewealth in a set of cases taken for analysis in Strathern, A. J. and A. M. 1969:146).[3] It is important, then, to have closely-related clansmen who are likely to live near each other, share some garden-land, and occasionally cook pork together and who are thus willing to co-operate in raising bridewealth on one another's behalf. The groom himself, if it is his first marriage and his situation is not unusual, does not contribute much, except perhaps nowadays in the way of Australian cash, nor does he take any active, formal part in negotiations before and at the actual transfer of wealth. His sponsor and senior clansmen do all this for him, and the occasion is seen at least partly as a matter of representation of the clan to an outside clan, that of the wife-to-be. Speeches at the ceremony of transfer frequently refer to inter-clan relations. Competitive arguments over the amount of bridewealth being displayed echo competition over ceremonial exchange. Many of the items the groom's people provide are met with items given from the bride's side, and disputes can easily arise both over the total size of the bridewealth and over the equivalence or otherwise of particular items to be exchanged. This competitive, demanding context requires that the groom should have forceful sponsors and representatives, and underlines his dependence on these for successfully obtaining his wife. After the marriage, moreover, the girl may run away or refuse to live at her husband's place, and further wealth and effort may have to be expended in order to recover her from her own kin.

If a marriage is a man's second or third, and especially if his father or other sponsor is now dead, he is much more likely, as he is by this time an adult man of some status, to pay a considerable part of the bridewealth himself, and to conduct the negotiations himself also. This is particularly so if he is an established big-man; in such a case men of his sub-clan or linked sub-clans may offer him only token contributions, as he is considered 'strong' enough to obtain the extra bride with his own resources. Such contributions are offered with an apology and an excuse that wealth is short at the time, and the big-man accepts them with special thanks.

Material on ten bridewealths observed during 1964 is given in Table 15. The items in the payments were all reduced to monetary equivalents according to rates of exchange prevalent in 1964, in order to facilitate direct comparisons. (Since 1964 cash values of pigs have risen more than five-fold and amounts of money given as a

**TABLE 15: MATERIAL ON TEN BRIDEWEALTHS OBSERVED
DURING 1964 TO EARLY 1965**

	Self	Contributed by		
		Non-agnatic or non-patrifilial kin	Affines and step-kin	Agnatic or patrifilial kin
	£s	£s	£s	£s
Non-agnate cases				
A	—	130	22	54
B	42	104	6	15
G	—	180	5	10
Agnate cases				
C	130 or* 94	1	—	112
D	25	—	31	212 or 200*
F	37	10	—	129
H	—	—	2	155
I	—	7	—	196
J	—	10	28	208
K	27	—	30	169

*Some of the items displayed were not given. The lower total represents the amount actually given, the higher the amount at first raised. I have not converted the £s to Australian dollar currency, but this can be done by a simple doubling.

part of bridewealth have increased greatly also. I retain the sample, however, since it concerns the same period as is dealt with by my census of clan composition.) In the three non-agnate cases the sponsors were: mother's brother, with contributions from father (A), mother's sister's son (B), and adopting kin of unspecified degree (C). In the agnate cases the sponsors were the boys' fathers, who were also big-men, in cases I and J, the father plus an elder brother in K, the father in D and H, a putative elder brother in F (where the husband was himself beyond the usual age of marriage and had lived for some time as a mission evangelist away from his clansmen in a Kombukla clan-area), and the husband himself in C. All the marriages, except for C, were first marriages for both groom and bride. In C the groom married a young girl as his second wife.

The average bridewealth raised for the non-agnates is slightly smaller than that raised for the agnates (£189 as against £209), but it is uncertain whether this represents any significant pattern, because of the small number of cases analysed and because the methods employed to reduce the bridewealths to monetary equivalents contain some uncertainties.

Differences between patterns in the individual payments are perhaps more revealing. One obvious entailed difference between the 'agnate' and the 'non-agnate' cases is the preponderance of contributions from non-agnatic (sponsoring) kin in the case of the latter and from agnatic or patrifilial kin in the former. In the agnate cases, in fact, non-agnatic kin contributed very little; whereas in the non-agnate cases agnatic or patrifilial kin made more sizable contributions.[4] This is interesting. It shows that in these cases the non-agnate was not entirely cut off from his original patrifilial kin. In A the boy's father was alive, and both he and the mother's brother, Əndipi, a major big-man, contributed to the payment (see case 9, chapter six). In B the husband was a Kawelka Kurupmbo man by patrifiliation, who had been nurtured by his mother's brother and was now living with his mother's sister's son among the Tipuka Kitepi, neighbours of the Kawelka. He was well beyond the usual age of marriage—hence his personal contribution—and, although he was known as a Kitepi man, his old father, who was still alive, and three other patrifilial kinsmen produced contributions, as they were 'ashamed' and 'sorry' for him. In G the boy had been orphaned and taken in at an early age, so that his sponsors were 'like' agnates to him; nevertheless his original patrifilial kin sent a small contribution, not to retain any lien on him but, again, because they were 'sorry'.

It is clear that the non-agnate had been unfortunate only in case B. He was well over the normal age of marriage, and the eventual

bridewealth raised for him was rather smaller than in the two other
cases. In G the groom had been brought up as if he were a son of
his sponsors; and in A not only did both the mother's brother and
the father contribute but the mother's brother is also a noted big-man
who has incorporated many non-agnates into his settlement.

We can now look at further cases of non-agnates, within Kawelka,
to see to what extent in general they are likely to be unfortunate.
Meggitt's table cited earlier indicates that twenty out of forty-five
non-agnates of one Mae parish were bachelors. Although I am not
certain that my figures will be constructed in the same way as
Meggitt's, I give in Table 16 an account of men in the Kawelka clan-
groups at February 1965 who were slightly or considerably over the
usual age of marriage and had not yet obtained a wife.

**TABLE 16: UNMARRIED MEN IN KAWELKA CLAN-GROUPS,
FEBRUARY 1965, WHO WERE OVER THE USUAL AGE OF
MARRIAGE**

Clan-group	Men who have never been married:			
	Agnates		Non-Agnates	
	middle-aged to old	young to middle-aged	middle-aged to old	young to middle-aged
Kundmbo	3	6	—	5
Mandembo	1	4	1	1
Membo	—	5	1	6
	4	15	2	12

Agnates: 19 out of a total of 163,* = 11.7 per cent
Non-Agnates: 14 out of a total of 95, = 14.7 per cent

*Cf. Table 6(a). Note that this Table does not include unmarried youths of
the clan-group who were not of age to be married in February 1965.

Two points must initially be noted about this table. First, in other
publications (A. J. and A. M. Strathern 1969, A. M. Strathern *in press,*
A. J. Strathern 1971) census figures updated to September 1965 have
been employed, and these show slight discrepancies with the figures
for February 1965: some young men had become married, others
had gone out of association with Kawelka, and wives had been
obtained in a few cases for boys whom we had earlier rated as too

young to be included in the clan-groups. Second, it is in any case hazardous to decide either a person's age or whether he is considered to be over the usual age for marriage or not. There is no indigenous concept of a definite age, in numbers of years, beyond which a young man ceases to be an 'eligible youth' (*kang wuə kumndip*) and becomes an 'adult bachelor' (*wuə wangen* or *wengen*). Whether someone is actually called *wangen* or not depends on various factors: politeness, the likelihood of his obtaining a wife in the near future, and one's relationship to him. My decisions, therefore, have had to be based on impressionistic criteria rather than any single, clear standard. Particularly, I have taken note of instances in which people either directly referred to a clan-mate as *wangen* or mentioned that a wife had not yet been obtained for him. (*Wangen* can be applied also to a married man without children, to a widower, and to a man whose wife has left him. Table 16 does not deal with these categories.)

A slightly higher percentage of the non-agnates have never been married, but the difference between the percentages is small. Moreover, the table does not enable us to explain why men fail to obtain wives, whether they are agnates or non-agnates. One or a combination of the following factors may be involved:

(1) Parents or sponsors may be dead or themselves of low status and not able to raise bridewealth.

(2) Lineage kin may be dead or not vigorous, etc.; or they may have dispersed elsewhere.

(3) The man may have been away on contract-work and returned to find that potential sponsors were not interested in helping him; or he may still be away at work.

(4) He may have had disagreements with his father or other sponsor; for example, one young man was refusing in 1964 to give part of his cash wages derived from local plantation work to his father and the latter was delaying the son's marriage.

(5) A youngest brother of a set is most likely to be a child when his father dies; and thirteen of the men in Table 16 are youngest sons. The young man may then have to depend on his elder brothers to help him raise a bridewealth, and these may be dilatory.

(6) A man may have been away from his patrifilial clan until he

was past adolescence. Returning, he finds that it is hard to secure a sponsor for his marriage.

(7) He may have some physical defect which handicaps him, although this is likely to be only a subsidiary factor, since other men with defects do marry. One man in Table 17 is said to have no external male genitals and this, rather than any other factor, is the reason why he has not married. Some men are also asserted to be mentally deficient, but I am unsure whether in certain cases this is just a rationalisation or not. A few of the men in Table 17 are unusually mild and unprepossessing, but again this may be because of their unfortunate position rather than its original cause.

(8) His sponsor may be a big-man, but may not be hurrying to obtain a wife for him, perhaps because he is committed to raising bridewealth for his own sons first.

(9) His situation may be purely temporary, in that, for various reasons, negotiations over his marriage have broken down, possibly more than once.

(10) He may himself have refused to settle down with a single sponsor, and, because of his uncertain allegiances, clansmen do not help him to obtain a wife.

Many of these factors can and do apply to agnates as well as to non-agnates. In particular, it is worth noting that the agnates of a clan-group may include men who have spent crucial periods of their life away with non-agnatic kin—these are also men whose parents are likely to have died long ago. When they return there may be no-one who particularly cares to sponsor them. Some men seem to have missed the boat also through being away at contract work when their kin would otherwise have raised bridewealth for them; but this does not always mean that kinsfolk will not help them when they return. Nowadays a few young men, especially men whose fathers are dead and who lack a good sponsor or have quarrelled with their co-residential kin or have no close lineage kin at all, spend longer periods away from home in coastal towns, such as Port Moresby and Lae, and delay their return.

About a third of the non-agnates in Table 16 are men whose fathers joined one of the Kawelka clan-groups and who are thus patrifilial clan members. But whether a man is 'patrifilial' or not, we can say as a general rule that he is most likely to remain unmarried if his father is dead or feeble, and if in addition he has no immediate brothers alive and/or co-resident with him. His marriage may also be delayed if he is the youngest of a set of brothers whose father is dead. It is a help if he has a mother alive, who will rear pigs especially on his behalf; also if the bridewealth for a sister can be used to obtain a wife for him in turn. One young man was lucky in that his elder sister's daughter was ready for marriage when he returned from a long period of contract work at Goroka in the Eastern Highlands. The sister had been living at the place of her brother's own potential sponsor, a classificatory mother's brother, rather than at the place of her husband, so the brother was able to claim a larger share of the bridewealth for her daughter than he could otherwise have done. With the help of this he and his sponsor prepared a bridewealth pay-ment to obtain a wife for him; he was aided also by his own original agnates, with whom he maintained exchange partnerships.

If a boy's father is dead, he can hope to find a sponsor either among his close patrifilial lineage kin; or in one of the big-men of his clan, provided he attaches himself to the big-man's settlement and works for him; or in a mother's brother, or less frequently a mother's sister's husband or father's sister's husband. He does not need to depend on finding a sponsor who has no sons of his own and wishes to 'continue his line'. Often, as we have seen in chapter six, a host's motive is to increase the present or future work-force of persons dependent on him. He may have sons of his own, but be happy to accept his sister's sons (and daughters) also, if the sister chooses to return to him and manages to remove her children. Table 17 considers this point for the Kawelka clan-groups. Uncertain cases and cases in which the non-agnate is the son of an incomer and thus was not himself directly taken in by a sponsor are omitted. It can be seen that in many cases the host already had a son at the time when he accepted a junior kinsman as an incomer (perhaps along with the incomer's mother, in instances where a married sister returned to her natal place).

Having looked at the incidence of men who have never been

TABLE 17: WHETHER HOSTS OF INCOMERS HAD SONS OF THEIR OWN OR NOT

Incomer was	Host already had son	Host later had son	Host had no son or daughter at time of induction, or else had daughter only
Sister's son, wife's brother's son or cross-cousin of host	18	16	7
Wife's son by previous marriage or wife's sister's son	1	3	3
Other categories, where incomer was junior to host	10	—	1
Incomer was not junior to host	5	5	3
	34	24	14

married at all, I now consider the relative frequency of marriage. We have to take into account the number of wives each man currently has, the total number of marriages each man has contracted, and the number of men who in the past have concurrently had more than one wife. Even if a man is only a serial polygynist, he still has had to find the resources to obtain each new wife in turn, unless he takes over a clansman's widow or a divorced woman who may run away to him for nothing. (Even in this case her kin may demand payment later.)

Table 18 gives an account of married men in Kawelka Kundmbo clan-group and clan-unit in February 1965. Since married men of the clan-unit are included, some of the agnates are actually men who are currently away from the Kundmbo clan-group. Other agnates again are men who in the past have been away and who had returned prior to, or in, 1964. It must be remembered, too, that my category of agnates includes all men whose father's father appears to have been

TABLE 18: NUMBERS OF CURRENT WIVES OF KAWELKA KUNDMBO MEN, FEBRUARY 1965

	No. of wives		
	3	2	1
Clan-group, agnates			
FFF lived at Mbukl, or is not recorded as an incomer	—	—	10
FF lived at Mbukl, or is not recorded as an incomer	—	1	8
FFF was Kundmbo incomer from Wahgi area	—	1	1
FF was Kundmbo incomer from Wahgi area	1	1	7
F was Kundmbo incomer from Wahgi area	—	—	3
FFF was incomer from another tribe	—	—	4
FF was incomer from another tribe	—	—	2
	1	3	35
Clan-group, non-agnates	**3**	**2**	**1**
F was Kawelka incomer from Wahgi area	1	—	—
F was incomer from another tribe	—	—	6
Brought by M, MM, MB, or FZ	1	—	3
Sons of men brought in	—	—	3
	2	—	12
Non-agn tes, now weakly associated with Kundmbo			
Brought by M	—	—	2
	—	—	2
Clan-unit, agnates (i.e. away from clan-group)			
F left Kundmbo	—	—	3
F refugee at Wahgi	—	—	2
Left by self	—	—	2
	—	—	7

accepted as a member of the clan-group. The relevance of this point is that in some cases the stability of a non-agnate's attachment to his current clan-group may be practically indistinguishable from that of someone whom I list as an agnate. Figure 9 shows this situation.

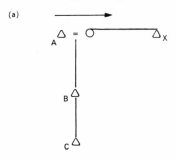

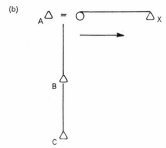

Figure 9. 'Agnate' and 'non-agnate'

In part (a) of the figure A moves into uxorilocal residence and is accepted into the clan-group of X, his wife's brother. (Alternatively, we could simply posit that A came as a refugee with no known kin-link to his hosts, but this is a rather less common situation.) B, his son, is born either before or after this move and is brought up as an *amb-nt-mei* ('woman-bearing') member of X's clan. In turn, his son, C, is a *wuə-nt-mei* ('man-bearing') member, and he is also an agnate according to my definition, since his father's father was accepted into the clan-group. Part (b) of the figure looks very much the same as part (a), but there is one difference. A does not join X; instead the mother of B comes to X, either leaving her husband or as a widow, bringing her young son with her. B is thus brought up as an *amb-nt-mei* member of X's group, and his son C becomes a *wuə-nt-mei* member; but in this case C is not an agnate, since his father's father, A, did not join X's clan-group. Nevertheless, C's attachment to the group of X is quite as firm and consolidated as in part (a).

These considerations show that simply because a man is labelled an 'agnate', it cannot be assumed that he has a more stable attachment to his clan-group than a 'non-agnate', since these two labels cover a number of possible situations. A case-history illustrates this.

16.* The father of a Kundmbo man came from the Nønda tribe, now extinct as a corporate group. He had married the sister of a Kundmbo big-man and came to live at her place, probably as a refugee. His son, X, born on Kundmbo territory, became an *amb-nt-mei* Kundmbo clansman, and the son's sons in turn also grew up with the Kundmbo. X himself sponsored the marriage of a sister's son who was brought up among the Kundmbo and has since become a major big-man. However, quarrels arose between X and 'other Kundmbo men' (my account did not specify which men), who were allegedly stealing his fat pigs. His wife was particularly upset when hard words were spoken to her for collecting some banana leaves for cooking purposes from someone else's tree. She cut her finger to indicate her anger (*popokl*), and took her children off to the place of her eldest daughter's husband among the Roklaka. Her husband, X, went with her. Their second daughter was married to a Roklaka man, and both sons received help from their Roklaka hosts to raise bridewealth and obtain wives. The elder of the two sons was still living with the Roklaka in 1964. The youngest son, however, eventually returned to the Kundmbo and made a house for himself at the nascent Lutheran Mission-sponsored 'house-line' next to a clan ceremonial ground. He was accepted as a Kundmbo clan-group member, although he made no gardens for his subsistence and seems to have bought food with money earned by intermittent spells of work at the nearest local plantation. He planted a few coffee trees at the place of his matrilateral cross-cousin among the nearby Minembi Engambo clansmen. When the Local Government Council system was introduced, he was actually elected Councillor for Kundmbo clan, ostensibly on the grounds that he was a young man who knew white men's ways, but perhaps also because no Kundmbo man of established status was willing to risk taking on such an uncertain position. He remained Councillor for a term, but was deposed at the next election, as his money debts to his clansmen were high and remained unpaid. By the end of 1964 he was losing his allegiance to the Kundmbo and was making plans to move for a while into uxorilocal residence with Kope tribesmen. It was said that in 1965 he would go back to the Roklaka. On the assumption that his father's father was accepted as a Kundmbo man and because he himself was accepted as such during 1964–early 1965 I have counted him as an agnate of Kundmbo in my list; but it can be seen that his chequered history precludes regarding him as a more stable clan member than non-agnatic members of it.[5]

This case is unusual, but not all elements in it are unique. At least three other agnates of Kundmbo have spent periods of time out of association with their clan-group, and others were still out of association, and almost certain to remain so, in 1964. However, most of the agnates and the non-agnates of the clan-group had spent their whole lives as members of Kundmbo.

In order to show the pattern of continuity in residence and affiliation more clearly than can be indicated by a simple division into agnates and non-agnates, I list married men of Kundmbo according to whether their ancestors are said to have been immigrants into the Mbukl territories of the Kawelka tribe or not (Table 18). In constructing this table, I have taken the genealogical record back as far as it goes. It may be remembered (from chapter two) that Kundmbo clan, unlike Membo, has no overarching genealogical framework linking its segments together. Informants of one sub-clan, Kiklpuklimbo, suggested, with an air of improvisation, that the putative earliest ancestor of their particular segment was actually the clan founder, but this was done specifically in answer to my question 'Who was the father of all the Kundmbo?' and the ancestor, Maninge, was not recognised as theirs by men of the opposite clan-section. There is, then no extensive linking of different lineage sets in the clan by means of an ordered, hierarchical, genealogical scheme; although ancestors are sometimes placed together with the assertion that they were brothers. It is consistent with this that the apparent depth of genealogical continuity revealed in Table 18 is not great. However, the majority of Kundmbo clan-group agnates are men whose father's fathers are said to have been Kundmbo men by birth also; only six men can be traced to ancestors who are said to have belonged originally to another tribe. (Of course, given the fact that little weight is placed on the precise memory of genealogical details, it is possible that some of the lineage sets which nowadays have few members or are out on a limb from others are also actually descended from incomers.)

The marriage figures for non-agnates of the clan-group are strongly influenced by the marriages made by two non-agnatic big-men, both of whom were brought up on Kundmbo territory from an early age but who belong technically to the non-agnate category. Each currently had in February 1965 three wives (and was likely to retain these), while all the other non-agnates had a single wife each. The great majority of agnates also had only a single wife (thirty-five out of thirty-nine men); three were duogynists, and one had three wives. This last was Ndamba, an eminent major big-man, and it is interesting to see that two of the duogynists were men who stood in the position of son to him: one, Pangk, is his eldest immediate son by his first wife, the other is his step-son. By 1969 Ndamba had also obtained a second wife for his next eldest son, Nykint, and a wife each for two more of his sons, both probably less than twenty years old. An established polygynist can, then, both increase his own connections and ensure the prosperity of his sons by endowing them with wives before his death.

Because of the wives held by the two non-agnatic big-men, the non-agnates have an average of $c.1.3$ wives each, the agnates only $c.1.1$, within the clan-group. (I omit men in the clan-unit and two non-agnates whose affiliation to Kundmbo is now partially severed.) Table 19, which considers the numbers of marriages made by Kundmbo men, introduces another perspective. Married agnates of the clan-group have made $c.1.4$ marriages each, non-agnates $c.1.6$.

TABLE 19: NUMBERS OF MARRIAGES MADE BY KAWELKA KUNDMBO MEN, FEBRUARY 1965

Clan-group, agnates	No. of marriages made					
	6	5	4	3	2	1
FF or FFF not an incomer	—	—	1	—	5	13
F, FF, or FFF a Kundmbo incomer	—	—	1	—	4	11
FF or FFF incomer of another tribe	—	—	—	—	1	5
	—	—	2	—	10	29
Clan-group, non-agnates						
F was Kawelka incomer	—	—	—	1	—	—
F or FF was incomer of another tribe	—	—	1	—	—	8
Brought by extra-clan kin	1	—	—	—	1	3
Sons of men brought in	—	—	—	—	—	3
	1	—	1	1	1	14
Non-agnates, now weakly associated with Kundmbo	—	1	—	1	—	—
Agnates of clan-unit only	—	—	—	—	1	9
	—	1	—	1	1	9

(The addition of the two weakly associated non-agnates would raise this figure further.) But more agnates have been married at least twice: twelve of forty-one, or c.30 per cent, compared with four of eighteen non-agnates, or c.22 per cent. The cause of this higher incidence of men making more than one marriage among the agnates is not, I think, to be found in the fact of agnation itself, especially since there are no jural bars on the non-agnates' holding land rights such as are actively employed by Enga agnates as a tool of discrimination within the clan. Nor is it simply that non-agnates, as I have defined them, always lack supporting extra-clan kin: this is true only in cases where a mother brings her son back to her own natal group or where a man's father came to live with his wife's people. In these situations a man's mother's clansmen are his own, and they cannot fulfil the role of extra-clan kinsmen as well. I do not know the exact circumstances for each of the Kundmbo non-agnates who are, or at some time have been, married, but their situations are roughly as given in Table 20. For seven, the situation of 'deprivation' holds, for eleven men it does not. Moreover, among the seven 'deprived' of

TABLE 20: WHETHER NON-AGNATES HAVE LOST LINKS WITH EXTRA-CLAN KIN OR NOT

	No. of men
1. Probably deprived of extra-clan help	
(a) F was uxorilocal refugee	2
(b) Orphaned and fetched by, or came to, MB	2
(c) M died, and taken by MM to MB's place	1
(d) F was refugee; maternal kin unknown	1
(e) M's people are extinct	1
	7
2. Probably not deprived of extra-clan help	
(a) Adopted by FZ and her H	1
(b) F was with Kundmbo; no necessary disruption of ties with maternal kin	7
(c) Son of an incomer	3
	11

extra-clan help is the major big-man who has made the most marriages of all Kundmbo clan-group members.

A further point relevant here is that when a man makes a second marriage, while still retaining his first wife, he is likely to pay a higher proportion of the bridewealth by himself: his sub-clansmen do not help him in the way they often do when a father is paying bridewealth for his son's first marriage. The husband must rely on his own production of wealth and its acquisition through exchange partnerships. Thus the man who obtains two wives is often on his way to becoming a big-man, unless he is simply a son well-endowed by a big-man father. The same is not necessarily the case for a man whose wife dies or leaves him and who, after a while, remarries. We have to see, then, how many men, of those who have in the past made more than one marriage, have held more than one wife simultaneously.

Three men have had three wives each for most of the period of their adulthood. All are major big-men. Of the others who have made more than one marriage, seven have had at some time, or still have, two wives concurrently, while six have been serial polygynists only. One non-agnate had, in February 1965, been married four times, but had lost all of his wives, and it was also said that the wives had come to him for nothing: he had not paid bridewealth for them. Perhaps, then, the theory of easy come, easy go might be applied in this case. Two of the men who have had more than one wife at a time are non-agnates, eight are agnates; four of those married more than once but only serially are agnates, two non-agnates. These figures reveal no obvious pattern of non-agnates marrying only serially.

Some men manage to marry only by taking on a widow who is inherited within their clan-group (polygynists also often pick up an extra wife in this way), or by accepting a runaway woman, for whom they may eventually pay a reduced amount of bridewealth.

Table 21(a) suggests that Kundmbo agnates had paid bridewealth for their wives in rather more instances than had non-agnates (some cases where information on marriages is not available have been omitted): c.88 per cent of the marriages they had contracted, compared to c.80 per cent for the non-agnates. The difference is caused not by a higher rate of inheritance of widows among the non-agnates, but by a higher number of marriages with divorcees; and this in turn is influenced by the four marriages of a single non-agnate. It is plain that for the majority of men, agnates and non-agnates alike, the usual road at least to a first marriage is to obtain, by payment of bridewealth, a previously unmarried girl (*ambokla wentɔp*) (Table 21(b)).

Finally, I have left out of consideration in Tables 18 to 21 those adult men of the clan-group who appear not to have married at all. Their numbers were given in Table 16. Nine, in February 1965, were agnates (out of a total of fifty-four agnates in the clan-group); five were non-agnates (out of a total of twenty-six). 17.5 per cent of those

TABLE 21: PAYMENT OF BRIDEWEALTH FOR, AND PREVIOUS MARITAL STATUS, WIVES OF KAWELKA KUNDMBO MEN

(a) NUMBER OF WIVES

Married as:	By agnates	By non-agnates*
Previously unmarried girls	48	21
Widows	6	2
Divorcees or runaways	3	7
	57†	30†

(b) NUMBER OF MEN WHO HAVE MARRIED WIVES IN (a)

Status of wives	Number of men‡	
	Agnates	Non-agnates§
Previously unmarried girls	42	17
Widows	6	2
Divorcees or runaways	3	3
	51	22

*Seven uncertain cases omitted.
†Agnates paid bridewealth in 50 cases, non-agnates in 24.
‡A man may appear more than once, through marrying, e.g., both a widow and a divorcee.
§Three uncertain cases omitted.

whom I included in the clan-group were thus men who were either clearly adult bachelors or were at least rather over the usual age of marriage. The non-agnatic bachelors (in this sense) comprised 19.4 per cent of the total number of non-agnates; the agnatic ones 16.4 per cent of the agnates. These figures reveal a slightly greater tendency for non-agnates to remain unwed than agnates; but, once again, the figures need to be examined in more detail. Of the agnatic bachelors, three were old men, attached to major or minor big-men, whose prospects of obtaining a wife were nil; none of the non-agnates was in a comparable position. One agnate's father was still alive and could be expected to obtain a wife for him when they resolved their quarrels with each other; two had living fathers who seemed unlikely to be able to raise the wealth required to obtain wives for them; two had lost their fathers and were dependent on immediate fathers' brothers;

and one had no close lineage kin at all and was dependent on a big-man of his clan (Nendipa, see case 9). None of these six men appeared to be over thirty years old, and all had some hope of eventually obtaining a wife. Among the non-agnates three had living mother's brothers, who seemed, however, to be making no moves on their behalf. One of the three worked at a local plantation as a work-overseer and drew a reasonable wage. He was not estranged from his maternal uncle, but perhaps it was felt he was away from clan affairs and a wife would be obtained for him only if he took a more active part in them. The two others had attached themselves to another man within the same sub-clan as their immediate mother's brother, who himself had gone to join a big-man in a different settlement. It was clear that neither their settlement-mates nor the mother's brother himself had plans to raise bridewealth on their behalf.[6] The fourth non-agnate lived with his father's sister's sons: I do not know whether they planned to help him, as they themselves lived in a settlement-place within the Wahgi territory which I rarely visited. The fifth non-agnate was actually a patrifilial member of the clan-group. His two married elder brothers were dilatory about helping him to obtain a wife (the father and a big-man eldest brother were both dead). In 1969 the son of a major big-man within the same clan-section was making moves to help him instead, and it looked as though he would be married soon.[7]

It can be seen from these cases that the point I have mentioned before holds: a young man needs an effective sponsor. To the extent that first generation non-agnates have lost kinsfolk or are neglected by kinsfolk who might be expected to help them, they are likely to be unfortunate. But the same can hold for agnates. It is interesting, also, that six out of the fourteen bachelors (two non-agnates and four agnates) come from the same lineage set within the clan-group. Since the clan-group can be divided into approximately twelve line-age sets, this number represents an incidence far greater than that which would occur by chance. Yet the same set includes one man recognised by many as a minor big-man, and another who is a duogynist; so I am uncertain whether it can be said that this is a 'depressed' lineage in terms of its married men's social status or not.[8]

This examination, then, of the marital status of Kawelka Kund-mbo men produces no clear-cut picture of fortunate agnates and unfortunate, jurally or economically deprived, non-agnates. It suggests, instead, that the pattern is more complicated and that the two categories need to be broken down to a point where we can see both the workings of individual case-histories and the circumstances running through these. Two clear conclusions which emerge are that a man can become a big-man, even if he is a first-generation incomer and is with his maternal clansmen (the evidence for this is the case of the big-man who has married six wives and retains three of them, and who was brought to the Kundmbo by his mother's mother), and a man may be unfortunate if he lacks an effective, and usually immediately related, sponsor, either his true father or his true mother's brother. It is best, also, if his sponsor is a man who has brought him up from an early age and has therefore taken on many of the functions, and come to approximate in the domestic sphere to the role of, a father in relation to him. Then he is likely to take on the duty of raising bridewealth for him, if he can, and thus of turning him into a clansman who has a chance of achieving some status within his group. Last, it is best of all if the sponsor is not only closely related and has brought the boy up, but is also a big-man who is keen to attach supporters to himself and build up a following.[9]

CHAPTER 8

CONCLUSIONS

In this final chapter I review some of the main concepts which I have been deploying in the analysis of Melpa group structure, summarise the ways in which I think they are applicable to my material, and suggest some problems for further investigation.

DESCENT, RESIDENCE AND FILIATION

Marie de Lepervanche (1968:169), after illustrating the disagreements among social anthropologists on how the term 'descent' should be defined and used, points out succinctly that in some Highlands societies 'descent is not a necessary principle of recruitment to groups at all. Therefore, in what sense can these be spoken of as descent groups?' She answers that descent, as a construct of the Highlanders themselves, 'is a way of talking about groups', and that 'the people use an agnatic idiom...to express...group solidarity—to conceptualise local group unity *vis-à-vis* other like groups' (1968:181; cf. Barnes 1967:39, and Watson 1964:14). At the same time she maintains that 'common residence and working together, rather than descent group membership ascribed at birth, are the bases of group solidarity' (1967:143), and stresses that the Highlands ideology differs from that of African lineage systems in that 'the emphasis is on brotherhood', not on lengthy pedigrees. She relates this emphasis to the competition for adherents and the vicissitudes of warfare in the Highlands (1968:181).

My examination of the descent idiom as it is employed by Melpa speakers clearly confirms de Lepervanche's analysis of its functions in

other Highlands societies. Her suggestion that there are also differences between the form of descent ideology in the Highlands and
African counterparts is pertinent, too, although block contrasts
between 'the Highlands' and 'Africa' can quickly become too cum-
bersome to manage in discussion. It is important, in fact, to stress
that it is primarily the assertion of descent from a common ancestor
and the use of this assertion to construct symbols of group unity and
plurality that one wishes to label in saying that Highlanders 'have'
dogmas of descent. Most Melpa speakers are less concerned with
their ability to trace sets of individual pedigrees up to named ancestors
as group founders than with simple statements of the order 'we are
all descended from one father, we are one semen people'. Nevertheless, it is clear that we cannot convincingly label these assertions as
anything but descent-constructs, even if the constructs vary between
a cognatic and an agnatic emphasis. It is worth considering further
here why there is less stress on genealogical pedigrees in some of the
Highlands societies than in classic Afrcian cases, such as the Tallensi.
De Lepervanche has given a partial functional explanation of this.
Her explanation rests on the fact that in practice recruitment to
groups does not, in the Highlands, depend on long genealogical
demonstrations of ancestry. Warfare scatters people, and big-men
try to obtain adherents by appealing to and using a number of kinship ties. *De facto* patterns of changes in affiliation go hand-in-hand
with a lack of stress on the necessity to show one's jural credentials
by documentary descent. Instead there is stress on all clansmen being
brothers, whatever the vagaries of their actual genealogical inter-
connections or the lack of these. To this I would add two further
points, which imply, I think, real structural differences between some
Highlands societies and the African Tallensi. These are, first, that
problems of and rules for the inheritance of material property,
although they certainly exist, do not seem to play critically decisive
roles in structuring Highlands groups (an exception to this statement
is Mae-Enga society as portrayed by Meggitt 1965)—it is hard to
imagine oneself writing a companion volume to Goody's *Death,
property and the ancestors* on Highlands material; and the second point
is that there is, similarly, a lack of stress on succession to offices of

headship over groups, at succeeding structural levels. Where there is such succession, as within the Siane lineage, it does not appear to be modelled on devolution from a single ancestor but on relationships between eldest, middle, and younger siblings—on brothers again. In African systems such as that of the Tallensi, where inheritance and succession are both important, it is the genealogical calculus which provides an essential internal order for these processes. In the Highlands, as is well known, instead of succession to offices of headship we find emphasis on the self-made big-man who by acts of will and energy gathers resources and supporters and who exploits and creates a wide variety of ties in order to do this. These differences in turn lead to a rather different self-conceptualisation by the Highlanders from the impression one gains of some African lineage-based societies. Fortes (1969:291-308), in discussing the differences between definitions of 'corporateness', plumps for Maine's original concept of perpetuity through 'universal succession' and the related notion that corporations are single juristic persons. He argues that these concepts most accurately correspond to the concepts which are entertained by members of unilineal descent groups (just as Maine first developed his idea of perpetuity in the analysis of the Roman *gens*), because in these 'the essential idea is that the living plurality of persons constitutes a single body by reason of being the current representation and continuation of a single founder' (p.304). While this 'essential idea' is certainly present and employed as a political dogma within their clans by Melpa-speakers, it is not underpinned at all structural levels by an emphasis on genealogical connections, and I suggest that this is related to a lack of stress on inheritance and an absence of succession to offices of headship. Perhaps such stresses are most likely to come about in societies where stability and order are, for ecological or whatever reasons, given high priority, rather than in those characterised by endemic warfare, competitive leadership, and continuous processes of territorial migration, expansion and decline of groups, with accompanying fission, segmentation, assimilation of persons from outside, and so on. So agnatic descent constructs, among the Melpa and perhaps some other Highlanders as well, are not made the basis of rigidly maintained jural rules determining inheritance and succession. Rather they are employed as moral symbols, as assertions of stability and solidarity in a world of flux, drawing men together against the divisive pulls of their extrapatrifilial ties.

I now return to the second part of de Lepervanche's propositions, the issue of locality *versus* descent. She has told us that Highlanders in some cases do not use descent dogmas as the basis for recruitment rules. Now she maintains that 'common residence and working together' are the 'real' bases of group solidarity 'rather than descent group membership ascribed at birth'. But this opposition is redundant, for if there is no descent group ascription and descent dogmas do not even ideally prescribe membership but have other functions, then there is little point in setting up 'descent group membership' as a straw man in order to contrast it with 'common residence'. If descent idioms are used to give moral value to the facts of 'common residence and working together', then surely they do form one 'basis of group solidarity'? Moreover, in her formulation, while opposing common residence to descent as a recruitment principle, de Lepervanche appears to imply that residence takes the place of descent as the basis for entry into group membership. But, if so, this is puzzling also, for she is not specifying in this statement how people do come to share residence and to work together, and without such a specification we are perhaps left to assume that *anyone* who offers to share residence and to work with a host is likely to be accepted. This is manifestly untrue for many of the Highlands societies. De Lepervanche herself quotes Firth's statement that 'in optative systems choice is never unrestricted' (Firth 1963:28). Moreover, much of de Lepervanche's analysis is devoted precisely to examining the strategic contexts in which choices are made.

The strongest case which de Lepervanche advances for the importance of 'locality' itself is that of the Korofeigu among the Bena Bena of the Eastern Highlands. She quotes Langness's argument that in Korofeigu rights conferred by residence (i.e. presumably residence alone) are as secure as those established by birth, that friends as well as cognates and affines may be admitted, and that they are accepted because the group needs to maintain its strength in the face of others. Those admitted are at once called by kinship terms, no doubt to mark and consolidate their new allegiance and to mask their external origins. Groups need manpower, and no questions are raised about entitlement by ancestry.

There are probably objective differences between the Korofeigu, as they were during the pre-contact period and for some years after it, and certain other Highlands societies, as Langness himself has suggested (Langness 1968:196); and patterns of warfare and alliance seem to offer keys to explaining aspects of these differences (Strathern, A. J. 1969b:44). In addition, Langness (1964:169-70) draws attention to the abundance of land among the Bena Bena and to the fact that individuals do not maintain long-lasting claims in fallow areas, although sons do inherit recently-cultivated plots from their fathers. An important point here is that land rights do not seem to be dependent on local group membership. Thus, two of the non-agnates in Nupasafa local group were uxorilocally resident husbands who 'still claimed land in their own area', that is the area from which they had come (Langness 1964:167), and in general 'land is owned by the individuals who have cultivated it and who reside on it plus those who have rights in it but do not reside on it' (p.170). What, then, gives a man entitlement to own land where he is not currently residing and co-operating? One wonders if previous residence and tillage are sufficient for this purpose and what limits are placed on this. In listing some theoretical limits on affiliation, Langness states that a man has rights in 'the group into which he was born, equivalent rights in a group in which he was raised', or in which his father was raised, or his mother's natal group, or the one in which she was raised (1964:170). Reducing these rules to the principles behind them, we might suggest that either filiation or quasi-filiation by nurturing are the important criteria. Perhaps it is a tie of this kind that enables one to claim land even if one is not co-resident and 'working together' with a particular local group. It would be particularly interesting to know what ideological statements Highlands peoples themselves make with regard to co-residence, what significance they themselves attach to locality by comparison with descent or filiation. I suspect myself that in many cases we would find an ideological fusion of the notions of locality and descent, such as, I have argued, is found in the

Melpa concept of the tribal creation-place or *kona wingndi* (chapter two). Such a fusion could explain why the Bena, for example, use kinship terms for all those with whom they are co-resident as a group; and why they equate rights in one's natal group with rights in a group in which one has been raised. Langness has pointed out that for the Bena, in a sense, residence creates kinship. It is a surprising statement, when put so strongly, but, in slightly weaker forms, probably applies to many other societies as well. Re-phrasing it, we might say that the Bena re-cast relationships of co-residence into a kinship idiom. One wonders, then, whether they have built out of this process some explicit ideology linking kinship and co-residence together—for example, as we find in the Mae concept of a man's blood 'remaining where he is reared and tying him there' (Meggitt 1965:28-9). Glasse and Lindenbaum (1969:324) have compared Bena to the South Fore and conclude that the two make similar use of kinship dogmas: 'The pressure to amalgamate for defence and security is . . . opposed by suspicion, challenges of sorcery, and the freedom to depart. . . . This contradiction seems to have led the South Fore to develop certain distinctive political forms. Chief among them is the use of "descent" as a means of conceptualizing relations of co-residence. . . . Descent is not a principle of recruitment but rather a symbol of group unity'.

While, then, it seems established that patrilineal descent is not the principle by which entitlement either to land rights or to membership of local groups is determined among the Bena Bena, it may be that filiation is important. Moreover, the Bena Bena do make statements about their groups which Langness initially interpreted as 'descent dogmas' of a kind, i.e. assertions which underpin the solidarity of local groups by claiming that their members are agnates, or at least 'brothers' (Langness 1964:165, 171).[1]

In his later re-study of this problem, Langness urges that the difficulty lies, not in resolving a supposed discrepancy between ideology and behaviour, but in finding out 'more accurately what the ideology is' (1968:195). I agree with this view, and it was to this end that I took up the question of idioms in terms of which the Melpa people describe their own groups in the first chapter of this book.

Chapters five, six, and seven have made it clear that with regard to the recruitment of individuals to clan-groups Barnes's generalisation (1962) is correct: the main pattern that can be discerned statistically is that of cumulative patrifiliation. Here it is necessary first to specify exactly what Barnes means by this term and second to relate it to Melpa concepts. Barnes employs the term as a label for empirical, statistical processes emergent from rules of recruitment to groups. Where there is a rule of recruitment by patrifiliation and this is largely followed, over a period of generations there will be a constant adding to or cumulation of patrifilial links within groups. Such a cumulation of links can occur whether there is also a strong/weak ideology of descent or not, and Barnes further argued that in Highlands societies descent dogmas are only weakly present.

It is not only that in Melpa group genealogies there is a regular recurrence of patrifilial links, for there are also matrifilial links at numbers of points in the genealogies as well. It is also that, because Melpa-speakers define recruitment rules in filiative terms, there is a very rapid 'conversion' of links. Sisters' sons who join a group or are brought up within it are known as *amb-nt-mei* members, but their sons, who belong by patrifiliation, are *wuə-nt-mei*, just as are those whose agnatic male ancestors belonged to the group. In time a whole segment founded by a sister's son may come to be known as *amb-nt-mei*, 'the woman-bearing' segment, but the individual patrifilial members of it are all *wuə-nt-mei*, 'man-bearing'. 'Woman-bearing' membership is continually converted into 'man-bearing' membership, and thus the pattern is cumulatively one of patrifiliation. Moreover, as I have pointed out earlier, although sisters who return to their natal kin with their children are usually spoken of as attaching themselves to their brothers, they do so by virtue of their own patrifiliation. It is because of their mother's patrifilial ties that sister's sons can be described as 'owners' (*pukl wuə*) of their mother's brothers' land. Melpa-speakers imply that a sister's son's claims are stronger than those of other men, for example unrelated refugees or uxorilocal husbands, although in practice the efficacy of such ties is rarely tested in disputes. Ideology, within the sphere of individual recruitment, is thus quite clearly not patrilineal, so that no question of discrepancy between ideology and behaviour arises. Statistical material indicates that filiative ties are the ones most usually employed in justifying and explaining clan-group membership, although residence and land use may be granted on other bases as well. Filiation is thus a mechanism, from a formal point of view, which guides and restricts access to membership in clan-groups. As Langness has stressed, a formulation in these terms presents only a part of the picture: we must find reasons for people changing membership as well as labelling the ties which they can exploit to do so (Langness 1964:171). Again, case-material in chapters six and seven may have helped to supply reasons.[2] Before returning to this point, however, I want to look at the question of ideology further.

If recruitment ideology is filial, what do we make of the rest of the ideology, in which clansmen assert that they are 'of one father', sub-clansmen that they are 'different men's houses' descended from the wives of a polygynous clan-founder, and so on? Filiation and individual rights of membership are not in question here. Instead we are in the realm of assertions about identity, continuity and unity. These are assertions which create and use a 'native model' of group structure. Further, they are assertions which mirror critical delimitations of rights and duties between clansmen. All clansmen respect the rule of exogamy; different clan-sections must pay reparations to each other for men they have lost in acting as mutual allies during warfare; sub-clansmen expect to co-operate closely in *moka* prestations and to help each other with bridewealth payments; and lineage kinsmen expect to be involved even more closely in financial enterprises and in land-use. The clansmen's common identity and their further sharing of identity at a higher level with other clans of their tribe is both symbolised and expressed actively in situations of conflict by the *mi*, mystical divination substance proper to their tribe. The *mi* substance is consumed by an accused man as a test of his innocence, or as a mark of an outraged person's oath, and is supposed to 'eat' (i.e. kill) its consumer if he is swearing falsely or subsequently breaks his oath. It operates precisely in the politico-jural domain which Fortes has stressed as the domain in which descent is important (Fortes 1969). It is not surprising, then, to find that idioms which resemble the patrilineal dogmas identified by Africanist anthropologists are utilised by Hageners as symbols of group structure. The difficulty is that they do not relate to recruitment; they relate only to obligations of membership once membership has been obtained.

As I have also suggested in the first chapter, the native models are not entirely easy to understand. Although Melpa-speakers seem to hold the question of recruitment and composition separate from the question of models for group structure, I suggest that there is actually 'interference' between these two levels which produces a 'mixed' ideology. In recruitment, matrifiliation is accepted as an, albeit secondary, mode of affiliation. It has to remain secondary, since it is out of harmony with other factors, such as normative patrivirilocality, and husbands' control over wives, but it is accepted because it meets certain interests, for example it enables big-men to increase their following, or it provides an avenue of refuge in warfare. Descent dogmas posit that clansmen share the 'grease', or semen, of an original male ancestor, and this fits with the notion that men contribute semen to the making of their children, while women contribute blood. In fact, however, these ideas cannot be comfortably entertained along with the fact of matrifilial recruitment to clans, and dogmas are modified. Parallel with the notion that clansmen are 'of one father' is the idea that they are 'of one blood', that is, that they share a maternally-given substance. In most contexts 'one blood people' are actually extra-clan non-agnatic kin. Calling clansmen by this term thus confuses the initial distinction between agnatic and cognatic kinship and accommodates the facts of recruitment to the native model which is the symbol for clan unity and one of the means of articulating clans within the tribe (cf. Gluckman in Meggitt 1965: xii).

As I have stressed also, it is important to notice that the descent idiom is not the only one which Melpa speakers employ as a symbol of group solidarity, segmentation, continuity, and so on. Two other important idioms are used. The first is that of the 'men's house group' (*manga rapa*) which is applied most regularly to the level of sub-clan divisions within the clan. This draws its force from the fact that men who live together and share either a dwelling house or a ceremonial house at the head of a dancing ground are likely to plan prestations together. Sub-clansmen do not literally all live together, but in discussions they are expected to congregate and to act jointly on the basis of decisions which they make. The idiom thus stresses what one might call the ideal of synchronic co-operation within sub-clan groups, whereas the descent idiom represents their corporate dia-chronic extension. Second, there is the image of the whole clan as a 'garden division' (*pana ru*) and the idea that persons who change membership 'plant' themselves, or are planted by big-men sponsors in a new 'garden division'. The emphasis here is on the territorial nature of land-holding and on a symbolisation of residence which states that joining a group implies making 'roots' with it, as a plant roots itself in a garden. This idiom becomes fused at certain points with the Melpa concept of kinship, since the lexeme *pukl* can mean both a physical root and a kinship link. Hence sister's sons have a particularly strong 'root' with their mothers' clan groups.

Each of these idioms thus plays a part in symbolising different aspects of Melpa social groups. The metaphor of 'planting' expresses the importance, for the individual, both of connection with territory and of the need to develop 'strong roots', that is, group identity and loyalty, while also indicating that individuals can change residence and group affiliation by 're-planting' themselves. The *manga rapa* idiom stresses the importance of co-operation arising out of co-residence. Finally the descent idiom is the rationale for the extension of kin terms within the clan and provides a logical model for relations of exclusiveness and inclusiveness between group segments and for the notion of their internal continuity. I suggest, then, that in the case of the Melpa, examination of the interplay of idioms as symbols is more informative than an attempt to determine whether 'the system is really patrilineal or not'. At the same time it must be clear from my account that 'the system' is not 'really patrilineal' in any simple or holistic way. Melpa clans are not internally structured in the same way as are Tallensi lineages, for example.

ALLIANCE

The wider context in which recruitment to groups operates has to be considered, as well as the narrow definition of recruitment rules themselves. Thus Langness has argued that recruitment to Bena local groups was 'open' because of the prevalence of warfare and the need for group strength, and de Lepervanche has charted the activities of big-men in recruiting supporters (Langness 1964:173; de Lepervanche 1968:177ff.). These considerations certainly applied, or apply still, in Hagen. In addition, I have argued (chapter six) that patterns of inter-group alliance must be taken into account.

First, the idiom of descent, agnatic or otherwise, goes hand in hand, at all levels of group structure, with idioms that symbolise alliance. Indeed, what is a descent idiom from one point of view is also an alliance idiom from another (Criper 1967). Brothers can be seen either as united because of their common parentage or divided, but linked, as separate members of a sibling set. In Hagen there is a special idiom employed which states alliance relations: the idiom of pairing. Pairing indicates either a former or a current special linkage between two groups; and groups can be paired together in this way at any level from the sub-sub-clan up to the tribe. Paired clan-groups intermarry fairly closely and are more likely to share territory with each other than with other groups. From their close association disputes also arise, in which their separateness is temporarily emphasised. They may be implicitly in competition for members, as Kawelka Kundmbo and their pair-clan Minembi Kimbo seem to be. In any case the density of their ties of intermarriage gives rise to a fairly high incidence of interchange of personnel between them, since a person is most likely to join his mother's group if he does not join his father's.

This book has concentrated on the descent idiom, on filiation as 'a mechanism of recruitment' (Barnes 1962) and on the situations of choice which arise in the lives of individual people, but this is not because I believe that these facts give an adequate total picture of Hagen society. Such a picture can be obtained only by a direct study of the structure of inter-group alliances, the medium in which they are expressed (*moka* exchanges) and the activities of the big-men who generate particular sequences of exchanges between groups. *The rope of moka* attempts to give such a picture and I hope that the account in that book will help to underpin and give fuller meaning to my references to big-men and alliances in this one.

The only point I wish to add here is that the pattern of inter-group alliances is congruent enough with a reduced stress on opposition between patrifilial and matrifilial ties. By contrast, the Mae-Enga stress this opposition sharply, and I suggest that this is directly related to the lack of development of inter-clan alliances among the Mae. Whether this point, as well as the factor of land shortage, also helps to explain the Mae people's emphasis on agnation as a rule of recruitment to clan-groups is a question which I can do no more than raise. In any case, to point out that the Mae political system differs from that of the Hageners is merely to raise the further question of why this should be so; and perhaps Meggitt would relate this in turn back to the basic situation of land shortage: when land is short, alliances sometimes go by the board. But this would not be equivalent to arguing that land shortage must inevitably generate clan exclusiveness (cf. the Chimbu, Brookfield and Brown 1963, Kelly 1968); or that abundance of land generates a development of stable alliances between groups (cf. the Bena Bena, Langness 1968).

PATRIFILIATION AND MATRIFILIATION

Glasse, in his study of South Fore marriage, suggests that 'what needs to be explained in the Highlands is not the absence of unilineal emphasis but the distinctive features such as patrifiliative recruitment and strong sibling bonds' (Glasse 1969:20). This is a point well taken, for many of us in writing about the Highlands have taken patrifiliative recruitment as a matter of course and have concentrated our attention on the (sometimes considerable, of course) range of variation in recruitment patterns.

In one sense this procedure can be justified. Patrifilial recruitment is a part of a normative system in which the elements all fit together. Once this system is given, one is not surprised to find that the statistical pattern approximates to it. However, it may be useful to attempt to derive patrifilial recruitment as an outcome from certain other factors, rather than as a principle which is itself given great or uniform normative weight. One of the features of many Highlands societies is the theoretical dominance of men over their wives. This is a feature subject to considerable variation, and in some contexts is more a myth than a reality; but it is enough for my purposes that it is an aim of men to achieve this dominance. It is easier to control wives if one gains specific claims over them by payments of bride-wealth and if the wives come to live in one's own settlement. Control is important, not only sexually but economically: men depend on women for productive labour, in gardening, child-bearing, and pig-rearing, and an adult man expects to depend most heavily on his wife or wives for this work. If we add to this another feature, that local political groups consist of sets of males who hold, or attempt to hold, their territory against other similar groups,[3] it can be seen that women must move on marriage from one of these groups to another, given that the men of each group may not marry their own females. Patrifilial recruitment of men to such local groups is not absolutely entailed by these features, for other arrangements would be possible. For example, the men of a local group could be related to each other matrilineally, and wives could come to live with their husbands in viriavunculocal residence, as they do in the Trobriands (Malinowski 1935). However, the problem with such an arrangement is that it entails men gaining control over their sisters' children when these grow up, or at least over their sisters' sons. The sisters' sons would have to move regularly, on approaching adulthood perhaps, to their mother's brother's place. If relations between the groups involved are both competitive and segmentary, as they are in most parts of the Highlands, this arrangement could be difficult to operate. For one thing, it would mean that boys were brought up within one political community and then moved to another, perhaps opposed to the first. This again would not be an impossible situation; but, given the nature of inter-group relations and given the male ideal of control over wives, patrivirilocal residence and patrifilial recruitment are simpler and more obvious arrangements to adopt. The outcome, however, is nowhere a pattern conforming rigidly to this set of arrangements; and the reasons for variation in outcomes have, then, to be sought. I will summarise what I think are the most important reasons, in the case of the Melpa-speakers, in the next section. Here I shall hazard a subsidiary argument about matrifiliation.

It has been a noticeable point about many of the cases cited or examined in more detail here that mothers sometimes succeed in removing their children from their husband's group, and take these back with them to their own natal group. Their success depends on a range of factors external to the domestic relationship between themselves and the children; but this relationship itself is likely to be relevant also.

When children are very small, of course, or perhaps even still suckling, it is expectable that they will go with their mother. However, this is not an absolute proposition: foster-mothers, even wet-nurses can be found. When a man pays bridewealth he has in mind obtaining rights over his wife's children as well as over the wife herself: it is specifically not regarded as a woman's jural right to remove her children from the husband's place, but the likelihood that women may do so, in the event of widowhood or divorce (separation poses a rather different problem) is recognised. Children may be looked on as jural minors, but this does not mean they are without effective volition. What case-histories suggest—although I can say no more than that they suggest this—is that children up to the age of five, and perhaps a little over this, are likely to go with their mothers because they are more strongly attached to these than to their fathers. From birth they sleep in their mothers' own pig-houses along with them, and are suckled, unless this is impossible, only by the mothers themselves. Breast feeding is permissive, and weaning does not take place until a child is two to three years old. During this time husband and wife are supposed not to have intercourse. (In any case, a man does not regularly sleep in his wife's house even while he is free to have sexual relations with her; he has intercourse with her beside gardens, in fallow land.) Further, the mother carries her child out to the gardens with her in a netbag slung over her back, so that an unweaned child is rarely separated physically from its mother either by day or night. I think that all these factors are bound to increase the strength of a child's attachment to the mother, and that this may last even after weaning is completed (cf. Bowlby 1969). A father, by contrast, is likely to spend much more time associating with other men away from his very young children. There is in fact a formal taboo on his holding a child for at least several weeks after it is born, since he would be polluted by such an action: the child has still its 'first skin', Melpa men say; only later when its good, clean skin, not affected by the blood of its mother's menstruation and parturition, has grown does he take the child in his arms. I would not wish to over-stress this argument. Fathers are generally fond of their children, and show their affection by carrying them around and giving them special foods, after they have been weaned. They stress that they are 'sorry' for their children, and one young man generalised that men care for their children more than they do for their wives. Certainly I have known instances in which fathers have tried to stop their wives from running away, ostensibly not to retain the wife, in the long run, but to keep their children. In a dispute one man declared passionately to me that 'children are our hearts', in explanation of why he would not let his wife go back with their children to her place when she was threatening to ask for divorce from him. These examples indicate, then, the attachment of fathers to their children, but they do not reveal the feelings of young children themselves. Judging by Melpa patterns of domestic residence, male-female separation based partly on notions of menstrual pollution, and the long period of post-partum taboo during which a child sleeps with and regularly suckles its mother, I am inclined to think that there may be some likelihood in the suggestion that the mother-child bond is strongly reinforced among the Melpa and that this fits with the value placed on maternal ties and the willingness of children to go with their mothers to a new place and settle there.

TRANSACTIONS, BIG-MEN, AND CHANGE

Discussion of group-membership and group structure in terms of descent and filiation gives us little insight unless it is set into its situational context and proper weight is given to the activities of big-men, especially the major big-men, who most significantly excel in ceremonial exchange and influence group decisions. While it is not true that big-men are regularly the ultimate arbiters on whether incomers should be accepted into their clan-group or not, it is true that they themselves are quite likely to be the ones who do not just accept but actively welcome and even recruit such incomers (cf. de Lepervanche

1968:175ff.). In relating normative statements and idioms to their context, as de Lepervanche urges that one should do, it is also necessary to recognise that complete consistency is unlikely to be met with. Instead norms and idioms are embedded, are actually used, in transactions, as Scheffler would put it (Scheffler 1965). They are invoked when social relationships are activated for some particular purpose. This is especially true of the descent idiom among the Melpa. Literal agnatic descent is not an important criterion for determining jural rights in corporate groups; but assertions that the men of such groups are all descendants (in some way) of a single founder and hence are all 'brothers' are a means of conceptualising corporacy and unity in relation to outsiders.

But the term transaction should mean rather more than this. Barth (1966:4) defines transactions as 'those sequences of interaction which are systematically governed by reciprocity'. In the Highlands the context in which transactions, thus defined, hold greatest sway, is that of inter-clan relations. The men who activate such transactions are, to a considerable extent, the big-men. The maintenance of normative rules governing marriage and the affiliation of children is itself dependent on particular transactions being successfully completed. Although this is not emphasised by informants when they give their formal statements about such topics as inter-group alliance, what should happen at the payment of bridewealth, and how children are affiliated to groups, case-histories regularly show the importance of big-men in guiding the transactions which underpin actual alliances, bridewealth payments, and affiliation patterns. The premises which affect their actions are two: first, it is to their advantage to have a say in the formation and maintenance of inter-group exchange ties; second, it is often useful for them to increase their following of supporters and actual workers by accepting incomers. Since big-men are continually seeking to excel in the exchange system, and to do so requires more control over exchange networks and pig-production than ordinary men are likely to have, we would expect to find that they try to extract value out of, and manipulate, marginal situations. They may require a son-in-law to join their settlement; or take in more married sisters (with their children) than ordinary men do;[4] they may take it on themselves to pay off debts in order to bind men to them as followers, or they may 'ransom' children by paying fees for their nurture by another group and so obtain the children for themselves. They may also move into pioneer areas, or establish more than one settlement, and use their non-agnatic co-residential kin to help them work land as well as mobilising occasional sets of non-co-residential kin for bridewealth occasions and pig-cookings.

The effectiveness of matrifilial ties in establishing clan membership, and ideological pronouncements about sisters' sons must be seen, at least partly, as belonging to this context. It is true that women have no jural right, for example, to remove their children. But if they wish to leave their husbands they can offer the children to their own natal kin in return for protection and support against the husbands, and where this is to the kinsfolk's advantage they will give protection. On the other hand, I am not convinced that the kinship ideology is nothing but an expression of people's interests in concrete situations, or that it has no reality except in relation to some material good, such as land, and rights over it. I see the force of kinship as an idiom and as an ideology arising to some extent out of the experience of bonds of attachment within the field of familial relationships. It is this experience which is transposed and written large on jural and political affairs so that it becomes a symbol of relationships between segmentary groups. Moreover, the structure of relationships in the narrower context of the family fits the structure of those in the wider context to which the symbols are applied. Just as brothers are to a certain extent rivals, so are sub-clans within the clan. It is this 'fit' which can, in fact, be exploited by big-men in declaring that their clansmen are all one because they share a 'single father', or are divided because the sub-clans are descended from 'different mothers'.

One can see the perception of situational advantages underlying the attitudes of groups and big-men to incomers in other Highlands societies. Reay (1959), Langness (1964), Meggitt (1965) and de Lepervanche (1967-8) have all emphasised this point. Kaberry (1967), in an overview of descent ideology in Highlands societies, has similarly stressed that 'the element of optation in affiliation . . . must

be examined in the context of the elaboration of extra-clan ceremonial exchanges . . . [and] . . . the competition among ambitious men to
become leaders and attract a following' (pp.121-2). And most recently
Watson (1970), making a plea which echoes the earlier one of Langness (1964) that we must look at Highlands societies in their own
terms, has developed the attractive concept of society as 'organized
flow'—an approach which focuses directly on the question of in-
flows and out-flows of personnel to and from local territorial and
political groups.[5] Without arguing that there is any particular merit
in selecting any one label to characterise Highlands societies, we can
suggest that in many parts of the Highlands, 'open-ness', both in
terms of the recruitment and loss of persons to groups and in terms
of who attains to positions of leadership within groups, is a strikingly
prominent feature. Watson has stressed this for the Tairora, while
pointing out further problems and arguing that we should look for
variability in this feature as well. Taking the feature of open-ness, we
can construct models of feedback processes in the growth and decline
both of groups and of the careers of big-men. Within groups
expanding in size there are opportunities for new big-men to obtain
followings, increase their power, and create new group segments.
At the same time other groups are declining, and their members
eventually disperse or are swallowed up by more powerful hosts or
neighbours. But competition between big-men, or the development
for other reasons of internecine disputes, splits the successful groups
apart again, so that group size returns to a previous level; and the
positive feed-back processes can then begin again. Whatever the
exact applicability of such a model, it is at any rate clear that Highlands societies were in the recent past subject to vigorous ongoing
processes of competition and change—whether entirely cyclical or
also in some long-term ways directional needs to be further worked
out. Over a span of several hundred or thousands of years these
processes of competition may have both engendered and been facilitated by continual expansion and movement of Highlands populations over the entire area which they currently occupy. Possibly the
availability of areas for expansion fostered continual replication
of the feature of structural open-ness; until in certain parts, such as

that of the Mae-Enga, when population expanded considerably, firmer control over recruitment to groups became necessary. (This last conjecture corresponds to that made by Meggitt himself, 1965: 263.) We can suggest also, as I have earlier done, that given an empirical state of flux in movements of persons, coupled with an emphasis on co-operation between current group-members in defence of, or in increasing, their material possessions, some kind of ideology is needed to act as a symbol for group-allegiance, whether such allegiance, or the group itself, is permanent or otherwise (cf. Salisbury 1956). The descent ideology provides one such symbol; and, at least among the Melpa, the men's house idiom provides another.

Given that all this is so, or approximately so, we should expect that Highlanders have quickly adapted to changes caused by the imposition of colonial peace in the 1930s and the later introduction of new economic opportunities. This suggests in turn that there should be excellent opportunities to study social changes in Highlands societies from this perspective. The difficulty here, of course, lies in the complexity of changes, even in cases where the history of contact with Europeans goes back no more than thirty years. However, at least the study of change enables us to cast synchronic hypotheses into a diachronic mould, even if it specifically precludes us from testing them in isolation from complicating factors. For example, if the Bena Bena in the pre-contact past accepted immigrants largely because of the need to maintain group strength in order to defend territory in warfare, what has become of this need since warfare was stopped? Similarly, if the Mae-Enga discouraged immigrants in the 1950s, has this attitude increased in sharpness during the 1960s, given greater population density as a result of medical services, etc.? (Cf. Reay 1967 on certain changes among the Kuma since the 1950s.) The answers to these questions will always depend on intergroup transactions which have developed during the contact period and on people's perception of their advantages. Thus, group strength may still be an ideal among the Bena if they have re-channelled their competitiveness into corporate ceremonial exchanges (cf. Salisbury 1962)—hence they may still welcome incomers. Certainly, this consideration holds among the Melpa, and groups keenly compare their size, strength, and ability to raise wealth for use in prestations. The continuing importance of prestations also underlines the fact that, although there is an overall governmental authority, relations between clan-groups are still segmentary in many contexts and that traditional-style big-men continue to be important as pivotal links between the groups. Given this fact, many of the considerations affecting the recruitment of non-patrifilial clan-group members still apply. Groups are still competitive, and big-men are still keen to attract adherents (although, since these can now go off on wage-labour they may find it harder to keep them). Scheffler, in his analysis of change among the Choiseulese, provides some suggestive parallels for what could perhaps occur in Hagen society in the next few years. He argues that 'leadership had been established . . . in activities . . . associated with intergroup conflict, and with the conflict suppressed ambitious men lost the sanctions previously available to them' (1964b:400). Leadership had in the past been linked to opportunities of making contractual alliances for warfare, and when warfare was ended by the imposition of colonial peace, this avenue for young men to enter the system was closed; while at the same time the avenue of cash-cropping, through the copra trade, was opened, and provided an alternative attraction to young men. In time the significance of segmentary groups and their leaders crumbled. It became possible to be rich without holding political power, and, Scheffler adds, 'the Choiseulese are quite aware of and disconcerted by these facts; they see that one of their major problems is that everyone is a big man and that consequently no one is' (p.401). These processes of change have not occurred in Hagen up till 1971. The *moka* system has survived, albeit under pressure and with predictions from big-men that soon it 'may have to go' (*mana mba*), and this has meant that segmentary inter-group relations and competition between big-men are still important. Correspondingly, big-men remain keen to recruit both agnates and non-agnates as their supporters. Further changes are likely to emanate from the growth of cash-cropping and potential accompanying shortages of land. At present groups and individuals are exploiting ties of various kinds in order to increase their plantings of coffee trees. In this phase, colonisation and the use of non-agnatic ties are likely to remain prominent. At the same time, as I have mentioned earlier, entrepreneurs who are living in enclave areas outside of their own group territories are likely to be criticised by, and to arouse jealousy among, their hosts. They may settle this by partnership arrangements, or an 'agnatic ideology' may be quoted at them in order to make them move back into their own group areas. *Moka* transactions between themselves and their hosts might stabilise their situation; or they might decide to give up *moka*-making altogether, obtain land on an individual lease-hold basis from the Administration and concentrate on cash and entrepreneurship. The directions for social change, and correspondingly for the decisions of individual men, are for the time being still open. But at all events it is clear that a changing external social and economic situation provides an opportune framework for investigation of the strength of ideologies, rules, and processes which were developed within earlier political and ecological contexts.

APPENDIX

SICKNESS DIAGNOSIS MADE BY TWO DIVINERS

(a) NORTHERN MELPA DIVINER

Status of victim	Whether F and M alive or not	Sickness sent by
1. Male, adult	alive	FF; FM; elder B; Z
2. Male, adult	alive (at this time)	FF
3. Female, adult	alive	FF; MF; MM
4. Male, old	dead	B; M
5. Female, old	dead	M
6. Female, child	alive	F elder B
7. Male, adult (informant)	dead	M
8. Male, adult (informant's B)	dead	M
9. Male, adult	dead	F; M
10. Female, adult	F alive M dead	M
11. Female, adult	dead	F and M together
12. Female, adult	dead	F and M together
13. Male, old	dead	M; F
14. Male, adult	dead	M

(b) GAWIGL DIVINER

Man	No. of time expert has divined for him	Ghosts responsible for sickness
1	occasionally	D (died young)
2	occasionally	F + dead children of both sexes
3	twice	F
4	seven times	F + M; dead children of both sexes
5	twice	1st wife; dead sons
6	once	F
7	twice	dead daughter (married before she died)
8	once	M
9	once	F
10	once	M
11	once	1st wife
12	twice	M + F
13	twice	M + F
14	twice	wife + F
15	twice	D; M + F
16	twice	1st wife; F
17	twice	M; married Z
18	twice	F; wife
19	four times	eB; M; dead children of both sexes; M + F

NOTES

PREFACE

[1] I was involved in this series as anthropological consultant to Mr John Percival, the film director, while he and his team were in New Guinea. We filmed and interviewed some of the families I know best at Mbukl.

INTRODUCTION

[1] This was an argument developed in an earlier version of this book, completed in July 1965. I first distinguished idioms in which people describe their groups from both their jural norms and statistical patterns of affiliation, then stated that my interest was to see whether at different levels of structure the descent idiom was dominant, and if not what other idioms were, and concluded that 'whereas the Hageners tend to conceptualise their clans as agnatic genealogical structures, nevertheless with regard to recruitment they make no rigid prescriptive statements' (1965:ix-x). My distinctions thus owed something to that which Barnes made, in his 1962 article on African Models, between filiation as 'a mechanism of recruitment' and descent as 'a sanctioned and morally evaluated principle of belief' (p. 6). They are similar also to those made by Sahlins (1965) between descent as a criterion of recruitment and descent as a political arrangement and by Barnes again in 1967 between 'structure' and 'recruitment' in relation to Mae-Enga groups.

[2] There are, however, parallels between the way new local groups are actually founded among the Nuer and processes of segmentation in the Highlands. See Evans-Pritchard 1940:216.

I. IDIOMS

[1] For criticisms of 'lineage theory' see Buchler and Selby 1968, chapter 4. Their discussion is especially interesting, since they explicitly compare two Highlands societies, the Mae-Enga and the Chimbu, with each other and with two African societies, the Tiv and Tallensi. Their treatment, however, follows Barnes's earlier (1962) article rather than the distinctions which have subsequently been developed by Barnes (1967), Sahlins (1965), Scheffler (1966), and myself (1969).

[2] It is interesting to see that other ethnographers of the Highlands have had difficulties in finding translation labels for native concepts. Thus Salisbury, after explaining that among the Siane 'the individual has a direct relationship with the original clan ancestors, sharing their material essence . . . most of

which is acquired through ceremonial and growth', adds 'I feel, however, that it is appropriate to call such a relationship with the ancestors one of descent, and that if existing definitions of descent do not fit the Siane case, then the definitions should be modified' (1964:170).

³ *Tepanem-nt kongon elinga manem-nt nim mitim.* 'Your father did his work and your mother bore you'.

⁴ Somewhat humorously, one informant (Kawelka Kundmbo Nykint) contrasted pigs and men in this context. Boar-pigs, he claimed, could impregnate sows in one act of intercourse, because the amount of semen they produce in a single ejaculation is much greater than that which a man can achieve. Nykint thus accommodates his observation of the mating of boars and sows with his culturally-given dogmas about the conditions of procreation; and, while contrasting men and boars in one respect, he asserts that the conditions of procreation are really the same for both.

⁵ There are terms in Melpa for abortion, miscarriage, and premature birth. The last is called *kangambokla roka ropa metim*, a phrase derived from the action of banana fruits in pulling over the stock. If the stock falls over to the ground before the fruit is ripe it is said to *roka rui*; and this image is applied metaphorically to the premature birth of children.

⁶ Compare Schwimmer's account of Orokaiva statements about conception: 'The male is believed to have a special quality (*ivo*), not shared by the female. This is a strength or power enabling the male to play his distinctive roles and it is transmitted by a man to his son in the "male blood" . . . . This is the *ivo* of the lineage. As women do not receive this type of blood, they cannot carry on the lineage' (Schwimmer 1969:132).

⁷ This again was Ru, who has a much more intellectualist approach to his own culture than perhaps is characteristic of the ordinary Hagener.

⁸ It can be seen that I am not here simply pointing to a discrepancy between ideology and practice but to ambiguity in the ideology itself—an ambiguity which, I think, can be adequately explained.

⁹ Marriage prohibitions are discussed in more detail in Strathern, A. J. and A. M. 1969.

¹⁰ A related idiom is *poklpa paka maka etepa mepa ponom*, 'it grows and makes forks and the line is carried on'. The metaphor here is derived from planting types of cane-grass, which put out numbers of shoots and grow in different directions (informant Nykint).

¹¹ I have here combined two texts given to me by Ru on different occasions: (a) 'wend ape-nga kaklp təp mep yand urumun e-nga akop tin morimon, wend ape-nga int purum-e-nga apop pongon nim motn, tin mema tenda morimon.' (b) 'wamb mon kandək etimin e-mil mon, tin wamb mbo tenda nitimon, tin mema pukli morimon, kaklk mek int int puklngena kona mba akop kakna etepa morom. Nim akop mon kandekin kona ile ui nøui, niminga mema pukli oronga pilikin un-e-nga akop mel mat ngopon mondamona mekon pøn nitimon.' For the idea here cf. Read 1955:278, and Fortes 1969:234.

¹² In a paper for a symposium on Highlands kinship systems, edited by E. A. Cook and Denise O'Brien.

¹³ The Manga, who live in the Jimi Valley to the east of Melpa speakers, and

whose language appears to share 36 per cent cognates with Melpa (Bunn and Scott 1962:4) make cross/parallel distinctions of Seneca type, a special case of Iroquois (Cook 1970; cf. Kay 1967; Lounsbury 1964, quoted by Kay). Some responses of Melpa informants clearly conform to this type; however, variability and uncertainty in responses indicate that they can hardly be consciously aware of so precisely-phrased a rule as Cook (1970, p.193) has constructed as a key to Manga usage. I am grateful to Gehan Wijeyewardene for discussion on this point; but he is not responsible for any errors in my statements here.

[14] Or they may be regarded as one's parent's one blood people rather than one's own (informant Nykint). A term for distant kin in general is *wamb pundun* or *pundun kngan*.

[15] Cook (1970:194-5) has shown how a similar set of terminological usages among the Manga can operate to obliterate distinctions between agnatic and non-agnatic lineage members, if the non-agnates are initially sister's sons of the agnates. In Ru's formulation also, which parallels Manga usage, the choice of sibling terms for FFZSch depends specifically on their living near to ego or actually belonging to his group.

[16] These, briefly defined, are sequences of gifts between individual partners, acting in concert with or separately from their group mates. The main items employed are live pigs, pork, and pearl shell valuables. An initiatory gift from a partner draws a larger main gift in return after a period of delay. Only if the main gift exceeds the initiatory gift in value is its donor said to 'make *moka*' and to gain prestige. After one such sequence the direction of gifts between the partners may be reversed. The *moka* is the major traditional vehicle for competition between individual men and groups in Hagen; and it is thus the institution which, in the terms of Wynne-Edwards (1962), fulfils the function of legitimising and channelling conventional competition in the society.

[17] In fact, this idiom is also sometimes applied to pairs of lineages, one of which is said to descend from a male, the other from a female member of the larger group of which they form segments. These could be described as male-founder and female-founder lineages. For an example see chapter two, note 8. The explicit recognition of women as lineage founders parallels the recognition of matrifilial recruitment.

[18] Thus I have on two occasions heard the big-man Ongka using a string of three terms for lineal ancestors, *anda kokoma*, *anda ror*, and *anda kouwa*, to express long connection with a territory.

[19] These are listed in Strauss and Tischner (1962:88-90). The term *eta* means 'axe-handle' and its sense here is that the weak refugees join the strong land-owners as an axe-handle is attached to the strong axe-blade. Ryan (1959:265) gives an interesting short list of Mendi terms. Particularly interesting is the Mendi category 'born to the land', *shu moria*, for those who have a full claim to residence within a clan territory and to membership of the clan. This phrase seems to stress place of birth as a criterion of entitlement to group-membership. Ryan notes that a non-agnate's child would deny being a newcomer (*ebowa*) and claim to be *moria*, if he had been born on the land of the clan with which he was currently identified.

[20] For views *pro* and *contra* this statement see Meggitt 1965 and Barnes 1967.

²¹ *Tin kang kel-mil moklmona wamb elpa mat tin tembokl-nt ri na roromin, tininga mam tepam rakl mendepukl mint etimbil, ee-mel tipu raklk koromin e-kin tin kui-nt roromin nitimon*. The use of the phrases *tembokl-nt roromin*, 'they strike with sticks', i.e. beat, and *kui-nt-roromin*, 'they strike with sickness' emphasises the parallelism between the actions of living parents and dead ones.

²² For fuller discussions of sickness and frustration see Strathern, A. J. 1968; Strathern, A. M. 1968.

2. THE KAWELKA

¹ Hagen tribal names often end in *-ka*, *-ke* or *-kae*. These forms seem related to the Maring *kai*, as it appears in the phrase *yu kai*, 'a root of men' (Vayda 1968 [1969], and Rappaport 1967:17). Cook (1970:191) reports that among the Narak-speaking Manga, neighbours of the Maring, the phrase *yua ka* means 'man rope' and is the general term for the named groups into which the Narak are divided. *Ka* is thus a cognate of the Melpa *kaan* or 'rope', although the Hageners do not nowadays use *kaan* to refer to their groups (cf. also Reay 1959:39 on the Kuma word *kan*). The Kawelka census point is Mbukl (underlined on Map 1). Variants are Buk, Bugl, Bugal, and Bukul.

² In 1970 Ongka told me the story again, this time beginning 'in the middle', and rearranging the names of the mythical ancestors a little. Thus the original migrant from Kuma to Mbakla he now called Tilkang (whom he mentioned as an after-thought in the 1969 version), and his two sons were Kipilya and Klaem. Klaem was dark-skinned and founded the Pøndimbo, Kipilya light-skinned and founded the Kundmbo.

³ The relationship between the two tribes is, I was told by Ongka, alluded to in ceremonial oratory: 'The Tipuka say of the Kawelka that they came down from Kuma like the spreading vines of the wild *Pueraria* plant (*kaan koeka-mil nggoi nimba urum*); that they took off all their Kuma-style decorations and replaced these with ones appropriate to their new area, given to them by the Tipuka; and that now the Kawelka give to the Tipuka pigs and shells, fight battles for them, and support them in disputes, so that they are pleased to have found them as allies.'

⁴ This was the information I was given in 1964. In 1970 I decided to re-check. Asked whether the sub-clan names were recent, Ongka said no and gave me an orthodox descent model of the groups as deriving from the wives of specific male Kundmbo ancestors; thus a woman of Kiklpukla tribe was married to a Kundmbo man and from her descend the Kiklpuklimbo, and so on. Nykint, however, who is himself of Kundmbo, said that some of the names *were* recent: only Kumapei, Roklambo, and Kumbambo were ancient. Ongka then said that if the sub-groups were 'founded', as Nykint claimed, by a Tipuka affine of the Kundmbo who called out new names for the Kundmbo 'men's house divisions' at a festival, then at any rate the occasion could not have been one as recent as Nykint suggested; and he suggested an alternative time, further back in the past. Finally, Ndamba (father of Nykint and a big-man), when asked the same question, claimed genially that in fact it was he who had invented the new set of sub-clan names, altering them from a previous set, and that he had instructed the Tipuka affine to call out the names in the

new way in order to ensure that his group-mates obtained a larger share of pork at a funeral distribution. Faced with discrepancies in their versions, Ongka and Ndamba (who are both big-men and are relatives-in-law) quickly declared that in fact the stories were the same (*ik tenda*). Whatever the actual history of segmentation in this clan, then, it is clear that big-men are likely to lay claim to inventing and altering sub-clan names, in accordance with their aims in particular exchange transactions.

⁵ This information was taken from a middle-aged man, of ordinary status, belonging to Kumbambo sub-clan, in 1965. In 1970 Ongka, my big-man informant, again gave a different version, as follows:

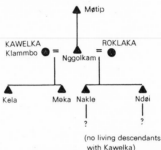

(no living descendants
with Kawelka)

Possibly the discrepancy can be resolved by suggesting that Nggolkam is another name for Nawe.

⁶ Membo clan and the Klamakae are neighbours and there are many *moka* partnerships between their members; so that it is interesting to see the Klama-kae cast collectively into the role of mother's brothers of the Membo in this origin story.

⁷ The genealogical relationships correspond to Ongka's 1970 version; but in this Ongka billed Kipilya as founder of Kundmbo clan and Klaem as founder of Membo + Mandembo together.

⁸ Confirmation of this, and some details not obtained earlier, was given by Ongka in 1970. He told me that Ndat, Mbe, and Raplka were all Kawelka men who came down from the Wahgi (Kuma) territory; and that their descendants are sometimes known as Oyambo Kundumbo or as *amb-nt-mei*, 'the woman-bearing members', by contrast with the sons of Tui and Toakl who are the *wuə-nt-mei*, 'man-bearing members'. Evidence from the migration-history of the Kawelka and other groups which have at some stage occupied parts of the Wahgi Valley appears to offer clues to the question of the previous occupation of the Wahgi, its drainage and agricultural exploitation. The major issue which has to be settled by research work is 'How much of the swampy areas was cultivated and what agricultual techniques and crops were employed in achieving this?' (See Allen 1970:177-83; Lampert 1967:307-9.)

⁹ Professor Ralph Bulmer has mentioned to me that among the Kyaka Enga, western neighbours of the Melpa, the term 'one men's house' refers to the men's house in which the founders of a current sub-group jointly lived. Strauss (1962:78) gives a similar account of the *rapa* concept among the Central

Melpa. He adds that the people themselves say that *rapa* divisions are necessary because of requirements of meat division at festivals, but opines that 'das ist aber naturlich nur ein sehr vordergrundiger Anlass'. As my discussion indicates, I see these 'pragmatic' reasons given by the Melpa themselves for their *rapa* divisions as correct and not as 'a superficial view', as Strauss here appears to do. Strauss also points out (ibid.) that the *rapa* are important in the calculus of marriage rules. This is true, and I would relate these rules in turn to the exchange system (cf. Strathern, A. J. and A. M. 1969). It should perhaps be noted here that sub-clansmen do not *literally* share a single men's house for living in. Each sub-clan contains a number of such men's houses. But they are thought of as *gathering in* a single men's house for discussions.

3. SETTLEMENT PATTERNS

[1] Waddell, however (1968:47), in arguing that this supposed contrast between the Eastern and Western Highlands has limited validity, points out that among the Siane 30 per cent of the women's houses are dispersed outside the main village; also that in the Chimbu situation men tend to be 'nucleated' while women are 'dispersed', so that one cannot characterise Chimbu residence patterns overall in these terms. On limitations of the East-West contrast see also Berndt 1964:201-2.

[2] I am grateful to Dr W. Clarke for pointing this out to me in the field and drawing my attention to Stanhope's proposition.

[3] In 1970 he was still living with the Kawelka Membo.

[4] In one of these cases, at the settlement Mina among the Kawelka Kundmbo, a single men's house was in 1970 shared by: two married sons of the settlement head (each of whom has two wives), two unmarried attached kinsmen, now old, and one unmarried son. The head, Ndamba, slept in his own house nearby, where he also kept his belongings and sometimes held discussions with visitors. One of the sons criticised the third married son for not sleeping in one of the men's houses but staying with his wife in the pig-house which he had built for her. Since the wife had not yet borne a child, the implication was that the husband was having regular intercourse with her, and this, according to Hagen ideas, brings with it dangers of menstrual pollution. It is safer to have intercourse with a wife during the day, when her condition can be more readily ascertained, and at night to sleep separately from her along with one's kinsmen in the men's house.

[5] In Kawelka Kundmbo clan ownership figures for pigs in January and November 1965 were as follows:

	No. of owners	Sows	Barrows	Piglets	Unspecified	Totals
January 1965	31	44	19	58	48	169
November 1965	38	66	20	60	51	197

Average pigs per man: January 5.45; November 5.18.
Comparatively few men had twice as many pigs as the average number. Among those censused, Ndamba was the only big-man. He had been impoverished by a bridewealth payment in January, but by November he had twenty-one pigs and three of his sons had thirty-two between them.

4, SETTLEMENT AND WARFARE

[1] Now (1970) deceased. His son has gone to live with an extra-clan kinsman and big-man who has recently obtained a wife for him.

[2] This story is also told, to illustrate a different point, in *The rope of moka*, chapter four, pp.72-3.

[3] The structure of warfare relations in the Məka Valley area has been examined in *The rope of moka*, chapter four. The basic points relevant to this chapter are that alliances between pairs of clans are of great importance, in Kawelka tribe Membo and Mandembo are paired and used to aid each other in war, among the Tipuka, Kitepi, and Oklembo clans are paired (although occasionally they also fought), the Tipuka-Kawelka alliance was most strongly realised in relationships between Membo-Mandembo and Kitepi-Oklembo, and Tipuka and Kawelka never fought each other as major enemies, only as minor enemies, whose battles resembled feuding.

[4] This friendship between Membo clan and the Klamakae had further repercussions when in 1965 a number of Klamakae, mostly close kin of the Kawelka, tried to gain permission to pay taxes along with the Kawelka at Mbukl and so to align themselves even more closely with the latter. This move was largely a result of rivalry between the leader of the splinter-group and the then Local Government Councillor, who was alleged to have seduced a number of men's wives and to have imposed, and himself pocketed, fines on his men for not turning out to Government road work. The move was scotched by the then vice-President (now President) of the Council, a Tipuka leader, who told the Klamakae magisterially that they had no business seeking to pay tax with the Kawelka, since 'Minembi and Klamakae have always been together, while the Kawelka are with the Tipuka. The names are there in the taxbooks and the government in Port Moresby knows about them, so we can't change the situation. If we do we'll be in trouble.'

[5] See *The rope of moka*, chapter eight, where the Eltimbo's difficulties in a series of prestations are discussed and the importance of their big-men in maintaining the clan's identity is detailed. Chapter four, p.57, also mentions the special linkage of Eltimbo with Kitepi, but adds, incorrectly as I have since established, that 'some Eltimbo men say they can no longer intermarry with Kitepi, there are so many marriages between them'. In actual fact, there are only three contemporary marriages between the two groups and these are all regarded as in some sense wrong, although none of the marriages has been broken up. The current dogma is that Kitepi and Eltimbo together form the Andakomonembo group and hence may not intermarry. In that sense, then, they are close to being a single clan. Yet Eltimbo leaders struggle to maintain themselves as in some ways separate from Kitepi leaders.

[6] When Kitepi-Oklembo clansmen presented two steers to the Kawelka as part of a *moka* gift in 1965, Ok was the only Kitepi man among those who live near Mbukl to be given a share of the meat by the Kawelka. This was done specifically to mark the fact that he had helped them in warfare against Kitepi clan thirty years previously.

[7] By 1970 the land of Raporong had acquired a cash value, in the sense that

one of its occupants had started a business of buying local people's coffee and re-selling it, after careful drying, to coffee factories in Mount Hagen township and Banz. His previous savings and profits from his new business enabled him to buy a Toyota Landcruiser truck, which he used to extend the range of his coffee-buying activities. Predictably, there was considerable jealousy of his success on the part of the original land-owners and there were rumours that they intended to expel him and send him back to his agnatic place—despite the fact that his lineage kin had been living at Raporong for two generations.

[8] One man described his dilemma (whether to stay in the Jimi or return to Mbukl) as follows: 'Where my "fathers", Kur and Anggi, were buried, there I said I would stay. I was sorry for them and felt pain in my stomach; but finally, not wishing to desert my "brothers" of Klammbo, I decided to return and did so, only recently.' I was told that such a feeling of unwillingness to move from the place where one's father has been buried is common enough.

5. AFFILIATION

[1] The etic/emic contrast has its limitations, of course, since even a statement of 'who is the son of whom' depends on a prior definition of 'son' and thus on the way in which different societies conceptualise paternity. I implicitly recognise this limitation when I speak later of the succession of *pater*-child links.

[2] Bohannan (1963:59) has made some rather different distinctions from those I wish to use. He defines 'agnatic' as follows: 'a descent link from a man to a child is called an *agnatic* link'. And he adds 'Many anthropologists call these patrilineal . . . links. I hesitate to do so because in some contexts the emphasis on lineality obscures the point.' I find Bohannan's definition confusing because he uses the term 'descent' for what is perhaps better referred to as a 'filiative' link (Fortes 1969). It is because he applies the term 'agnatic' in his definition only to this filiative domain that he finds it necessary to distinguish 'agnatic' from 'patrilineal'. I shall use 'agnatic' to refer to descent ties which contrast with, while subsuming, certain filial ones, which I call patrifiliation (Cf. also Meggitt 1969:3.)

[3] Moreover, there is always open to them the possibility of returning to their original agnatic kinsmen. One such case occurred in 1970 when a man and his sons returned to the Kawelka Klammbo group after a dispute in which their social status in a Tipuka clan was impugned. The man's father had originally joined the Tipuka as a refugee at his wife's place. The host to these returned agnates, as to most of the non-agnates in Klammbo, was the major big-man Ongka.

[4] The terminological problem here is similar to that presented by Newman (1965:35-7) on Gururumba. Newman distinguishes the clan-village, membership of which may depend on either birth or residence and changes whenever residence changes, and the sib, membership in which depends on birth, in fact on patrilineal descent, only. As de Lepervanche (1968:165) has pointed out, there is some awkwardness in the definition of the sib adopted by Newman, since he himself says that 'if a man resides most of his life in a clan not of his own sib his descendants become members of the clan sib rather than his natal

sib'—which shows that sib membership is not always determined strictly by agnatic descent. It, too, depends in certain cases on residence. A more detailed analysis might reveal whether in all respects original sib-affiliation is lost by descendants of a man who lives away from his natal sib's area. Cf. also Bulmer's distinctions between 'clan' and 'parish' (Bulmer 1960:221).

⁵ See, however, note 7, chapter four.

⁶ A. M. Strathern (*in press*) is examining this topic in detail. I give a brief summary here.

⁷ Note that in terms of the now defunct dispute on 'strong' and 'weak' patriliny, this fact would enable one set of theorists to argue that the Daribi are 'strongly patrilineal'—a conclusion that Wagner would certainly reject!

⁸ Membo Kont. He is now (1970) Councillor for a large regional ward in Dei.

⁹ See chapter seven.

¹⁰ Cook (1970:192) reports a similar pattern for one clan among the Narak-speaking Manga: 'Of the 76 genealogical non-agnates . . . 62 are descendants of 9 female agnates who had returned to their natal patrilineage.' Hence most of the Manga non-agnates become terminologically assimilated and indistinguishable from agnates. Looking at the system from outside, Cook concludes that 'as the generations pass, continuing influxes of non-agnatic kinsmen are subsequently pressed into service as agnates' (p.195). My only reservation here is to wonder whether the Manga also see the process of assimilation in these terms. Compare also figures given by Ryan for the Mendi, 1959:266.

¹¹ I am not suggesting that this definition is a cross-culturally valid one. Carroll and Goodenough at the beginning and end of a volume on adoption in Eastern Oceania (Carroll (ed.) 1970) have shown the complications here. Carroll concludes that the task of providing such a definition may be a hopeless one. Goodenough distinguishes a number of different 'transactions in parenthood' as an alternative to a block term such as adoption. My definition here, Carroll would argue, probably shows some ethnocentric bias. It is similar, however, to that given by Meggitt (1965:25-6) on the Enga and by Fortes (1969:256). In terms of a locally-discriminated set of categories we can distinguish, as Meggitt does, between adoption, in which the adopted person becomes fully filiated to the adopter, and fostering, by which a child is brought up by substitute parents but its original filiation is not annulled and is still recognised. Presumably these distinctions are important to the Enga themselves. In Hagen, children taken over by their maternal kin as orphans may not fall clearly into either the 'adoption' or 'fostering' category; but they are best spoken of as fostered, for their original patrifiliation is not forgotten and they are usually referred to as sister's children rather than children of their hosts. An orphaned sister's son may be at first brought up as a son, but later told of his original filiation, to forestall the possibility of his wishing to marry into his first father's group.

¹² Of the non-agnates in Table 6, thirty-four middle-aged to old men had made an average of two residence-moves (from one clan-area to another) in their lifetimes, while thirty-four young to middle-aged men had moved on average 1.56 times. These averages are not high, and they suggest that men do not make residence and affiliation switches very often. The figures are not

conclusive, since conceivably a man may change affiliation without changing residence; conversely a residence-move does not by itself indicate a change in clan affiliation. By residence here I refer to where a man has his house and the bulk of his gardens; I do not include visits.

[13] Cf. note 5, chapter three.

[14] Similarly, in 1969, when Kawelka men in the Waghi were embroiled in disputes over land-use and ownership with neighbouring Ndika tribesmen, one big-man at Mbukl (Membo Kont) commented 'Let them all come back here to me. I am short of men.'

[15] However, by 1970 he had returned to the Kawelka fold and had his own house at the settlement-place Maepna (cf. chapter three). His mother's second husband belonged to a lineage ('the sons of Rongnda') whose men now live chiefly at this settlement-place.

[16] The letter-writer was Kawelka Kurupmbo Ru. He wrote in Pidgin, which I translate. Ru lives near to the old settlement-place of the subject of his story, at location G (Map 3).

[17] Briefly, the basis of belief in ghostly attack seems to lie in emotional attachments formed in lifetime. Sons are emotionally attached to their fathers, and brothers to one another. When the father dies the son experiences a loss. To overcome this he supposes that the father's ghost survives death. At the same time the death arouses Oedipal guilt in him. He assumes that his father will show aggression towards him as well as solicitude for him. Here the subject seems to have experienced a loss also when his brothers left him and to have interpreted his sickness initially as a sign of his father's pity. Then, when he himself transgressed what he supposed was his father's will, he interpreted the sickness as caused by the father's anger. Cf. Fortes's classic treatment (1949: 234ff.) of father-son relations among the Tallensi.

[18] Cf. note 8, chapter four.

[19] Bulmer gives a comparable, but slightly lower, figure for a Kyaka group (Bulmer 1960:226). Cook states for his Manga clan that he has traced only three instances of uxorilocal residence resulting in only three descendants out of a current total of 358 men (Cook 1970:192).

[20] Asked in 1970 about this case, Ongka commented: 'the children associate all the time with other Eltimbo children, but who knows if they will later become Kitepi or not? It does not matter. These two groups live in the same place, they are a single "line" (reklaep), Pørwa, their Councillor, looks after them both.'

[21] There may be some doubt about the impropriety of such a marriage: if the mother's clan is large and divided into separate sections and the man marries a girl from the opposite section to that of his mother, he can argue that the marriage is allowable after all.

[22] Further, some of the men who at one time had all their gardens at their wives' places subsequently did return to their own clan areas. In one case, while the man himself gardened only at his wife's place, some of his married sons resided at his agnatic place and gardened there.

[23] An uxorilocally-resident husband may sometimes be called an *eta* or *elta*, a term indicating disparagement of someone who is a 'refugee', dependent on

the good-will of his hosts for his land-claims. But whether a man is actually called this or not depends on the situation. When a big-man 'pulls' his son-in-law into residence with him or a number of men encourage a sister's husband to join them, the term is not likely to be heard. The affiliation of the children of the uxorilocal husband whose case I have discussed here was still uncertain in 1970. Ongka remarked that even if the father should die, perhaps his children would be 'sorry' for the place where they had been brought up and decide to stay living there, as they were so firmly established, even if their father's people called them back (*kaemb koromen kona ile pek nggi ningk ya wøi namona na ok tøk iting nda*).

²⁴ On the other hand we have also seen that Hageners may encourage their married sisters to return to them, 'pulling' their husbands if necessary as well as bringing their children, if their group is short of adult males.

6. CHOICES

¹ I.e. in the sense that they had no direct 'root' (reason) of war with Kundmbo. See *The rope of moka*, chapter four, p.55.

² The rest have been taken from more distant tribes or from new neighbours in the Wahgi area. See Table 10.

³ There are some mistakes in my account of Tipuka and Minembi segmentation on pp.57–8 of *The rope of moka*. First, Tipuka Eltimbo and Kitepi should not intermarry, not because there are 'so many marriages between them' but because they are regarded together as Andakomonenbo (see chapter four, note 5). Second, Kelmbo-Waembe are not one exogamous unit. The large Kelmbo clan has in fact split into two exogamous units. Moreover, Waembe and Kelmbo can still intermarry, although it is true that in other respects Waembe is incorporated into Kelmbo. Third, in Minembi tribe, Ropkembo is simply regarded as a sub-clan of Nambakae clan, although it is true that Ropkembo and Øyambo, the other sub-clan, are socially rather separate. Each now has its own local government Councillor.

⁴ See *The rope of moka*, pp.91–2. In 1970 tensions between the Tipuka-Kawelka alliance and some clans of the Minembi tribe rose again, as a result of poisoning accusations and of complications surrounding a physical attack on the local Council President, who belongs to Tipuka Kitepi clan.

⁵ I do not include this lineage in the Kundmbo clan-unit, as its current members are 'minimum depth' agnates of Kimbo by my definition.

⁶ By 1970 the Kundmbo had recovered the balance of their bridewealth payments and found a new wife for their sister's son. However, the other sister's son had in the meantime seduced his cross-cousin, a daughter of his mother's brother, who had come home dissatisfied with her marriage. He was told to leave, and returned to his father, who soon obtained a wife for him.

⁷ I am most grateful to Karl Heider for raising and discussing this question, which he deals with for the Dani in his book, *The Dugum Dani* (1970:132). Cf. also Vayda, A. P. (1968).

⁸ Two cases are cited in *The rope of moka*, chapter four, pp.86–7. One shows clearly that the migrant was forced out through the influence of one big-man and saved by another, whose 'helper' he became.

⁹ As in this and following sections of this chapter I shall be giving a number of cases and stories, I shall number them from 1 onwards. The asterisk indicates that the story relates to the past and its events were not witnessed by me. Some stories relating partly to the past, partly to situations or events of 1964-5, are not asterisked.

¹⁰ Stick fights over the distribution of meat occur quite frequently. It is clear both that pork is highly valued as food and that to be left out of a distribution is to be socially insulted. On both counts, anxieties arise over its division and these can lead to fighting.

¹¹ The ordinary term for sexual intercourse in Melpa is *ronom*, the identical word which is used for physically striking an adversary. Accounts of raids are likely to tell how men went out *wuə rok*, *amb rok*, *kng rok*, 'killing men, raping women, and slaughtering pigs', where the same verb is used for each action.

¹² By 1964 he was old and surly and was known as a rubbish-man. He had gone to live at the settlement of his sister's son, a major big-man. There, on one occasion, he attempted to hang his wife from the rafters of their house, accusing her of commiting adultery and refusing to work. He was committed to court for this, but appears to have returned before his case was actually heard, and went to live with his daughter's husband, whose clansmen in 1969 claimed that he had now joined their group. He and his wife now live in separate houses.

¹³ This point has been discussed in *The rope of moka*, chapter ten, pp.223-7.

¹⁴ In 1970 the father and both his sons had gone to live with kinsfolk in another clan near to the Baiyer Valley which has been depleted in warfare and so has plenty of land for immigrants.

¹⁵ He was still unmarried in 1970. Annoyed at his brother's neglect of him, he seduced a clansman's wife in 1969 and was unfortunately required to pay as a fine the one pig which he was raising as a nucleus for a bridewealth payment. After this he migrated to a new settlement in the Baiyer Valley.

¹⁶ In 1970 I learnt that he had stayed for abour four months only with his mother's people. His hosts had helped him prepare gardens and planned to secure him as a group member, but he had been restless and was always visiting other clan areas to play card-games for stakes of money. Eventually his maternal kin realised that he might be poisoned by enemies while on his cards-circuit and they would then be blamed by his patrifilial kin, so they warned him, and he then returned to his clan and settled down again.

¹⁷ In fact, this boundary was at one time pushed back in warfare; and numbers of Membo men in 1964 gardened on the far side of the Piling without any complaints being made by the Klamakae. Checking on this matter indicated that one recognised boundary in the past was not the river Piling itself but the ridge beyond it which runs up towards Tiyapana.

¹⁸ An interesting part of the history of Kawelka re-colonisation in the Wahgi is Nggoimba's aim of establishing himself as a big-man with supporters in his own territory. It is interesting also, and possibly significant, that many of the men of Membo clan who joined him are non-agnates, either themselves incomers or the sons of incomers—men who may not have felt the same bonds with the Mbukl territory as other Kawelka men appear to feel. Perhaps, also,

Membo clan took in too many incomers, thus taxing the capacity of its territory; but this I cannot demonstrate.

[19] One sub-group of Yelipi men in 1970 purchased a Toyota Scout pick-up vehicle, which considerably eased their commuting problems.

[20] By 1970 the situation appeared to have worsened. See chapter four, note 7.

[21] It would be interesting to speculate further on the advantages and disadvantages of hillside or valley and of forest and grassland areas for settlement. Kawelka men themselves speculate in this way, many saying that they dislike the heat of the Baiyer and Jimi Valley areas but they like the variety of crops and fruits which these areas produce, and hence they maintain links of marriage and exchange with men who live in them.

[22] By 1970 Raema had returned to live within his own clan area; Ruk had gone as a migrant to a new settlement, occupied by both Kurupmbo and Membo men, in the Baiyer.

[23] As can be seen from my account, the question of Ai's genealogical links with the Kundmbo by comparison with those of his assistant is quite irrelevant to a discussion of their social status. Ai is the non-agnate; the agnate is a rubbish-man who 'helps' him as his *kintmant*.

[24] The end of this man's story came in 1970. He had gone to work for the husband of a daughter of Ai, in a nearby clan, and had stayed for two years without receiving any pay from his affine. One day he dug some sweet potatoes from a plot belonging to the daughter, and the married couple chided him for this. 'Where can I go now?' he said, 'you have given me no money or pigs, and I am ashamed to go home without these'. He went into his house, poured decorating oil from a gourd over his skin, smashed the container, cut his blanket and sleeping mat into pieces, pushed his bush knife into the fire, left the house and hanged himself. Ongka, the Kawelka Councillor, went to the erstwhile hosts and demanded compensation for his death, as they had mistreated him; but none was given.

[25] However, he stayed with Ai, who subsequently found him a new wife and paid bridewealth for her.

[26] Instead of doing so, he had by 1970 moved again, to his maternal kin among the Kombukla Andakelkam.

[27] I.e. immediate sister. My implication here is that immediate kin ties are important, for example that women prefer to return to their 'true' brothers and that affective as well as jural components of women's relationships are involved here. Table 13(c) purports to show that 'sister's son' relationships are also important in the cases where a host was not a big-man.

[28] That is, women do not go to a whole range of kinsfolk: they return to their own patrifilial clan-group. Thus what is matrifiliation for their children results from their own patrifiliation. Are we, then, to regard the system as strongly or weakly patrifilial? The conundrum echoes that posed by Leach in his article on Kachin and Lakher marriage (Leach 1957; cf. also Barnes 1967:42).

[29] Men also sometimes 'marry' a widow not in order to procreate children or even to have a further sex-partner but simply to gain extra 'woman-power' for looking after pigs and gardens; perhaps also to gain children the woman may have borne already.

[30] Strauss (Strauss and Tischner 1962:107-8) gives a useful summary on the situation of widows, and adds a point which I do not make in the rest of my discussion: that a woman who has lost children or has had miscarriages at her husband's place feels that this signifies 'religious disharmony' between her and the place and is likely, when her husband dies, to flee from it. By 'religious disharmony' Strauss probably means that the husband's ancestral ghosts are not helping her or are actually attacking her. He gives also relations between the husband and a woman's kin and possible suspicions that she has poisoned the husband as further factors influencing a widow's choices.

[31] This, and the other points alluded to in this section, are explored more deeply in A. M. Strathern (*in press*).

[32] In the event he did not retain the wife, but he did keep his child by her.

[33] Cf. Meggitt (1965:28-9) on Mae-Enga ideas.

[34] It is also true, as Schneider points out, that in a patrilineal system if 'the criteria for establishing paternity are ambiguous, then multiple claims might well obfuscate membership lines' (1965:63). Or, one might add if there is more than one way of claiming a child as 'one's own', this gives the recruiters in such a system some options. An example would be the Yakö, among whom adoption is frequent (Forde 1963). Possibly Schneider, in his assertion about choice and structure, is thinking of the distinction quoted by Buchler and Selby (1968) between 'ground rules that structure the basic framework within which decision-making occurs, and rules that guide choices among the options this framework allows' (p. 100; the distinction is quoted from Atkins and Curtis 1969). However, if so, he does not make this explicit.

[35] An attempt to make the kinds of distinction needed to analyse the operation of cognatic descent constructs was made by Peranio in 1961. Peranio distinguishes between descent, descent lines, and descent groups. His discussion partly anticipates the later clarification made by Scheffler. It is interesting also to note that the basis of Scheffler's own distinction, between cultural constructs and social processes, is partly to be found in the distinction between culture and social structure emphasised by British structural anthropologists in the 1950s (Fortes 1970:73).

[36] Ties with, e.g., mother's mother's clan, father's mother's clan, and father's father's mother's clan, while remembered as a basis for calculation of marriage prohibitions, are much less significant for providing avenues of affiliation. Herein lies the difference between the Hagen system and those of societies in which cognatic descent is given more emphasis.

[37] On the other hand it is acceptable for a man to act as an intermediary between two groups if he has close ties with both. Such a man is said to be 'on one side like the *oim* snake, on the other like the *ndal*'. (The two snakes are of markedly different hues.)

7. STATUS

[1] Bachelors and widowers are dealt with by Meggitt in Table 22, p. 41. I am not sure whether this table is based on the same parish as Table 21, p. 40. If it is, there is a slightly higher proportion of agnates who are widowers than

non-agnates; and this raises the question of whether widowed (and un-remarried) men are of lower status than currently married men or not.

[2] I have reviewed the question of status-stratification in Hagen, in relation to Vicedom's analysis, in *The rope of moka*, chapter nine, so I shall not present Vicedom's views in detail here.

[3] This figure includes some contributions by the groom himself and a few by men of clans paired with the sponsoring clans.

[4] Data on the distribution of bridewealth payments for girls by their own kin show that in almost all cases something is given to the girl's maternal kin. A mother's brother usually endows his sister's daughter with decorations and ornaments which are said to help her fetch in a good bridewealth, and he is repaid for this. The pattern for the distribution of payments thus differs from that for contributions.

[5] In 1970 he had been back for a few months with the Kundmbo, and attached himself to the big-man of his sub-clan. He made no gardens of his own, although he helped others in the big-man's settlement to make theirs and they supplied him with food. He had also obtained a new wife, with the help of a Kundmbo clansman.

[6] An important point is that neither man had taken in the two non-agnates as children. They were probably born on Kundmbo territory as sons of an uxorilocal husband, and their father was now dead.

[7] The situation in 1970 was as follows. The three old unmarried agnates remained as before. Four of the others were married, one was dead (killed in an accident while working at a saw-mill near Goroka), and one (Nendipa) had left the Kundmbo and remained a bachelor at the place of his mother's people. Of the non-agnates, three were now married, one had left his sponsors and gone off as a 'cargo boy', remaining unmarried, and one, also unmarried, had become a worker (*kintmant wuə*) for a big-man, Membo Kont, who had paid his local government tax for him and so saved him from a spell in jail.

[8] Three of the six were married by 1970.

[9] The range of material I have considered in this chapter is rather narrower than that which Meggitt presents in his chapter on 'The Status of Non-Agnates' (1965: chapter three). This is partly because I cannot match all of Meggitt's data, and partly because I have been to some extent concerned with a different point and a different situation: first, questions of land were not, in 1964-5, a very restrictive influence on the intake of non-agnates into the Kawelka as they are among the Mae; and, second, I have been interested in exploring patterns below the level of an agnate/non-agnate distinction in a way which differs from Meggitt's treatment. Again, since the definition of 'agnate' which I have adopted is probably not the same as Meggitt's, it might be unwise to compare my tables too directly with his. By some definitions there would be no agnates at all in Kundmbo clan-group, since none of its men is connected unambiguously and in an agnatic line with a single accepted male founder of the clan. For further discussion and examination of status differences among the Kawelka see Strathern, A. J. 1971, chapter nine; and of bridewealth and polygyny Strathern, A. M. *in press*, e.g. chapters three and five.

8. CONCLUSIONS

[1] Langness has emphasised to me his doubt as to whether concepts such as patrifiliation, descent, etc. adequately represent Bena ideas relating to groups and recruitment. My suggestions here, then, must be regarded as strictly tentative.

[2] In particular one may note the recurrence of statements such as 'He was *popokl* (angry and frustrated) and left'. Withdrawal from a clan-group is often a symbolic act of protest against being baulked in some way or shamed by one's clansmen, and a man takes revenge by removing his support from them and lending it elsewhere.

[3] It is important also to note that these may be groups which are holding particular ecological niches and expanding into new ones, so that they are sometimes independent of, sometimes directly in competition with each other. Territorial boundaries stabilise this situation.

[4] In both of these cases they thus 'break' the rules of proper residence at marriage in order to gain supporters for themselves.

[5] Watson rightly points out in this article that it is analytically unhelpful to label Highlands societies as 'loosely structured', 'optative', etc. Instead of seeing group composition in terms of deviations from some kind of ideal, in static terms, we need to develop models of actual dynamic processes and see to what extent these can be described systematically.

REFERENCES

ALLEN, J. 1970. Prehistoric agricultural systems in the Wahgi Valley—a further note. *Mankind*, **7**: 177-83.

ATKINS, J. and CURTIS, L. 1969. Game rules and the rules of culture, in *Game theory in the behavioural sciences*, edited by I. R. Buchler and H. G. Nutini. Pittsburgh: University of Pittsburgh Press.

BARNES, J. A. 1962. African models in the New Guinea Highlands. *Man*, **62**: 5-9.

—— 1967. Agnation among the Enga: a review article. *Oceania*, **38**: 33-43.

BARTH, F. 1966. *Models of social organization*. London: Royal Anthropological Institute, Occasional Paper No. 23.

BERNDT, R. M. 1964. Warfare in the New Guinea Highlands, in New Guinea: the Central Highlands. *American Anthropologist*, **66**: (4, part 2) 183-203. Special publication, edited by J. B. Watson.

BOHANNAN, P. 1963. *Social anthropology*. New York: Holt, Rinehart and Winston Inc.

BOWLBY, J. 1969. *Attachment and loss*. Vol. 1: *Attachment*. London: The Hogarth Press, in association with the Institute of Psycho-Analysis.

BROOKFIELD, H. C. 1964. The ecology of Highland settlement: some suggestions. *American Anthropologist*, **66** (4, part 2): 20-38. Special publication, edited by J. B. Watson.

—— and BROWN, P. 1963. *Struggle for land*. Oxford University Press, in association with the Australian National University.

—— and —— 1967. Chimbu settlement and residence: a study of patterns, trends and idiosyncrasy. *Pacific Viewpoint*, **8**: 119-51.

BROWN, P. 1962. Non-agnates among the patrilineal Chimbu. *Journal of the Polynesian Society*, **71**: 57-69.

BUCHLER, I. R. and SELBY, H. A. 1968. *Kinship and social organization: an introduction to theory and method*. New York: Macmillan Company.

BULMER, R. N. H. 1960. Leadership and social structure among the Kyaka. Ph.D. dissertation, Australian National University.

BUNN, G. and SCOTT, G. 1962. *Languages of the Mount Hagen Sub-District*. Summer Institute of Linguistics, published by the Department of

Information and Extension Services, Port Moresby, Territory of Papua and New Guinea.

CARROLL, V. (ed.) 1970. *Adoption in eastern Oceania*. Association for Social Anthropology in Oceania Monograph no. 1. Honolulu: University of Hawaii Press.

COOK, E. A. 1970. On the conversion of non-agnates into agnates among the Manga, Jimi River, Western Highlands District, New Guinea. *Southwestern Journal of Anthropology*, **26**: 190-6.

—— and O'BRIEN, D. (eds.) in press. Symposium on New Guinea Highlands Kinship Systems. Paris: Mouton and Co.

CRIPER, C. 1967. The politics of exchange. Ph.D. dissertation, Australian National University.

DE LEPERVANCHE, M. 1967-8. Descent, residence and leadership in the New Guinea Highlands. *Oceania*, **38**: 134-58 and 163-89.

DURKHEIM, E. 1961. *The elementary forms of the religious life*, transl. by J. W. Swain. New York: Collier Books.

EVANS-PRITCHARD, E. E. 1940. *The Nuer*. Oxford: Clarendon Press.

—— 1951. *Kinship and marriage among the Nuer*. Oxford: Clarendon Press.

FIRTH, R. W. 1963. Bilateral descent groups: an operational viewpoint, in *Studies in kinship and marriage*, edited by I. Schapera. London: Royal Anthropological Institute, Occasional Paper No. 16: 22-37.

FORDE, C. D. 1963. Unilineal fact or fiction: an analysis of the composition of kin-groups among the Yakö, in *Studies in kinship and marriage*, edited by I. Schapera. London: Royal Anthropological Institute, Occasional Paper No. 16: 38-57.

FORTES, M. 1949. *The web of kinship among the Tallensi*. London: Oxford University Press.

—— 1953. The structure of unilineal descent groups. *American Anthropologist*, **55**: 17-41.

—— 1959. Descent, filiation and affinity: a rejoinder to Dr. Leach. *Man*, **59**: 193-7 and 206-12.

—— 1967. Totem and taboo. *Proceedings of the Royal Anthropological Institute of Great Britain and Ireland for 1966*: 5-22.

—— 1969. *Kinship and the social order: the legacy of Lewis Henry Morgan*. Chicago: Aldine.

—— 1970. *Time and social structure and other essays*. L. S. E. Monographs on Social Anthropology No. 40. London: Athlone Press.

GLASSE, R. M. 1959. The Huli descent system: a preliminary account. *Oceania*, **29**: 171-84.

—— 1968. *Huli of Papua: a cognatic descent system*. Paris: Mouton and Co.

—— 1969. Marriage in South Fore, in *Pigs, pearlshells and women: marriage in the New Guinea Highlands*, edited by M. J. Meggitt and R. M. Glasse.

New Jersey: Prentice-Hall.

—— and LINDENBAUM, S. 1969. South Fore politics. *Anthropological Forum*, **2**: 308-26.

GLUCKMAN, H. M. 1965. Introduction in *Lineage system of the Mae-Enga*, by Meggitt, M. J. Edinburgh: Oliver and Boyd.

GOODY, J. R. 1962. *Death, property and the ancestors: a study of the mortuary customs of the LoDagaa of West Africa*. London: Tavistock.

HARRIS, M. 1969. *The rise of anthropological theory*. London: Routledge and Kegan Paul.

HEIDER, K. G. 1970. *The Dugum Dani: a Papuan culture in the Highlands of West New Guinea*. Viking Fund Publications in Anthropology No. 49. New York: Wenner Gren Foundation.

KABERRY, P. M. 1967. The plasticity of New Guinea kinship, in *Social organization: essays presented to Raymond Firth*, edited by M. Freedman, pp. 105-23. London: Frank Cass and Co.

KAY, P. 1965. A generalization of the cross/parallel distinction. *American Anthropologist*, **67**: 30-43.

—— 1967. On the multiplicity of cross/parallel distinctions. *American Anthropologist*, **69**: 83-5.

KEESING, R. M. 1967. Statistical models and decision models of social structure: a Kwaio case. *Ethnology*, **6**: 1-16.

—— 1970. Shrines, ancestors, and cognatic descent: the Kwaio and Tallensi. *American Anthropologist*, **72**: 755-75.

KELLY, R. C. 1968. Demographic pressure and descent group structure in the New Guinea Highlands. *Oceania*, **39**: 36-63.

LAMPERT, R. J. 1967. Horticulture in the New Guinea Highlands—C 14 dating. *Antiquity*, **41**: 307-9.

LANGNESS, L. L. 1964. Some problems in the conceptualization of Highlands social structures, in New Guinea: the Central Highlands. *American Anthropologist*, **66** (4, part 2): 162-82. Special publication, edited by J. B. Watson.

—— 1968. Bena Bena political organization. *Anthropological Forum*, **2**: 180-98.

LEACH, E. R. 1957. Aspects of bridewealth and marriage stability among the Kachin and Lakher. *Man*, **57**: 50-5.

—— 1960. The Sinhalese of the dry zone of Northern Ceylon, in *Social structure in Southeast Asia*, edited by G. P. Murdock, Viking Fund Publications in Anthropology, No. 29, pp. 116-26.

—— 1962. On certain unconsidered aspects of double descent systems. *Man*, **62**: 130-4.

LEAHY, M. J. and CRAIN, M. 1937. *The land that time forgot*. London: Hurst and Blackett.

LEWIS, I. M. 1965. Problems in the comparative study of unilineal descent, in *The relevance of models for social anthropology*, edited by M. Banton, A.S.A. Monographs No. 1, pp. 87-112. London: Tavistock.

LIENHARDT, G. 1961. *Divinity and experience: the religion of the Dinka.* Oxford: Clarendon Press.

LOUNSBURY, F. G. 1964. The structural analysis of kinship semantics, in *Proceedings of the Ninth International Congress of Linguists*, edited by Horace G. Lundt. The Hague: Mouton, pp. 1073-93.

McARTHUR, M. 1967. Analysis of the genealogy of a Mae-Enga clan. *Oceania*, **37**: 281-5.

MALINOWSKI, B. 1935. *Coral gardens and their magic: a study of the methods of tilling the soil and agricultural rites in the Trobriand Islands*, 2 vols. New York: American Book Company.

MEGGITT, M. J. 1958. The Enga of the New Guinea Highlands: some preliminary observations. *Oceania*, **28**: 253-330.

—— 1964. Male-female relationships in the Highlands of Australian New Guinea, in New Guinea: the Central Highlands. *American Anthropologist*, **66** (4, part 2): 204-24. Special publication, edited by J. B. Watson.

—— 1965. *The lineage system of the Mae-Enga of New Guinea.* Edinburgh: Oliver and Boyd.

—— 1967. The pattern of leadership among the Mae-Enga. *Anthropological Forum*, **2**: 20-35.

—— 1969. Introduction, in *Pigs, pearlshells and women*, edited by M. J. Meggitt and R. M. Glasse. New Jersey: Prentice-Hall.

NEWMAN, P. L. 1965. *Knowing the Gururumba.* New York: Holt, Rinehart and Winston Inc.

PERANIO, R. D. 1961. Descent, descent line and descent group in cognatic social systems. *Proceedings of the Annual Spring Meeting of the American Ethnological Society*, Symposium on Patterns of Land Utilization, pp. 93-113. Washington: University of Washington Press.

PETERS, E. L. 1960. The proliferation of segments in the lineage of the Bedouin of Cyrenaica. *Journal of the Royal Anthropological Institute*, **90**: 29-53.

RAPPAPORT, R. 1967. *Pigs for the ancestors: ritual in the ecology of a New Guinea people.* New Haven and London: Yale University Press.

READ, K. E. 1955. Morality and the concept of the person among the Gahuku-Gama. *Oceania*, **25**: 233-82.

—— 1966. *The high valley.* London: George Allen and Unwin.

REAY, M. O. 1959. *The Kuma: freedom and conformity in the New Guinea Highlands.* Melbourne University Press, published for the Australian National University.

—— 1967. Structural co-variants of land shortage among patrilineal peoples. *Anthropological Forum*, **2**: 4-19.

RIVERS, W. H. R. 1924. *Social organization*, edited by W. J. Perry. New York and London: Knopf.

RYAN, D. J. 1959. Clan formation in the Mendi Valley. *Oceania*, **29**: 257-89.

—— 1969. Marriage in Mendi, in *Pigs, pearlshells and women*, edited by M. J. Meggitt and R. M. Glasse, pp. 159-75. New Jersey: Prentice-Hall.

SAHLINS, M. D. 1961. The segmentary lineage: an organization of predatory expansion. *American Anthropologist*, **63**: 322-45.

—— 1965. On the ideology and composition of descent groups. *Man*, **65**: 104-7.

SALISBURY, R. F. 1956. Unilineal descent groups in the New Guinea Highlands. *Man*, **56**: 2-7.

—— 1962. *From stone to steel: economic consequences of a technological change in New Guinea*. London and New York: Cambridge University Press.

—— 1964. New Guinea Highlands models and descent theory. *Man*, **64**: 168-71.

SCHEFFLER, H. W. 1964a. Descent concepts and descent groups: the Maori case. *Journal of the Polynesian Society*, **73**: 126-33.

—— 1964b. The social consequences of peace on Choiseul Island. *Ethnology*, **3**: 398-403.

—— 1965. *Choiseul Island social structure*. Berkeley and Los Angeles: University of California Press.

—— 1966. Ancestor worship in anthropology: or, observations on descent and descent groups. *Current Anthropology*, **7**: 541-8.

SCHNEIDER, D. M. 1965. Some muddles in the models: or, how the system really works, in *The relevance of models for social anthropology*, edited by M. Banton, A.S.A. Monographs No. 1, pp. 25-86. London: Tavistock, and New York: Frederick A. Praeger.

SCHWIMMER, E. G. 1969. Letter on virgin birth. *Man*, N.S., **4**: 132-3.

STANHOPE, J. M. 1970. Patterns of fertility and mortality in rural New Guinea, in *People and planning in New Guinea*, edited by Marion W. Ward, New Guinea Research Bulletin No. 34, pp. 24-41. Canberra: Australian National University.

STRATHERN, A. J. 1965. Descent and group-structure among the Mbowamb. Fellowship dissertation, Trinity College, Cambridge.

—— 1966. Despots and directors in the New Guinea Highlands. *Man*, N.S., **1**: 356-67.

—— 1968. Sickness and frustration: variations in two New Guinea Highlands societies. *Mankind*, **6**: 545-51.

—— 1969a. Finance and production: two strategies in New Guinea Highlands exchange systems. *Oceania*, **40**: 42-67.

—— 1969b. Descent and alliance in the New Guinea Highlands: some problems of comparison. *Proceedings of the Royal Anthropological Institute of Great Britain and Ireland for 1968*, pp. 37-52.

—— 1971. *The rope of moka: big-men and ceremonial exchange in Mount Hagen.* Cambridge: Cambridge University Press.

—— *in press.* Melpa kinship terms. To be published in a symposium on New Guinea Highlands kinship systems, edited by E. A. Cook and D. O'Brien.

—— and A. M. 1969. Marriage in Melpa, in *Pigs, pearlshells and women*, edited by M. J. Meggitt and R. M. Glasse. New Jersey: Prentice-Hall.

—— and —— 1971. *Self-decoration in Mount Hagen.* London: Gerald Duckworth.

STRATHERN, A. M. 1968. *Popokl*: the question of morality. *Mankind*, **6**: 553-61.

—— *in press. Women in between.* London: Seminar Press.

STRAUSS, H. and TISCHNER, H. 1962. *Die mi-kultur der Hagenberg stämme.* Hamburg: Cram, de Gruyter and Co.

VAYDA, A. P. 1968. Hypotheses about functions of war, in *War: the anthropology of armed conflict and aggression*, edited by M. Fried, M. Harris and R. Murphy. New York: Natural History Press, published for the American Museum of Natural History.

VAYDA, Cherry Lowman-. 1968 [1969]. Maring big men. *Anthropological Forum*, **2**: 199-243.

VICEDOM, G. F. and TISCHNER, H. 1943-8. *Die Mbowamb.* Hamburg: Cram, de Gruyter and Co.

WADDELL, E. 1968. The dynamics of a New Guinea Highlands agricultural system. Ph.D. dissertation, Australian National University.

WAGNER, R. 1967. *The curse of Souw: principles of Daribi clan definition and alliance in New Guinea.* Chicago and London: Chicago University Press.

—— 1969. Marriage among the Daribi, in *Pigs, pearlshells and women*, edited by M. J. Meggitt and R. M. Glasse, pp. 56-76. New Jersey: Prentice-Hall.

—— 1970. Daribi and Foraba cross-cousin terminologies: a structural comparison. *Journal of the Polynesian Society*, **79**: 91-8.

WATSON, J. B. 1964. Anthropology in the New Guinea Highlands, in New Guinea: the Central Highlands. *American Anthropologist*, **66** (4, part 2): 1-19. Special publication, edited by J. B. Watson.

—— 1967. Tairora: the politics of despotism in a small society. *Anthropological Forum*, **2**: 53-104.

—— 1970. Society as organized flow: the Tairora case. *Southwestern Journal of Anthropology*, **26**: 107-24.

WYNNE-EDWARDS, V. C. 1962. *Animal dispersion in relation to social behaviour.* New York: Hafner.

INDEX

Abortion, 237
Adoption, 106, 161, 244, 249
Adultery, 148-9, 151-2, 247
Affiliation: and alliance, 131-42; and
bridewealth, 125-7; attitudes to
incomers, 116-17, 119; cases of
change in, 148-83; changes of, in
Kawelka tribe, 102, 106-8, 141;
complications in changes of, 95-6;
distinction in, between clan-group
and clan-unit, 96; effects on of
orphanhood, widowhood, and
separation, 120, 169, 172-4; exchange between Tipuka and
Kawelka tribes, 75; in enclave
settlements, 159; incorporation of
sisters' sons, 17, 18-19, 20-1, 101,
106-12 *passim*, 142, 160-5 *passim*,
176, 177, 187, 244, 248; 'man-
bearing' and 'woman-bearing'
idioms, 18, 139, 149, 203, 219,
238; position of women in
relation to, 98-9; pressures to
change in enclave settlements,
159; structure and recruitment, 2,
91, 94, 221; relevance of kin-
terms to, 16-17; terms for persons
who change, 19
Affines, 138-9; *see also* Affiliation,
Husband-wife relations, Maternal
kin, *Moka*

African models and New Guinea
Highlands societies, 1, 2-4, 24-5,
41, 92, 213-16, 236
Agnation: among the Nuer, 3;
and beliefs in ghosts, 25-30;
definition of, 91-5, 243, 251;
'deprivation' of non-agnates, 208;
marriages made by agnates and
non-agnates, 206-12; relative stability of agnates' and non-agnates'
attachment to groups, 203-5;
return of men to agnatic place,
243; significance of agnation
among Mendi and Mae-Enga,
189-93; *see also* Patriliny
Ai, Kawelka Kundmbo, 78, 162-8
passim
Alliance, 14, 21, 73, 147, 179, 222-4;
affecting affiliation, 130-42, 176,
223; and marriage patterns, 133-
42, 157; and rivalry, 139-40, 223;
involving Tipuka, Kawelka, and
Minembi tribes, 40, 75, 77, 78,
80, 87, 89-90, 134, 159, 239, 242,
246; *see also Moka*, Warfare
Andakapkae tribe, 80
Assassination, 77, 175
Australian Administration, 1, 86-7,
90, 149, 158, 192, 231, 233
Autonomy, concept of, and the
noman, 144

Bachelors, 117, 149, 163, 164, 165, 190-1, 197-200, 209-11, 250

Baiyer Valley, 32, 116, 117, 133, 148, 158-9, 178, 180, 247, 248

Bena Bena, 216-24 *passim*, 223, 224, 231

Big-men, 5, 12, 14, 21, 38, 39, 47, 59, 61, 62, 108, 114, 116, 119, 149, 153, 212, 228; and group-segmentation, 42, 51, 240; and succession, 171-2, 206; conduct of disputes, 149-56; contract alliances through marriage, 77-8, 86; grant territory to incomers, 76, 80-1; importance of in recruiting or expelling group-members, 34, 67, 70, 72, 111, 142, 147, 149-51, 160-8, 177, 180, 181-2, 192, 213, 214, 227-33; pay bridewealth for others or for selves, 126, 161-2, 194, 200, 206, 208-9, 211; rise of, after arrival of Europeans, 86, 87; sacrifice to ghosts, 26, 38; use of 'helpers' by, 108, 115, 124, 148, 161-8 *passim*, 192, 210, 250

Bridewealth, 12, 98, 117, 150, 165, 172-3, 181-2, 204, 250-1; and affiliation, 125-7, 161-2, 177, 178-9, 180-1; contributions to, 193, 195-7; paid by agnates and non-agnates, 194-5, 209; sponsor needed to raise, 193, 199, 200, 211-12

Brother-sister relationship, 124, 176-7; *see also* Affiliation, Maternal kin

Brothers, 118, 147-8, 198, 211, 213, 214, 243; *see also* Disputes, Intra-clan relations, Kinship

Cash and cash cropping, 56, 57, 87, 138, 159, 194-5, 198, 232-3, 243

Chimbu, 32, 57, 224, 236, 241

Choice: and social structure, 4, 183-7, 249; of children to return to patrifilial clan, 182; relevant to affiliation of Kawelka non-agnates, 109-12; discussed generally, 129-30, 142-4, 183, 216; in uxorilo-cality, 120-8

Choiseulese, 4, 184, 232

Colonisation and migration, 32, 56, 75, 76, 89, 103, 114-18 *passim*, 144-8, 157-60, 247; *see also* Baiyer Valley, Wahgi Valley

Compensation payments: bride-wealth as, 125; extension of since warfare stopped, 139; for adultery, 148-9; for killing, 8-9, 179; for nurture of children, 179; for suicide, 248

Complementary filiation, 24-5, 176

Cordyline, as divination substance of Kawelka tribe, 36, 40-1, 155

Corporate groups, 8, 215

Culture, distinguished from social structure, 249

Cumulative patrifiliation, 2, 104-5, 219-20, 224-7

Dani, 247

Daribi, 22-4, 28, 224

Dei Council, 32

Descent: and locality, 3, 19-21, 40-1, 47, 100-1, 106, 216-20, 222, 243-4; contrasted with filiation, 8, 19, 22, 24, 187, 218-21, 243-4; definition of, as analytical term, 7-8, 23-5, 183, 213, 237, 243-4; descent-constructs, 8, 10-12, 24, 53, 184, 213-16, 249; descent dogmas (idioms), 2, 4, 24, 44, 48, 52-3, 105, 186, 213-16, 220-2, 228, 231, 236; unilineal and non-unilineal, 183-5, 249; *see also* Affiliation, Agnation, Patriliny

Dinka, 41

Disputes: internal to clan, 77, 148-56; over affiliation, 139-40, 169, 180; over bridewealth, 125, 150, 153, 178-9, 180, 194; over land, 157, 158; over *moka*, 150, 153, 154-6, 176-7; over pigs or pork, 116, 204, 247; over widows, 163; *see also* Land tenure

Divination substance, *see Mi*

Diviners, 27-30, 234-5

Division of labour, 59, 224

Divorce, 12, 168-9, 173, 187

Ecological niches, 251

Elti and Penambe tribes, 37, 169

Emic/etic statements, 91-5, 243

Entrepreneurs, 159

Epilke tribe, 117

Eta, 19, 192, 238, 246

Expansion of territory, 77-82, 90, 145-6, 230-1, 251

ɔndipi, Kawelka Membo, 160-2, 163-8 *passim*, 177, 196

Father-son relationship, 9, 154, 160-1, 165, 183, 198, 210-12, 243, 245; as shown in ghost attacks, 26-8, 118-19; as shown in residence patterns, 66-8, 70; in Kawelka origin story, 36-7

Filiation: matrifiliation, strength of, 225-7; patrifiliation and matrifiliation, 224-7; 'strong' and 'weak' patrifiliation, 249; *see also* Affiliation, Descent, Procreation

Flexibility: and rules, 6; in attitudes to group membership, 34, 129, 251; *see also* Choice

Fostering, 111, 149, 172, 226, 244

Frustration(*popokl*), 27, 28-9, 118-19, 126, 144, 149, 150-1, 152, 155, 187, 204, 239, 251

Gahuku-Gama, 55

Gardening, 46-7, 58, 62-3, 68

Gawigl language, 28

Genealogies: and group structure, 31, 52, 214-16; emic and etic, 91-5; of Kawelka clans, 44-52; of Minembi Yelipi clan, 45-6; Siane, 93-4; simplification of, 49; variation in, 44-6, 52; *see also* Descent

Ghosts, 9-10, 12, 21, 22, 25-30, 36-7, 116, 118, 126, 169, 234-5, 245, 249

Goroko, 200

Group segments: clan and territory, 54-72 *passim*, 73-90 *passim*; clan-sections, sub-clans, 42-4, 51; creation of new segments, 45-6, 51, 71-2, 239-40; lineages, 35-6, 44-5, 49-51, 93; terms for different levels of (*see also* -*mbo* idiom, Descent), 18, 42, 43

Gururumba, 244

House-building, 71

Huli, 74, 75, 102, 186

Husband-wife relationship, 20-1, 174, 177-9, 224-7, 241, 249

Ideology, 1-5, 186, 218-22, 228-30, 237; *see also* Descent

Inheritance, 214-16; *see also* Bigmen, Land tenure, Succession

Intra-clan relations, as shown in disputes, 148-56

Ivo (Orokaiva concept), 237

Jealousy, 28, 171, 173, 175, 177, 243

Jimi Valley, 32, 89, 133, 148, 160

-ka suffix, 239

Kachin, 249

Kaepa, Kawelka Klammbo, 37-8

Kawelka tribe: divination substance of, 36, 40; location and numbers, 32; origin story, 36-9, 239; non-agnates in, 102, 106-12; population of clan-groups, 64, 104-5; segments of, 35, 39-46 *passim*; settlements at Mbukl, 64-6; terms for segment-levels, 43-4; Wahgi Valley territory, 58, 67, 68, 76, 90, 103, 114-15, 116, 157, 158, 162, 205, 246, 248

Kawelka tribe segments: case histories relating to, 175, 180, 181, 196, 204-5; compared, 42-6, 48, 81-2; expansion of settlement by (Kundmbo clan) 76, (Membo clan) 78, (Kurupmbo clan-section) 88-9, (Mandembo clan) 103; genealogies of (Kundmbo) 44-5, 205, 239, 240, (Membo) 47-52, 239, 240, 248, (Kundmbo and Membo compared) 48; marital status of men in, 197-204 *passim*; marriage patterns of, 133-6, 201-4

Keme tribe, 148

Kiklpukla tribe, 239

Kinship: and affiliation, 19, 108, 248; and exchange relations, 17, 176; and friendship, 16, 237; as ideology, 229; ideas of procreation, 8-16, 237; terms, 16-21, 53, 106, 176, 217-18, 238; 'vegetable' model of, 19-20, 237; *see also* Affiliation, Agnation, Descent, Filiation, Maternal kin, Patriliny

Klamakae tribe, 42, 80-1, 133-42 *passim*, 160, 180, 240, 247-8

Kombukla tribe, 77-8, 133-42 *passim*, 163, 248

Kona wingndi, 40, 101, 218

Kont, Kawelka Membo, 47-8, 51, 157, 244, 245, 250

Kopalike Meake and Mandke tribes, 43

Kope tribe, 163, 205

Kopong, 10-11

Kor kil køi, 26

Korofeigu, 216-24 *passim*

Kotna mission station, 177

Kuk, Kawelka settlement-place, 37, 162

Kukilika tribe, 37

Kuma (Central Melpa area), 37, 38, 77, 239

Kuma (Wahgi Valley people), 18, 231, 239

Kurup tribe, 43

Kyaka Enga, 241

Lae, 199

Lakher, 249

Land tenure, 20, 67, 71-2, 97-8, 123, 160, 187, 217, 219, 246, 247-8; and group territories, 42, 78, 80, 82-9; and land shortage (disputes), 34, 157, 158-60, 189-93, 245; boundary demarcation, 87; provision of gardens to extra-clan kin, 58, 62-3, 175; tenurial status of incomers' claims, 73-88 *passim*

Lkalke (Klalke) tribe, 145

Local government councillors, 151, 154, 156, 177, 178, 204-5, 242, 244, 246, 250

Locality names, 60

Mae-Enga, 4, 13, 14, 18, 22-4, 25, 29, 30, 32, 74, 75, 92, 116, 146, 147, 189-93, 214, 218, 224, 231, 236, 244, 249, 250-1